TRACES
BEHIND
THE
ESMERALDAS
SHORE

TRACES BEHIND THE ESMERALDAS SHORE

◆

Prehistory of the
Santiago-Cayapas Region, Ecuador

WARREN R. DEBOER

THE UNIVERSITY OF ALABAMA PRESS

Tuscaloosa and London

Designed by Erin Toppin Bradley

∞

Library of Congress Cataloging-in-Publication Data

DeBoer, Warren R.
Traces behind the Esmeraldas shore :
prehistory of the Santiago-Cayapas Region, Ecuador / Warren R. DeBoer.
p.   cm.
Includes bibliographical references and index.
ISBN 0-8173-0792-3 (alk. paper)
1. Indians of South America—Ecuador—Esmeraldas (Province)—Antiquities.
2. Indians of South America—Ecuador—Esmeraldas (Province)—Material culture.
3. Cayapa Indians—Antiquities.
4. Excavations (Archaeology)—Ecuador—Esmeraldas (Province)
5. Esmeraldas (Ecuador : Province)—Antiquities.
I. Title.
F3721. 1. E75D43   1996
986.6´ 3501—dc20   95-8371
CIP

British Library Cataloguing-in-Publication Data available

96 97 98 99 00 — 5 4 3 2 1

To my mentors:
Donald Lathrap, John Rowe, and Paul Tolstoy,
who by disagreeing have kept archaeology more interesting.

CONTENTS

FIGURES

TABLES

FOREWORD

I don't recall the exact date (it was an evening in the spring of 1986), but the conversation remains clear in memory. Paul Tolstoy called from Montreal and asked if I would be interested in participating in his upcoming archaeological project in Ecuador. The target was the Santiago-Cayapas basin of coastal Esmeraldas, an area that was famous for its antiquities but poorly known from the standpoint of scientific archaeology. Although I had heard of La Tolita—the site having a somewhat notorious reputation for the large quantities of gold and other preciosities looted from its mounds—I otherwise knew nothing about the area or its prehistory. Nestled away in the northwestern corner of Ecuador, Esmeraldas Province was *terra incognita*. "It's lowland tropical forest," Paul explained, "and, Warren, you're familiar with doing archaeology in such places." This was partly true. I had worked in the Ucayali and later in the Huallaga valleys of the Peruvian Amazon. In 1986, the prospect of continuing work in Peru was dim. The protean and sinister forces of Tupac Amaru, Sendero Luminoso, and assorted *narcotraficantes* made further work on the Huallaga unappealing—or, more frankly, downright dangerous. And, yes, a sabbatical was coming up. "Paul, thanks for the opportunity, I'll be glad to join you," I said. All sorts of wonderful things do occasionally ensue from such unheroically conditioned decisions.

During the period August through December 1986, the University of Montreal Santiago-Cayapas Project carried out an initial reconnaissance of the inland area backing the coastal site of La Tolita. More than eighty sites were recorded. Surface collections (dominated by durable potsherds) were made at all but three sites, and limited excavations were made at a few. More than fifty thousand artifacts were collected, as well as an array of carbon and soil samples from excavated contexts. A preliminary summary of this evidence, one primarily designed to sketch a ceramic chronology for the region, has been published (Tolstoy and DeBoer 1989).

Building on the initial work launched and implemented by Tolstoy, I returned to the Santiago-Cayapas during the summers of 1988, 1989, and, most recently, 1992. The archaeological survey was continued (more than two hundred sites are now recorded), and more specialized ethnohistoric and ethnoarchaeological studies dealing with the Chachi, the current Native American inhabitants of the Cayapas, were carried out (DeBoer 1989, 1991a; DeBoer and Blitz 1991). The decision to omit the results of the 1992 season from the following account stems, in part, from the fact that the recovered artifacts remain incompletely analyzed, but it is also based on the need for closure. In order to write, one has to pretend, at some point, that requisite knowledge is in hand. This pretense, of course, is a fiction. Ongoing doctoral research in the Santiago-Cayapas includes Claire Allum's analysis of contemporary Chachi land use patterns and Judy Kreid's fine-grained survey of the lower Santiago. Whether the following account survives these and future studies remains to be seen.

Speaking of all these precedent and continuing efforts, I must mention those colleagues who participated in, and thereby made possible, any accomplishments achieved. Although the following appears to be a mere list of personnel, it serves more to acknowledge a shared history of toil, thoughts, arguments, fun, and occasional discomfort.

1986 Season
Paul Tolstoy (University of Montreal)
Brigitte Chevalier (University of Montreal)
Warren DeBoer (Queens College)
Daniel Poulin (University of Montreal)
Line Rigazio (University of Montreal)
Sara Stinson (Queens College)
Elka Weinstein (York University)

1988 Season
Warren DeBoer (Queens College)
Claire Allum (University of Calgary)
Judith Kreid (City University of New York)
Sara Stinson (Queens College)

1989 Season
Warren DeBoer (Queens College)
John Blitz (City University of New York)
Joe Jimenez (City University of New York)
Judith Kreid (City University of New York)
Sara Stinson (Queens College)
David Syring (Cornell College)

1992 Season
Warren DeBoer (Queens College)
José Chancay (ESPOL—Escuela Superior Politécnica del Litoral)
Milton Herrera (City University of New York)
Arthur Rostoker (City University of New York)
Sara Stinson (Queens College)

Thanks to the entire crew.

The people of the Santiago-Cayapas were surprisingly kind and cooperative in the face of this small force of nosy foreigners who, armed with trowels, shovels, compasses, and other exotica, were obviously ignorant about how to live. Guillermo Ayoví and his family facilitated all aspects of the project. As *maestro de la marimba, sabio de la selva* [savant of the jungle], and raconteur extraordinaire, "Don Guillo" is one of those remarkable people who automatically enters long-term memory. At Guadual, Benito Palacios served skillfully as navigator and general caretaker, keeping us out of all sorts of trouble. The late Claudio Corozo was the hardest of workers and one of those individuals who instinctively understood the value of knowing about the past; his wife, Rosa Estupiñan, is the best cook of the region, making haute cuisine out of a range chicken and an imported jar of peanut butter. In Maldonado, Juana Ulloa graciously shared her house with a team of three archaeologists while her son-in-law Pedro Sanchez served as guide and general intermediary in the Santiago segment of our survey.

The patience of our Chachi hosts was extraordinary. We thank the late Perdomo Añapa for permission to excavate in his *finca* (farm in local Spanish) and for introducing us, however fleetingly, to the world of the Chachi shaman. Many thanks to Vicente Añapa, Milena Cimarrón, Lucho Cipriano, and Atanasio Cipriano, who arranged for our use of Jesusito's house as an archaeological basecamp. Vicente is the best field archaeologist on the Cayapas, more skillful at "reading" and moving dirt with a machete than we are with trowels. Many others helped in important ways: Benedicto Sandoval gave us the royal tour of Punta Venado; Pedro Tapuyo welcomed us to the community of Zapallo Grande; Adolfo Chapiro taught us much of the Chachi way; and Domingo Acero negotiated our stay at Herradura. At Zapallo Grande and at Borbón, Lester and Sharon Meisenheimer extended many courtesies (most memorable was the cold lemonade). Among other expatriates, perhaps the most engaging was Stephen Tarjanyi, who threw Molotov cocktails against Soviet tanks in 1956 Budapest, fled to Chicago to drive a Holsum Bread truck, and later kayaked to the Esmeraldas shore to set up a farm and tourist lodge at the mouth of the Onzole.

A special debt must be expressed to the dedicated and constantly underfinanced community of Ecuadorian archaeologists. Jorge Marcos, the late Presley Norton, Francisco Valdez, Josef Buys, Maria Clara Montaño, the late Pedro Porras, Vicki Dominguez, Monica Bolaños, and Lenín Miño—all shared their ideas and enthusiasm, and many assisted us in the process of acquiring permits. And special thanks to Leon Doyon and Megan Criley whose apartment became a *segunda casa* for many archaeologists passing through Quito.

Archaeology is expensive. We are extremely grateful to the following for supporting our investigations in Esmeraldas: the Social Sciences and Humanities Research Council of Canada, the National Science Foundation, and the Professional Staff Congress of CUNY Research Foundation.

My sister, Ainsley DeBoer, designed the illustration for the cover. Somehow, without reading the book, Ainsley captured and condensed its contents in one montage. I drafted the remaining, less inspired figures of artifacts and maps.

Without Sandee Kotler, whose efforts at preparing the text as well as numerous tortuous tables can only be described as indefatigable, the book would not have been completed. Without Sara, this project would have been possible but joyless.

Warren R. DeBoer
Queens College

TRACES BEHIND THE ESMERALDAS SHORE

1
BACKWARD

If only there were even an old ruin someplace on the land, some indication that someone had been here before us and that we were part of a human chain; but only stone would last in this steaming vat of organic dissolution, and there is no stone here except river gravel. In the midst of my longing for human continuity in those first days, I found a broken fragment of a plate three feet underground in a hole we were digging for the foundation of my new house. I experienced a moment of elation, of belonging, but it didn't last. On the back of the plate was inscribed "Turin 1923" (Thomsen 1989: 22–23).

As a retired Peace Corps volunteer homesteading along the Esmeraldas river, Thomsen reminds one of a Conrad character slowly sinking into terminal tropical torpor. The insects bite, the midday sun burns, and nightly rains carpet the forest floor with knee-deep mud, but above all, the misplaced European is unnerved by the prospect that the jungle has no history. A major goal of this book is to lay foundations for a history or, more specifically, a prehistory of the Santiago-Cayapas region of northernmost Esmeraldas province, Ecuador. Pursuant to this goal, a chronological framework, one extending well before 1923, is needed.

This purpose may seem passé, even strangely antiquated, in an age when postmodern critiques invade all quarters. Yet it is a task that needs to be done, not merely to allay Thomsen's angst but to give archaeology some semblance of scientific footing. For much of Ecuador, basic chronological work remains underdeveloped and, as a result, processual—much less postprocessual (the postmodern in its archaeological guise)—concerns often resemble clever ruminations more than approaches anchored to any knowledge of what happened in the past.

Many years ago, my Shipibo friend and coworker, Manuel Rengifo (a Don Lathrap protégé), commented: "Well, Ricardo" [my name in Ucayali Spanish], "if you don't know how old it is, you're not a good archaeologist, but if you want to know what it means, my brother-in-law is a pretty good shaman." Wanting to be a good archaeologist, I here follow the first part of Manuel's advice. At the time, I regarded his second recommendation as more parody than prophesy, but today, of course, archaeologists-as-shamans are flying everywhere.

The construction of a space-time framework for prehistoric Ecuador is a particular challenge. Unlike Peru to the south, ancient Ecuador was largely free of those periodic "horizon styles" that serve to correlate regional cultural sequences. Except for a poorly defined "Chorreroid" horizon during the early first millennium B.C. and the brief Incan intrusion at the end of prehistory, Ecuador always remained a patchwork of local polities. Sometimes these polities emulated each other in terms of material culture, but, as often, they maintained a distinctiveness that obscures their interconnections. In this mosaic cultural landscape, the ar-

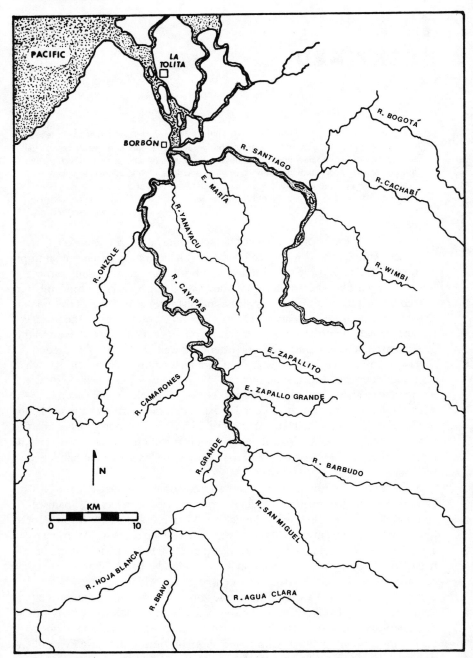

Fig. 1.1   *The Santiago and Cayapas rivers and their major tributaries. The same base map is used throughout the text.*

chaeologist is well advised to begin by documenting local sequences reliably. This we will attempt to do for the Santiago-Cayapas region.

Figure 1.1 maps this region. In addition to the major drainages, this map plots two landmarks of significance: La Tolita, the largest and most famous archaeological site of the region (of which more below), and the modern town of Borbón, which is connected by a road to the provincial capital of Esmeraldas. Borbón is the gateway to the Santiago-Cayapas river system. From this bustling and sweltering port, redolent of rotting fish, fruit, and other offal, one continues by boat, either downstream to the Pacific or upriver to the interior. It is toward this interior, a region that I frequently refer to as "La Tolita's hinterland," that our archaeological work turns. This inland concentration is based, to a certain extent, on a division of labor. Francisco Valdez and his team of Ecuadorian archaeologists have been carrying out a long-term project of excavations and survey at La Tolita; thus our inland focus is complementary in an areal sense. Furthermore, our wish to sketch a full sequence for the region's prehistory with an emphasis on changing settlement patterns over time calls for broad-scale coverage rather than intensive excavation at a few sites.

Although not to be found in any textbook, our survey procedures were geared to the environmental facts of the hinterland. As will be seen in the next chapter, vegetation is typically dense, and, except for trails and clearings, ground visibility often approaches zero. Away from rivers, the terrain can be rugged, consisting of knifelike ridges separated by ramifying *esteros* or creeks. This is not a landscape where one cheerfully undertakes random transects. Rather one hopes for trails along ridge tops or, if necessary, wades up esteros, hoping that water and mud stay below chest level. That this description is not total hyperbole is indicated by an observation made by John Blitz, who noted that our site discovery rate was somewhat higher when surveying upslope than downslope. The probable reason for this otherwise unexpected finding is that whereas one climbs cautiously up a mud-slicked slope—often one's nose is literally close to the ground—the descent can be a more hurried affair. We have not attempted, however, to correct for this anal-nasal distinction in estimating site frequencies.

But the physical environment is only part of the matter. While the interfluves may seem to the unknowing outsider to be largely unused wilderness, this is hardly the case. Although most land is still not legally owned, it is nonetheless claimed both by Native American Chachi and Afro-Ecuadorian residents of the region. In fact, land claims are an extremely sensitive issue at present, given the ongoing influx of land-seeking settlers from Manabí province to the south. This is neither the time nor the place for strangers to be trekking around the countryside, occasionally stopping to take compass bearings or to unroll a 50 m tape to measure sherd scatters. Brandishing a permit from the Patrimonio in Quito only heightens the suspicion.

One must work with the local inhabitants both in the sense of establishing a certain degree of rapport and in the sense of offering employment as guides, informants, and field-workers. The income is appreciated, and, as ignorant but

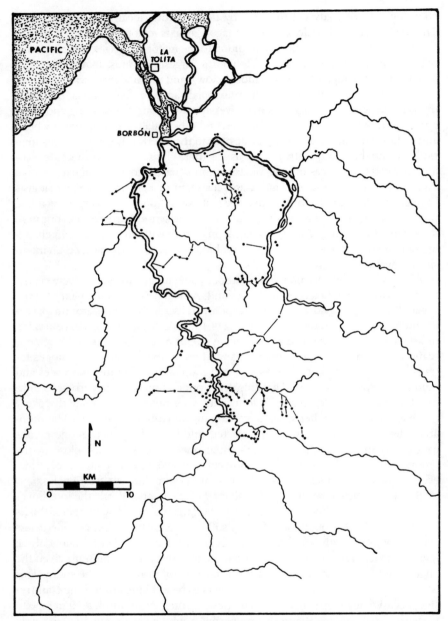

Fig. 1.2   *Distribution of archaelogical sites* (dots) *and major overland routes followed on survey* (lines connecting dots).

relatively wealthy foreigners, we have little else to offer. The people, of course, are a great store of knowledge concerning the location of archaeological materials. They have seen the telltale potsherds in their *platanales* (agricultural clearings), situated both near to and well inland from their river-based settlements, and once our horns were removed they were willing to take us to these sites. Nearly half of all sites were located on the basis of this local knowledge, although a significant minority were encountered while en route to the destinations targeted by informants.

In addition to overland survey, we also relied on motorized or paddled canoes, plying along exposed river banks and stopping at all settlements to inquire about archaeological sites. Today human population is overwhelmingly concentrated along navigable rivers, although interfluvial areas are utilized for farming, hunting, and the gathering of forest products. One might expect that prehistoric distributions were similar. In fact, it has been argued that "tropical forest culture" (*sensu*; Lathrap 1970) has always been primarily a river-oriented phenomenon. To be evaluated, however, this proposition requires a comparison of riverine and interfluvial site abundance. Oddly, the data for such an obvious comparison are rarely obtained. In this respect, the Santiago-Cayapas evidence, as mapped in fig. 1.2, is intriguing. Along navigable river banks, the linear density is 0.60 sites/km; this figure doubles to 1.31 sites/km in the interfluves. Not surprisingly, a river-based survey would miss much of the archaeological story. These results, however, do not apply to site area that, in contrast to site numbers, is somewhat higher along rivers—that is, riverine sites tend to be larger. Furthermore these composite figures of linear density are not too meaningful, as values for individual periods fluctuate wildly over time. But this anticipates a chronology to be developed in later chapters.

As is evident in fig. 1.2, our survey did not involve even coverage of the entire Santiago-Cayapas. Some areas, such as the Onzole and the far upper Santiago, have yet to be looked at, whereas other areas have been more intensively explored. The dense cluster of sites on the upper Cayapas, for instance, reflects the location of our 1986 base camp more than the facts of prehistoric settlement distribution. Similarly, the site cluster on the lower Estero María indicates the intensively surveyed "catchment" around our 1988–89 base camp at Maldonado. These base camps were essential fixtures of the survey. Here project personnel worked, ate, and slept. Here materials coming in from the field were washed, labeled, and submitted to preliminary analysis. The base camp also formed that "middle ground" (White 1991) in which visiting archaeologists and local folk got to know each other and to establish the rapport so necessary to carrying out archaeological or any other kind of research.

As outlined above, our survey procedures do not guarantee a representative sample of the archaeological past. They were successful, however, in documenting numerous sites in both riverine and interfluvial areas, and as an accommodation to the realities of the physical and social landscape of the Santiago-Cayapas, numbers of sites may be our best expedient guide to "representativeness." We will be in a better position to evaluate this optimistic possibility when Judith Kreid completes her ongoing systematic, auger-based survey of the lower Santiago.

The harbinger of a site was usually a sherd protruding from a river bank, lying on the surface, or exposed by the earth-turning involved in house building or agricultural activity. Invariably one sherd contagiously guaranteed others. That is, sites were almost always artifact clusters rather than "find spots." Site dimensions were estimated by tracking the extent of surface debris coupled with the sinking of probes to sterile soil. Usually midden was shallow, 10 cm or less overlying a hard clay, but in a few cases cultural deposits extended to greater depths. When feasible, these latter sites were revisited to carry out excavations designed to check for cultural stratigraphy. Surface collection procedures varied over the course of the project. In the 1986 campaign, an attempt was made to collect a "grab" sample of sherds (preferably a hundred or more) from each site. This procedure was designed to procure representative and comparable collections to carry out a quantitative seriation based heavily on paste types. Rims, decorated pieces, or other "diagnostics" were given no more value than the humblest of undecorated body sherds. A preliminary frequency seriation of the 1986 material is available elsewhere (Tolstoy and DeBoer 1989). Tolstoy and his students at the University of Montreal are currently working on a more refined version.

Beginning in 1987, I shifted collection procedures to emphasize the recovery of rims, decorated body sherds, or other diagnostic artifacts. Two factors prompted this change. By this time, for much of the sequence, the range of vessel and decorative forms was well enough known that a selected sample of artifacts indeed served to identify, in short order, the phase attribution of the collection. The second reason involved my own predilection concerning the most meaningful way in which to approach ceramic analysis, a bias that I acquired during my training by John Rowe and the "Berkeley school."

The starting premises of this approach are that good potters make pots, not potsherds; that pottery vessels, as the actual tools used in the past, are more meaningful units of analysis than fragmentary sherds; and that ceramic analysis, therefore, should begin by contextualizing sherds in the whole vessels from which they come. This contextualization is more readily accomplished in the case of rims and other sherds that are directly informative as to the form of their parent vessels. As illustrator during all seasons of the Santiago-Cayapas project, I began by sorting through the sherds of each lot collected in the field, checking for conjoins, and combining sherds that had a good chance of coming from the same vessel. All such vessel units were drawn with the use of conventional procedures for the illustration of archaeological pottery (e.g., Adkins and Adkins 1989). More than two thousand partially or, more rarely, totally reconstructed vessel profiles are now available for study, and it is this corpus that forms the major basis for the phase-by-phase ceramic descriptions presented in following chapters. I should emphasize that this vessel-oriented analysis by no means precludes the utility of sherd-based typological approaches. The latter, however, are not my preference.

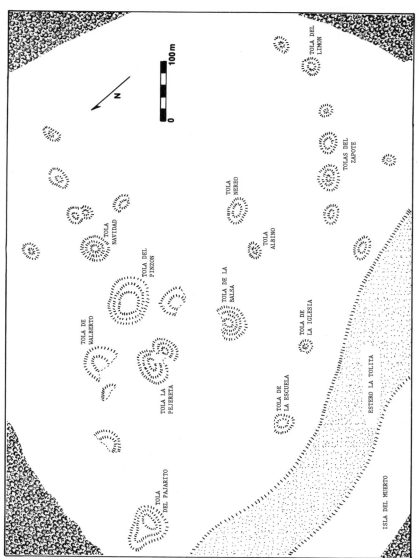

Fig. 1.3   Site of La Tolita showing major mounds and mound remnants.

In developing vessel shape categories, I have no particular classificatory theory to espouse. I prefer to draw pottery rather than to talk about it, and the shape distinctions made in this volume should be evident to even the most casual of viewers. (In fact, if I could get away with it, I would avoid words altogether and engage in the more "telling" medium of pictures.)

As indicated previously, our survey was ambitious in that we hoped to establish a full cultural sequence for the Santiago-Cayapas, not merely to understand the workings of La Tolita's hinterland. Yet clearly, as the largest archaeological monument of the region, La Tolita played an important role in regional prehistory, and a brief consideration of this famous site is in order. These comments are appropriately brief, for ongoing investigations at La Tolita will undoubtedly transform our knowledge of this prehistoric site in the near future (see Valdez 1987 for an anticipatory summary). Figure 1.3 plots some of the thirty or so mounds that define the center of the settlement. Modified from Valdez (1987: fig. 8), this map is, in turn, based on the plan given by Ferdon (1940: 267). Yet an earlier map was prepared by Uhle (1927: fig. 2). There are discordances among all these plans, a fact probably attributable to the destructive mining of mounds for gold that has taken place throughout this century. Despite the scale of destruction and the cartographic disagreements among archaeologists, a layout of mounds around a large rectangular plaza open to the east can still be detected (the scale in fig. 1.3 is in the center of this plaza). Excavations in these mounds, whether by looters or archaeologists, indicate that they contain burials. This is not to say that these tumuli are strictly mortuary in nature, for postholes indicating structures have been identified on the summit of at least one of them (Tola del Pajarito).

Before the investigations by Valdez and his coworkers, there was doubt about the dating of La Tolita and its associated mounds. In her overview of Ecuadorian prehistory, Meggers (1966: 103) suggested that the mounds themselves, although incorporating earlier materials, could well date to the Integration period after A.D. 500. A large and well-provenienced roster of radiocarbon dates, however, now makes it clear that mound-building at La Tolita began as early as 300 B.C. and completely ceased by A.D. 350 when the site was abandoned (Valdez 1987). New information also indicates that the central mound group at La Tolita (the area portrayed in fig. 1.3) is but part of the total extent of midden at the site. Valdez (1987: 11) estimates that total site size approaches a square kilometer (North Americanists may note that this rivals the size of Moundville, the second largest prehistoric site in the Eastern Woodlands), although it is not known whether this entire area represents one large contemporary settlement or a palimpsest accrued over centuries. There are many other questions about the nature of La Tolita that will surface in the narrative to which we now turn.

2
COAST, RIVER, AND FOREST

It is a powerful convention that the second chapter present the environmental background as if such presentation were obligatory and logically precedent to what follows. The "natural" backdrop of landscape and waterscape is always, in part, a product of the history of human utilization. However ardent the wish to be in pristine or virgin forest, nowhere in our inland treks from the river did we find an innocent landscape: there were sherds beneath our feet as seemingly primordial trees towered above; even in the most remote and apparently trackless areas, the flora always included anthropogenic relics—a spiny-trunked peachpalm or a feral *chirma* with its edible purple tubers. The river banks sport a truly international arboretum, including such recent introductions as the breadfruit. Among the local black population, surnames such as Johnson, Dunkelmann, and Stalín hardly suggest isolation from the great global forces of recent history.

As an archaeologist, I am not the one to review the recent political history of the Santiago-Cayapas basin, nor will I even attempt an adequate environmental description of the region. Much of the available evidence has been synthesized admirably in previous studies. Among these are Wolf's (1879) still excellent survey of Esmeraldas geography, which includes specific sections on the Santiago-Cayapas; Murphy's (1939) general description of the littoral of Colombia and Ecuador; West's (1957) majestic cultural geography of the Chocó, the southern border of which includes the Santiago-Cayapas; and Whitten's (1965, 1974) more recent and localized accounts. Selectively drawing on these studies, the following sketch begins with the coast, an area never touched in our archaeological reconnaissance.

The Mercurial Maritime

Murphy (1939: 14) sets the stage well, although perhaps with a bit of hyperbole: "This is the maritime Chocó, a flooded lowland of perpetual rains, of selva and morasses, of hundreds of streams, many or most of which pour into the Pacific through multiple mouths. The line between earth and ocean becomes tenuous, for the greater part of the shore is fringed with a maze of mangrove-covered flats and islands, separated by a network of *esteros* and grading into shifting bars and shallows which in many places extend for miles offshore."

This general description applies to the shoreline flanking the mouth of the Santiago. Behind a string of offshore spits that form a continuing hazard to navigation, and that until recently were the basking grounds for formidable crocodilians, stands the mangrove-fringed coast. As classically diagnosed by West (1956), this mangrove forest is a highly distinctive vegetation community that is saline tolerant and specifically adapted to intertidal conditions. Within this community, the stilt-rooted red mangrove (*Rhizophora brevistyla*) is dominant; the black mangrove (*Avicennia nitida*) with its pneumatophores, or aerial root tips, is also conspicuous. At high tide, the mangrove zone becomes a veritable labyrinth of canoe trails winding through the flooded forest. Local inhabitants claim that the earnest navigator can follow this protected network of channels from the Santiago northward to Tumaco.

In terms of human utilization, the mangroves are a source of fish, shellfish, edible crustaceans, and various tree products. Due to salinity and the tidal rhythm of flooding and draining, the agricultural potential of this zone is low, but this is not to say that farming does not take place. As West (1956: 114) observes:

> Within the swamp back from the seacoast for a distance of one-half to one mile, one frequently encounters along tidal channels small areas of sandy soil which rise slightly above the general level of swampy muck. These sandy spots are locally called *firmes*. They are sites of human habitation within the mangrove swamp; freshwater is usually found at a depth of three to four feet below the surface; and coconut palms, patches of maize, and other crops are grown. Some of these firmes appear to be remnants of old beach ridges that have been largely destroyed with the general seaward advance of the coast.

One might add that not only are such *firmes* sites of contemporary settlement, but they are often strewn with the telltale sherds marking ancient occupations.

From the archaeological standpoint, it is important to note that today's coast was not there in the past. In the short term, this inconstant coastline is reworked daily by current and tide and periodically is assaulted by tsunamis resulting from submarine earthquakes or volcanic eruptions. The last major tsunami, in 1906, destroyed coastal villages, drowned hundreds of individuals, and recontoured the shore from the Santiago to Tumaco and beyond (West 1957: 57). The fury of these events is etched in local memory and folklore. Time and time again, we were told of *the* great tsunami (*maremoto* in Spanish) that swept away the ancient civilization of La Tolita. In support of this theory, people allege that cobble deposits found far up the interfluvial hills are remnants of this legendary deluge.

In the long term, the coastline flanking the Santiago is expanding seaward. According to recent geomorphological research (Tihay 1988), the whole area seaward from the contemporary riverine port of Borbón (fig. 1.1) is a relatively recent landform resulting from the interaction between eustatic changes in sea level and the prograding buildup of the Santiago-Cayapas delta. In Tihay's, preliminary reconstruction, based on C-14 dates associated with relict strands, a beach paralleling the present shore stood at Borbón at about 5000 B.P.; by 4000 B.P. the vicinity of La Tolita was emerging as habitable land; and by 2000 B.P. the delta approached its modern form. As a consequence of this changing coast, it is unlikely that Early or Middle Formative sites will be found seaward from Borbón: the area was either under water or has been subsequently buried through alluviation.

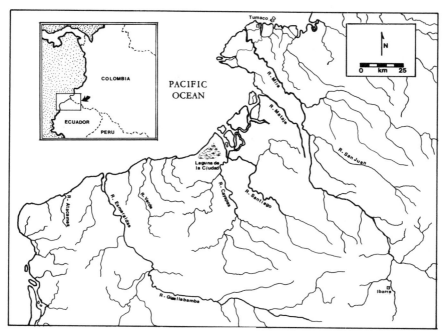

Fig. 2.1   *Northwestern Ecuador and southwestern Colombia. Santiago-Cayapas basins and neighboring Laguna de la Ciudad are at center of map.*

The stabilization of the essentially modern shoreline by 2000 B.P. not only created the current mangrove coast, it also created an extensive freshwater backswamp, today known by the provocative toponym Laguna de la Ciudad (lake of the city), that is located southwest of the lower Santiago (fig. 2.1). Elevated beach strands and *firmes* as well as artificial tolas and ridged fields, all strewn with sherd deposits, have recently been identified throughout Laguna de la Ciudad, a discovery that suggests that this seemingly inhospitable swamp was occupied and modified for agricultural purposes by prehistoric populations (Montaño 1991). The scale and timing of this modification remain to be detailed; however, once better understood, these earthwork projects may well recast our notions about the agricultural base of La Tolita. The preliminary verdict, however, is a familiar one: there is no fixed environmental potential that is independent of resource management, at least in the short run.

River in the Rain

In a satellite photo, the Santiago-Cayapas basins appear as an expanse of mottled forest broken by dendritic strands of water coalescing seaward. This coalescence follows two main branches, the Santiago and Cayapas respectively, that join at the modern port of Borbón. Below Borbón—to push this arboreal metaphor a bit further—a taproot of the combined flow of the two rivers directly seeks the Pacific while lateral roots skirt and define an archipelago of deltaic islands (fig. 1.1). However dwarfed by the surrounding forest when viewed from on high, these rivers are the lifelines of transportation and exchange, the sources of agriculturally valued strips of fertile alluvium, and accordingly the foci of contemporary human settlement.

Although to a considerably lesser extent than the Esmeraldas basin, the Santiago and Cayapas rivers still drain a formidable watershed that stretches from the foothills of the western cordillera across a coastal plain to the Pacific shore. This watershed encompasses some 6190 km², and downriver from Borbón, where the combined width of the two rivers exceeds 2 km even at low tide, the annual discharge is estimated at 8695 x 10⁶ m³ (Alcina Franch 1979: 29). Immediately above Borbón, in their lower courses, the Santiago and Cayapas are wide rivers with modestly sized floodplains. Tidal effects, which daily influence the navigability of a maze of side channels (esteros), are felt as far upstream as the mouth of the Bogotá on the Santiago and the mouth of the Camarones on the Cayapas (fig. 1.1). Within this tidal zone, river banks are low and backed by a scrubby secondary forest frequently broken by *platanales* (clearings dominated by plantains) and, increasingly in recent years, by *potreros* (cattle pasture). The human population of the lower reaches of the Cayapas and of the entire Santiago basin is dominated by Afro-Ecuadorian blacks whose recent history and lifeways have been portrayed by Whitten (1965, 1974).

Above tidewater, the river regime shifts dramatically. In the case of the Cayapas, the floodplain narrows between densely forested hills rising up to 70 m in height. Banks are high, and, in more entrenched sections, floods on the order of a 15 m rise in river level may occur after heavy rains. On these high-banked patches of alluvium, the Chachi build their stilt houses with floors elevated above all but the most severe of floods. The current is swift and the first rapids appear just below the mouth of the Zapallo Grande. The latter are an impediment to canoe traffic only during low water. More substantial rapids, at times resembling cascades, occur up the San Miguel and the Río Grande, the two headwater affluents of the Cayapas (fig. 1.1).

The Santiago presents a somewhat different aspect. It is wider and shallower than the Cayapas, with strong and capricious currents throughout its course. Upriver from the Bogotá, the channel often divides into a series of rapids that braid around cobble-strewn islands. In these stretches, upstream navigation requires pushing or dragging the dugout against a powerful current. Beyond Playa de Oro, canoe travel becomes infeasible altogether and further upstream travel is perforce overland.

Distances and travel times between major settlements on the Santiago and the Cayapas are given in figs. 2.2 and 2.3 respectively. Travel times pertain to the dugout canoe, the traditional watercraft in the area, and are estimated on the basis of itineraries collected in the field. These estimates are of the coarsest sort and apply to a 4 m dugout with two paddlers and a cargo consisting of two

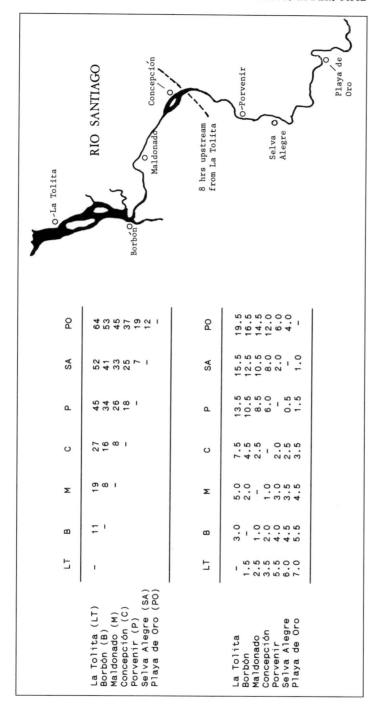

RIO SANTIAGO

O–La Tolita

Borbón O

Maldonado O

Concepción O

8 hrs upstream
from La Tolita

O–Porvenir

Selva
Alegre O

Playa de
Oro O

Distance matrix (kilometers):

	LT	B	M	C	P	SA	PO
La Tolita (LT)	–	11	19	27	45	52	64
Borbón (B)		–	8	16	34	41	53
Maldonado (M)			–	8	26	33	45
Concepción (C)				–	18	25	37
Porvenir (P)					–	7	19
Selva Alegre (SA)						–	12
Playa de Oro (PO)							–

Travel times (hours):

	LT	B	M	C	P	SA	PO
La Tolita	–	3.0	5.0	7.5	13.5	15.5	19.5
Borbón	1.5	–	2.0	4.5	10.5	12.5	16.5
Maldonado	2.5	1.0	–	2.5	8.5	10.5	14.5
Concepción	3.5	2.0	1.0	–	6.0	8.0	12.0
Porvenir	5.5	4.0	3.0	2.0	–	2.0	6.0
Selva Alegre	6.0	4.5	3.5	2.5	0.5	–	4.0
Playa de Oro	7.0	5.5	4.5	3.5	1.5	1.0	–

Fig. 2.2 Estimated distances and travel times in paddled dugout on Santiago River. Upper left, Distance matrix in kilometers. Lower left, Travel times in hours; numbers above the matrix diagonal pertain to upstream travel, those below to downstream travel. Right, Map of the Santiago with cited settlements.

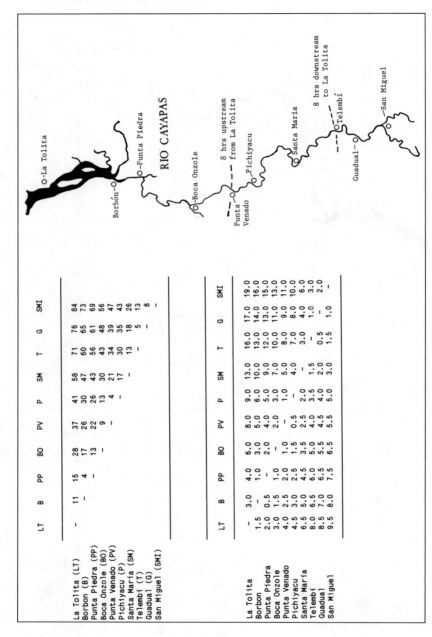

	LT	B	PP	BO	PV	P	SM	T	G	SMI
La Tolita (LT)	–	11	15	28	37	41	58	71	76	84
Borbón (B)		–	4	17	26	30	47	60	65	73
Punta Piedra (PP)			–	13	22	26	43	56	61	69
Boca Onzole (BO)				–	9	13	30	43	48	56
Punta Venado (PV)					–	4	21	34	39	47
Pichiyacu (P)						–	17	30	35	43
Santa María (SM)							–	13	18	26
Telembí (T)								–	5	13
Guadual (G)									–	8
San Miguel (SMI)										–

	LT	B	PP	BO	PV	P	SM	T	G	SMI
La Tolita	–	3.0	4.0	6.0	8.0	9.0	13.0	16.0	17.0	19.0
Borbon	1.5	–	1.0	3.0	5.0	6.0	10.0	13.0	14.0	16.0
Punta Piedra	2.0	0.5	–	2.0	4.0	5.0	9.0	12.0	13.0	15.0
Boca Onzole	3.0	1.5	1.0	–	2.0	3.0	7.0	10.0	11.0	13.0
Punta Venado	4.0	2.5	2.0	1.0	–	1.0	5.0	8.0	9.0	11.0
Pichiyacu	4.5	3.0	2.5	1.5	0.5	–	4.0	7.0	8.0	10.0
Santa María	6.5	5.0	4.5	3.5	2.5	2.0	–	3.0	4.0	6.0
Telembí	8.0	6.5	6.0	5.0	4.0	3.5	1.5	–	1.0	3.0
Guadual	8.5	7.0	6.5	5.5	4.5	4.0	2.0	0.5	–	2.0
San Miguel	9.5	8.0	7.5	6.5	5.5	5.0	3.0	1.5	1.0	–

Fig. 2.3   Estimated distances and travel times in paddled dugout on Cayapas River. The format is identical to that of fig. 2.2.

young children, a raceme of plantains, and a chicken or two. There is, of course, an inherent asymmetry in river travel depending on whether one is going with or against the current. This asymmetry has interesting implications for river-based interactions. For instance, from Telembí on the upper Cayapas, approximately eight hours of paddling are required to reach La Tolita near the coast. According to the Chachi, even the hardiest of voyageurs is unlikely to paddle for more than six to eight hours per day, so from the perspective of a resident of Telembí, La Tolita can be regarded as the limit of a day's travel. The return trip, however, takes sixteen hours or two days of travel. From the perspective of La Tolita, there-fore, Telembí is well beyond a day's striking distance. These asymmetries should be kept in mind when attempting to understand riverine settlement patterns in the past, particularly during the period when La Tolita reigned as the paramount center and port of the region.

Ultimately Andean drainages, the Santiago and Cayapas are also fueled by a substantial local precipitation. Whether in the form of generally brief morning or afternoon showers or as night-long torrents, rain is routine. At our base camp on the upper Cayapas, Morpheus announced himself nightly with a pelting of the roof thatch above. Moon and stars were rarely seen, and it is unsurprising that the Chachi make little of generally invisible lunar and astral movements. Regard-less of season, things get wet, particularly, it would seem, inside the plastic con-tainers favored by visiting gringos.

What strikes the outsider as uniformly excessive wetness is subject, however, to significant regional, seasonal, and year-to-year variation. Mean annual rainfall increases inland from the coast according to a clear gradient (see bioclimate in fig. 2.7). On the drier coast, 2000 mm/yr is average, whereas 5000 mm or more characterizes the upper reaches of the Santiago and Cayapas, where moisture-saturated clouds are driven against the Andean foothills. Although always in ample supply, rainfall tends to be greater in the months of March through May; how-ever, there is no consistent rainy season. In 1983, for instance, September was the wettest month (fig. 2.4). Mean values also obscure the great variability in total annual precipitation. For example, annual rainfall at Zapallo Grande on the upper Cayapas has ranged from 4300 to 7200 mm over a twenty year period (fig. 2.5).

The generally heavy rainfall and the absence of a salient dry season have an important bearing on local agricultural practices. Perhaps most noticeable is the replacement of a "slash-burn" approach to field clearance by what West calls a "slash-mulch" technique. In West's (1957: 129) words:

> For most of the humid tropics of the world, native shifting agriculture is usually described as "slash-burn" cultivation, implying the use of fire in clearing the plots. Throughout most of the Pacific lowlands, however, the heavy precipitation and lack of a dry season preclude the effective use of fire. Instead a peculiar system, which might be called "slash-mulch" cultiva-tion, of probable Indian origin, has evolved. Seeds are broadcast and rhizomes and cuttings are planted in an uncleared plot; then the bush is cut; decay of cut vegetable matter is rapid, forming a thick mulch through which the sprouts from the seeds and cuttings appear within

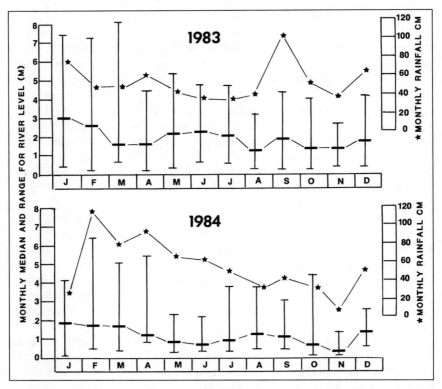

Fig. 2.4   *Monthly rainfall at Zapallo Grande and median river level at nearby Telembí on the upper Cayapas during 1983–84. Zapallo Grande data for figs. 2.4 and 2.5 provided by Lester Meisenheimer, a local Protestant missionary.*

a week or ten days. Weeds are surprisingly few, and the crops grow rapidly, the decaying mulch affording sufficient fertilizer even on infertile hillside soils.

Occupants of the Santiago-Cayapas, whether Chachi or black, continue to be faithful slashers and mulchers. In their view, only ignorant outsiders such as the recent immigrants from Manabí, resort to burning. As suggested by West, there is every reason to believe that the slash-mulch strategy is an ancient one. In the late sixteenth century, Cabello de Balboa (1945: 16) attributed it to the Barbacoas, as he called the inhabitants of what is today the northern Esmeraldas and neighboring Colombian coast. In this regard, it is interesting to note that our auger probes, when free of sherds, were equally barren of charcoal, perhaps an indication that fire was never an important technique among prehistoric farmers of the region (compare Sanford et al. 1985).

The river not only provides water for bathing, drinking, boiling plantains, washing clothes, and floating canoes, but it is also a source of food. No systematic inventory of riverine fauna is available, but Mitlewski (1985) records nearly

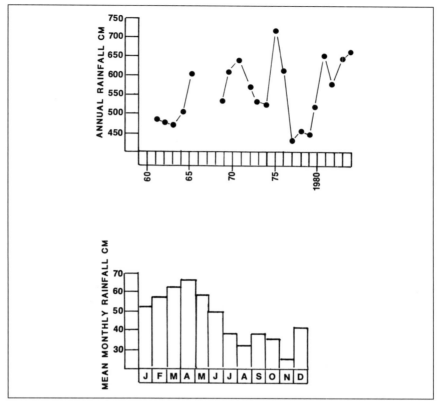

Fig. 2.5   Top, *Annual rainfall at Zapallo Grande during the period 1961–84.* Bottom, *Average monthly rainfall at Zapallo Grande during the period 1961–84.*

thirty species of edible fish, among which the *sábalo* figures prominently in the diet, and at least fifteen taxa of crustaceans including various freshwater shrimp and a crab that the Chachi call *jaihua*. Fished through an assorted technology of nets, harpoons, traps, hook and line, poisons, and even dynamite, the river's harvest, although declining and now often supplemented by canned tuna, is still a vital part of the subsistence economy. The forest is also an essential resource.

The Fabled Forest

On one trek inland from the upper Cayapas, I found a glass bottle with the label MINERAL WASSER, a relic from the turn of the century when the Germans were quite active in the area. This sort of "small thing forgotten" always energizes the archaeologist's imagination, and I wondered how many soldiers died on the fields of Europe with their uniforms buttoned by *tagua* palm nuts extracted from the forests of the Santiago-Cayapas. Tagua (*Phytelephas aequatorialis*), also an important source of roof thatch and other construction material, produces a so-called vegetable ivory that, until the mass production of plastics after World War II, was a major source of the world's buttons. Today, with natural products in fashion, the tagua industry is making a comeback (Barfod et al. 1990).

The imagined German who tossed his bottle along the trail may very well have been enchanted by the surrounding dark forest, the *Urwald* flanking zones of human settlement. The Chachi and blacks think in a related manner and populate their arboreal surroundings with all sorts of creatures: gigantic snakes, superferocious jaguars, anthropomorphic giants and dwarfs, ogres, and nymphs— generally sinister beings that devour the flesh, steal the soul, hurl death-dealing darts, or seduce the unwary away from cultural proprieties.

However magical and potentially dangerous, the forested interfluves are a regularly utilized landscape. Their corrugated topography is studded with modern agricultural clearings, ancient archaeological sites, and equally ancient but still-used trails that follow the tops of knifelike ridges. The highest exceeding 100 m in elevation, these ridges are remnants resulting from the erosional work of a maze of esteros. The esteros range from wide streams that are navigable by dugout in their lower courses to narrow, unnavigable creeks that are ankle-deep during low water but that become raging torrents after heavy rains.

The forest itself is typically composed of two to three stories or strata (West 1957: 40–41). Reaching up to 30 m in height, the upper stratum includes a variety of tree species that are often supported by buttressed roots. Among these are the *chanul* (*Humiriastrum procerum*) and red-barked *sande* (*Brosimum utile*), both favored for canoe construction; the *carrá* (*Huberodendron patinoi*); the *chalviande* (*Virola* sp.); the *damajagua* (*Poulsenia armata*), the source of bark cloth; the giant *ceiba* (*Ceiba pentandra*); the tropical cedar or *cedro* (*Cedrela odorata*); and the extremely hard-wooded *guayacán* (*Tabebuia guayacan*), the preferred wood for house posts. A second story, centering around 10 m in height, includes an assortment of slender-trunked trees among which the following palms figure prominently: *pambil* (*Socratea* sp.), *gualté* (*Wettiria utilis*), *milpeso* (*Jessenia polycarpa*), and the aforementioned *tagua* (*Phytelephas aequatorialis*). A third stratum consists of ferns, shrubs, vines, and seedlings that in closed forest form a relatively sparse undercover.

The substrate of rocks and soils that supports this dissected terrain of forested ridges separated by esteros has not been studied in fine-grained detail, but we do have the general survey prepared by the joint French-Ecuadorian team of ORSTOM-PRONAREG (Office de la Recherche Scientifique et Technique Outre-Mer Acuerdo Mag—Programa Nacional de Regionalización Agraria). The available ORSTOM-PRONAREG maps for the Santiago-Cayapas are reproduced in simplified form in the four panels of figs. 2.6 and 2.7. Following ORSTOM-PRONAREG terminology, these figures summarize the pedology (soils), geology, agricultural conditions, and bioclimate, the last largely a derivative of the previously discussed mean annual precipitation.

The coastal plain of Esmeraldas is part of the Bolívar Geosyncline, which stretches from the Darién southward to the Guayas drainage of southwestern Ecuador. The seaward margins of this great fold are now largely truncated or submerged by the Pacific, but the sequence of downward-sloping deposits is still evident on the mainland. As seen in fig. 2.6, the Andean foothills are banked by lutites (muds lithified to varying degrees) of Eocene age. Seaward, the deposits form a horizontally stratified record of subsequent Tertiary and Pleistocene sedimentation: Oligocene deposits extend just downriver from San Miguel; Miocene sediments extend downriver to Telembí; Mio-Pliocene deposits reach Borbón; and seaward from Borbón, as discussed earlier, is a series of geologically recent beach lines.

Not unexpectedly, soils display a significant, although not perfect, correlation with their geological underpinnings. The upriver early Tertiary deposits are weathered to a ridge topography characterized by steep (70°) slopes and generally shallow soils tending toward the acidic. Downriver, the Mio-Pliocene–derived formations have gentler slopes and are less subject to erosion. Further seaward, the terrain flattens and is capped by Quarternary deposits variably subject to water saturation and high salinity. Cutting through this banded progression of deposits are the ribbons of alluvium-enriched levees and floodplains flanking the major drainages— strips of real estate stolen from the Andes. Volcanic eruptions in the cordillera have also left their mark in tuffs and ashes intercalated with the local lutites. These volcanic imports, potentially of great significance to an understanding of soil variability, have not yet received the study they deserve, nor have the volcanic deposits that provide such useful stratigraphic markers for the Jama-Coaque cultural area to the south (Isaacson n.d.) been identified in the Santiago-Cayapas.

If geology and pedology are autocorrelated and if bioclimate is largely a reflection of mean annual rainfall, then the ORSTOM-PRONAREG "agricultural indices" represent the ultimate conflation of all these incestuous variables. Furthermore, these indices usually express negative conditions. One might get the impression from looking at fig. 2.6 and fig. 2.7 that farming is a rather hopeless enterprise in most of the Santiago-Cayapas: slopes are steep, and soils are acidic and subject to aluminum toxicity or waterlogging. In fact, however, *agriculture* comprises a host of human and plant interactions that are not directly determined by the physicality of rocks, soils, and water. The Chachi farmer on the upper Cayapas, for instance, does not plant on 70° slopes! Nor does he plant just anywhere within the general soil zones mapped in fig. 2.6.

When selecting a field for a *platanal,* a Chachi farmer sensibly avoids slopes conducive to erosion and, with equal sense, avoids the red to yellow-colored clays of low fertility. The preferred soils are described as either "sandy" or "black" (*tierra llena de humo* in the local parlance). These latter soils are said to occur in patches both along the river and inland. (Judging by the frequency with which archaeological sites occur in contemporary agricultural fields, I suspect that "black" soils are, in part, anthropogenic; this possibility is currently being investigated

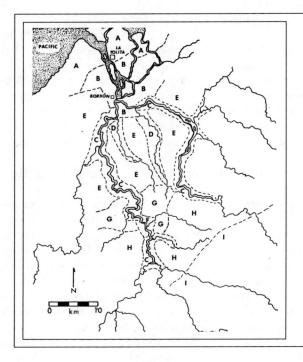

Pedology

A: Marine-fluvial deposits; sands and calcareous clays; mangroves, swamps, and braided esteros.

B: Dissected plain of marine-fluvial deposits; deep clayey soils with problems of water-saturation and salinity.

C: Fluvial deposits banking high terraces; sands, clays, and muds.

D: Fluvial deposits banking high terraces (otherwise as C).

E: Sandstones and conglomerates highly weathered in variegated clay matrix; clayey soil with problem of Al toxicity; pH 4–5.5; slopes >25°.

F: Sandstones and conglomerates; clayey soils with frequent rock outcrops; slopes ~70°.

G: Shales and clays intercalated with sands and tuffs; slopes variable but reach 70°; pH 4–5.5.

H: Mosaic of variability dominated by clays intercalated with sandstones; slopes generally > 70°.

I: Shallow soils with frequent rock outcrops; slopes often > 70°; silicified sandstones and quartxites.

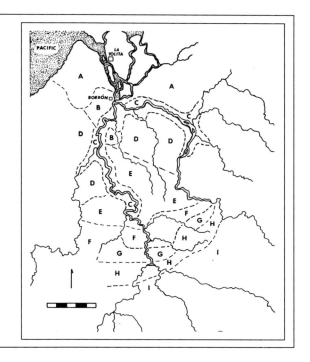

Geology

A: Quarternary littoral deposits.

B: Cachibí formation (Pliocene).

C: Recent alluvial and colluvial deposits.

D: Borbón formation (Mio-Pliocene); sandstones with con-
      glomerate and tuff lenses.

E: Onzole formation (Mio-Pliocene); stratified lutites inter-
      calated with volcanic ash and tuff.

F: Angostura formation (Miocene); fossiliferous, greenish
      sandstones

G: Pambil formation (Oligocene-Miocene); tabular, speckled
      sandstone containing shell fragments.

H: Playa Rica formation (Oligocene); lutites intercalated with
      sandstone conglomerates.

I: Zapallo formation (Eocene); hard gray lutites intercalated
      with sandstone; cherts common.

Fig. 2.6   *Pedologic and geologic indices as rendered in* ORSTOM-
PRONAREG *survey of Santiago-Cayapas.*

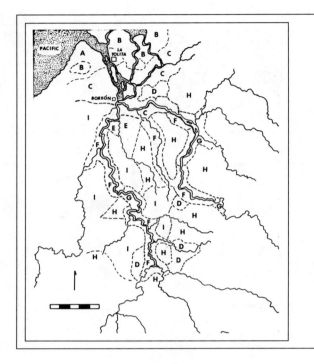

Agriculture

A: Sandy coastal soils.

B: Mangroves.

C: Alluvial clays; problems with water-logging and Al toxicity; pockets of volcanic ash.

D: Clays on moderate relief; volcanic ash locally; problem of Al toxicity.

E: Shallow clayey soils over undulating relief; problem of Al toxicity.

F: Alluvial clays.

G: Sandy soils on ancient beaches and terraces, flooding frequent.

H: Clay soils on steep slopes (40–70°); problem of Al toxicity.

I: Variable soils under forest; frequent rock exposures.

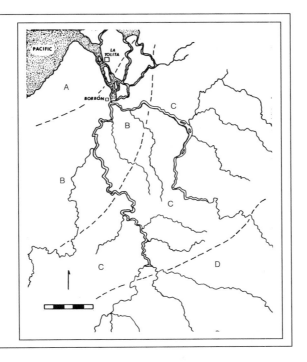

Bioclimate

A: Humid, 1300–2500 mm annual precipitation.

B: Very humid, 2000–4000 mm annual precipitation.

C: Super-humid, 3000–6500 mm annual precipitation; moderate solar deficit.

D: Super-humid with high cloud cover and high solar deficit.

Fig. 2.7   *Agricultural and bioclimatic indices as rendered in* ORSTOM-PRONAREG *survey of Santiago-Cayapas.*

by Claire Allum of the University of Calgary in dissertation research on Chachi land use patterns.) To be most effectively exploited, fields should be within an hour's travel time or so from the house or settlement—the two tend to be the same, as most of the Chachi continue to live in dispersed, single-house settlements. Beyond this radius, a *rancho* or field house is built at the site of the distant field (but see DeBoer 1989: 485).

As the words for agricultural field suggest (*platanal* in Spanish, *platano* meaning banana; *pandapala* in Chachi, *panda* meaning banana), the plantain is the focal staple throughout the Santiago-Cayapas. Coming in a number of varieties with varying edaphic requirements and culinary properties, plantains are indeed the staff of life, each adult consuming on the order of a *mano* or bunch per day. Depending on whether the fruit is eaten green or ripe, nine to eleven months after the corm or rootstock is planted, a "stem" of fruit is ready to harvest. After it bears fruit, the stalk is cut down, and new fruit-bearing stalks emerge. Depending on soils, a platanal may continue to produce for up to twenty years, with five to six years being cited as typical. Plantains are most commonly eaten boiled; they may also be processed into a heavy, stuffing-like mass called *bala.* Although connoisseurs will have lengthy discussions about the relative flavors and textures of various batches of *bala,* to me it was always monotonously tasteless.

Almost certainly a post-Columbian introduction, plantains now dominate the subsistence economy, yet the *platanal* or Chachi *pandapala* is hardly a monocultural field free of indigenous cultigens. Maize is often planted with the plantain rootstocks and matures in a quick three to four months. Two maize harvests may thus be obtained before the growing plantains block off sunlight. Among the Chachi, maize is ordinarily processed to *champu,* a drink particularly popular during Christmas gatherings at ceremonial centers (see chapter 9). Other native crops include *rascadera* or *badú* (*Xanthosoma* sp.), two varieties of manioc (*Manihot esculenta*), and a botanically unidentified root crop locally called *chirma.* Coffee and cacao are also widely grown as commercial crops.

In addition to the "outfields" where the bulk of the diet is produced, every Chachi settlement is also associated with a house garden (*rastrojo* in Spanish) in which a number of useful plants are carefully tended. Although variable in composition, these gardens frequently include papaya (*Carica papaya*), star-apple or *caimito* (*Chrysophyllum caimito*), *guayaba* (*Psidium guajava*), *guagua* (*Inga* sp.), avocado (*Persea* sp.), soursop or *guanábana* (*Annona muricata*), *madroño* (*Rheedia* sp.), *zapote* (*Achras* sp.), and *chontaduro* (*Bactris gasipaes*). In addition to these arboreal crops, a *rastrojo* also typically includes one or more *azoteas* or elevated garden beds (usually decrepit canoes potted with soil) in which various condiments and medicinal herbs are planted.

Chachi agricultural practices, therefore, are complex adaptations that produce and manage a series of interstices—pockets that escape from, insinuate into, or even alter the environmental fixture. A further example of this point is the fate of "abandoned" fields and house sites. In fact, such sites are not abandoned at all. They continue as sources of useful tree crops and a variety of successional flora.

Walking across a former house site with a local informant, my colleague Sara Stinson was introduced to a welter of plants, more resembling a pharmacopoeia than a weedy aftergrowth: *Santa María*—its leaves are good for headaches; *gualanga*—its flowers stop nosebleeds; *Doña Juana,* an herb, and *batatilla,* a liana—both snakebite remedies; *churco*—administered as an enema for intestinal ailments; *lengua vaca*—good for liver problems; and *cordoncillo*—another alleged snakebite cure. The list for this one plot exceeds forty useful plants. Clearly there is a system of floral knowledge at work in the Santiago-Cayapas that rivals those of the better studied Ecuadorian Amazon (e.g., Schultes and Raffauf 1990; also see Holm-Nielsen et al. 1983 and Holm-Nielsen and Barfod 1984).

Although fish are the major protein source, hunting in the forests is also avidly pursued, the shotgun being the universal arm (the blowgun, a traditional weapon of the Chachi, is no longer used). The sweet and fatty flesh of large rodents such as the agouti or *guantín* (*Dasyprocta* sp.), the capybara (*Hydrochaeris hydrochaeris*), and the paca or *guanta* (*Agouti paca*) is particularly prized. A more common catch, however, is the smaller spiny rat (*Proechimys* spp.), a nocturnal animal caught in traps set along trails. Forest dwellers that are no longer abundant are peccaries (both white-lipped and collared), Baird's tapir (*Tapirus bairdii*), and the red brocket deer (*Mazama americana*). Also very rare today, the black spider, red howler, and white-cheeked capuchin monkeys were formerly common game species (West 1957: 164). Other game includes sloths, armadillos, iguanas, and toucans.

Exploited for their oil and meat during the eighteenth and nineteenth centuries and more recently for their hides, the formerly abundant crocodile (*Crocodilus acutus*) and cayman (*Caiman sclerops*) have practically become extinct. Felines such as the ocelot or *tigrillo* (*Felis pardalis*) and the jaguar (*Felis onca*), also valued for their skins, are rare indeed. Two highly venomous snakes that are killed to rid the forest of their presence are the fer-de-lance (*Bothrops* sp.) and bushmaster (*Lachesis* sp.). This policy seems to have little impact on the snake population, however, and snakebite continues to be a significant cause of death.

Finally, to complete this geographical survey, mention should be made of the disease environment. Today, malaria, both of the vivax and of the falciparum varieties, is endemic throughout the Santiago-Cayapas and is a leading cause of death. Equally ominous is the growing incidence of onchocerciasis or river blindness. In the early 1980s, the infection rate exceeded 50% for both basins, with rates among the Chachi of the upper Cayapas topping 80% (Guderian et al. 1983). It should be remembered that both of these scourges, malaria and river blindness, along with a host of other diseases (such as cholera, which swept the area in 1991), are introductions from the Old World and did not figure in the prehistory of the Santiago-Cayapas.

3
SKETCHING THE SEQUENCE

The construction of a reliable chronology is a basic archaeological task. Without a sound chronology, any inferences about subsistence, settlement, or social systems in the past are likely to be historical monstrosities. The main mission of this chapter is to develop a cultural sequence for the Santiago and Cayapas basins on the basis of stratigraphy, seriation, and a set of not always friendly radiocarbon dates. The sketched sequence is preliminary and not without problems.

Before the actual material is confronted, a confession should be aired. The following is written, by and large, in a confirmatory mode. After surface collecting scores of sites, digging several stratigraphic probes, and drawing thousands of the recovered artifacts, I became fairly well acquainted with the range of artifact variability in the sampled archaeological record and, on the basis of this familiarity, formed some strong impressions about what the chronological sequence ought to be. It would be the conventional lie of the scientific method to suggest that the following exercises are "discovering" the chronology. Rather, they are evaluating (and rationalizing to colleagues) discoveries already made.

These hypotheses or hunches are phrased in terms of phases, those "practicable and intelligible units of archaeological study" (Willey and Phillips 1958: 22). In principle, a phase is a taxonomic unit that is tightly defined in terms of time, space, and cultural content; in practice, however, it is often used more loosely to refer to any resolvable "chunk" of culture history that is too localized to be a "horizon" and too short-lived to be a tradition. Felicity aside, the following presentation is geared to phases composed of formally similar assemblages derived from both excavated and surface contexts. Whether such phases are arbitrary slices of an essentially seamless continuum in which everything is "transitional" or whether they represent real disjunctures in the pace of change is an important issue best addressed once a sound relative chronology calibrated by independent chronometric dates is established. Now to the data, beginning with the stratigraphy of deposits and their encased artifacts.

Stratigraphy

Paul Bahn (1989: 62) provides a loose but otherwise permissible definition of stratigraphy: "The different layers encountered in a site, one above the other. In general, given a pair of layers, the upper one is younger than the one that lies beneath." I would amend Bahn's gloss by pointing out that, with exceptions, stratigraphic logic applies not only to layers but also to their associated cultural contents. The more serious should consult Harris's (1979) definitive treatment, although the spare and simple stratigraphic evidence from the Santiago-Cayapas does not require the complex wiring diagram of a "Harris matrix."

Of several sites where limited excavations were conducted, four furnish evidence for ceramic stratigraphy. These cases can be described quickly and are summarized in fig. 3.1. The details of excavation are given later. At C69, thick deposits of Guadual ceramics (see correlative chapters for the definition of this and other ceramic phases) are superposed over deposits containing a mix of Mafa and Selva Alegre sherds. Within the latter mix, however, Mafa sherds tend to have a deeper and probably precedent distribution. At nearby C36, deep Guadual deposits rest on a thin layer of Selva Alegre materials without Mafa admixture. As Mafa, Selva Alegre, and Guadual ceramics each occur repeatedly in single-component surface deposits, the combined evidence from C69 and C36 suggests a temporal sequence that runs from Mafa through Selva Alegre to Guadual.

A third stratified site is C55, where a substantial Herradura midden covers a scatter of Guadual sherds including an associated pit filled with only Guadual materials. A fourth and final case is R30, where deep deposits of Las Cruces ceramics are separated from an underlying Selva Alegre midden by a virtually sterile clay layer. Although the R30 stratigraphy demonstrates the precedence of Selva Alegre to Las Cruces, it does not specify the temporal placement of the latter with respect to Guadual or Herradura. Such specification requires additional evidence.

To anticipate such evidence, return to fig. 3.1, where a composite sequence, one only partly determined by stratigraphy, is presented. A seriational argument to be developed later places Tumbaviro after Herradura, while a number of specific features shared by Herradura and Las Cruces suggests that the two are essentially contemporary phases centering on the Cayapas and Santiago, respectively. Bouchard's (1985) ceramic sequence from the Tumaco region (just across the Colombian border), outlined in the right-hand column of fig. 3.1 along with associated radiocarbon dates, provides an additional and independent cross-check. At this point, no major contradictions emerge in the proposed chronological ordering, but perhaps they are waiting to happen.

Seriation

By seriation is meant the placement of sets of associated artifacts in a series based on their similarity wherein the order of the series is believed to represent change over time. Phrased as such, seriation commits itself to culture as a learned, even quasigenetic, entity that is transmitted with considerable fidelity, but never flawlessly, from generation to generation. In the seriational scheme of things, any contemporary constellation of cultural traits embodies simultaneously legacies

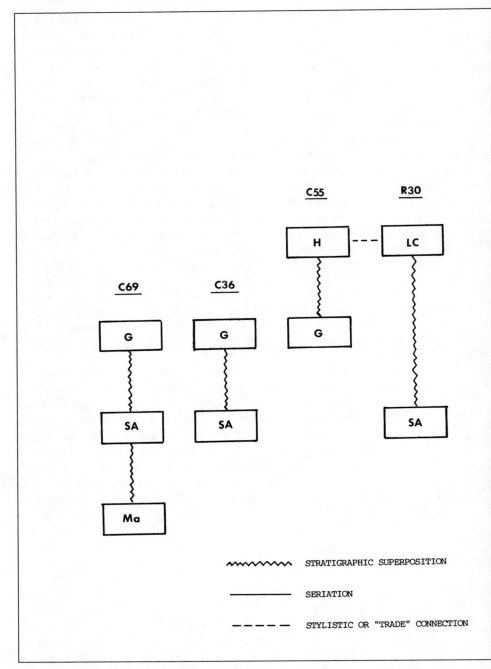

Fig. 3.1   *Stratigraphic relations among phases at four sites* (left), *derived composite sequence* (center), *and comparative sequence from Tumaco* (right).

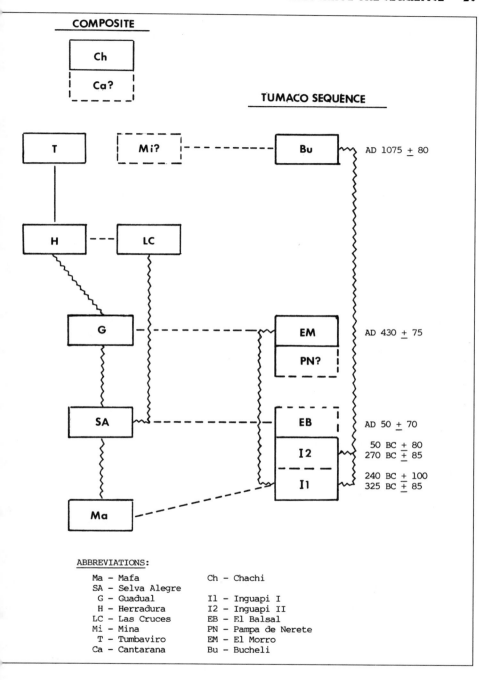

COMPOSITE

Ch

Ca?

TUMACO SEQUENCE

T

Mi?

Bu — AD 1075 ± 80

H — LC

G — EM — AD 430 ± 75

PN?

SA — EB — AD 50 ± 70

I2 — 50 BC ± 80 / 270 BC ± 85

I1 — 240 BC ± 100 / 325 BC ± 85

Ma

ABBREVIATIONS:

Ma — Mafa   Ch — Chachi
SA — Selva Alegre
 G — Guadual   I1 — Inguapi I
 H — Herradura   I2 — Inguapi II
LC — Las Cruces   EB — El Balsal
Mi — Mina   PN — Pampa de Nerete
 T — Tumbaviro   EM — El Morro
Ca — Cantarana   Bu — Bucheli

from the past and harbingers of the future. In general, this is a plausible premise, although any particular seriation is always a hypothesis, one to be evaluated against independent stratigraphic or chronometric evidence.

The following seriational exercises are eclectic. With common artifact categories, such as ceramic bases, a frequency seriation is possible. In the case of rarer categories, such as spindle whorls or figurines, a presence-or-absence approach is more appropriate.

Paste

Of the more than sixty-five thousand sherds collected during fieldwork, some are decorated, some are rims and provide clues to vessel shape, but all possess a fabric of color and texture. For some time now, Paul Tolstoy and his students at the University of Montreal have been developing a paste typology designed to seriate this class of abundant ceramic evidence. An initial rendition of this seriation has been published previously (Tolstoy and DeBoer 1989: fig. 2) and will not be repeated here.

Wall Thickness

Sherds not only have a paste but also a thickness that may have both functional and chronological significance (e.g., Braun 1983). Wall thickness (a measurement best taken on uninflected body sherds) has not yet been tabulated for most of the Santiago-Cayapas collections, and the following results pertain to a sample of about twelve hundred measurements. As seen in fig. 3.2, there is a clear trend from thin to thick vessel walls beginning with Mafa and ending with Tumbaviro. Between these poles, the thickness data display a directionality that conforms to the independent testimony of stratigraphy. A similar trend toward increasing wall thickness over time has been noted by Guinea Bueno (1988) for the Esmeraldas-Atacames area.

Pigmentation

The percentage of sherds bearing traces of paint or pigmented slip also varies systematically (fig. 3.2). Pigmentation is relatively rare in Mafa, increases dramatically to reach its greatest frequency in Guadual, and subsequently diminishes to virtual absence in Tumbaviro.

Bases

A wide variety of base forms is represented by more than five hundred complete or fragmentary specimens. This variety can be reduced to several categories, for which site-by-site distribution is given in tables 3.1 and 3.2. These categories are as follows:

1. annular or ring base;
2. *pata* (Spanish for foot and leg of an animal): in sets of three or more, patas, as Ecuadorian archaeologists regularly call these vessel supports, come in the variety of forms illustrated in fig. 3.3;

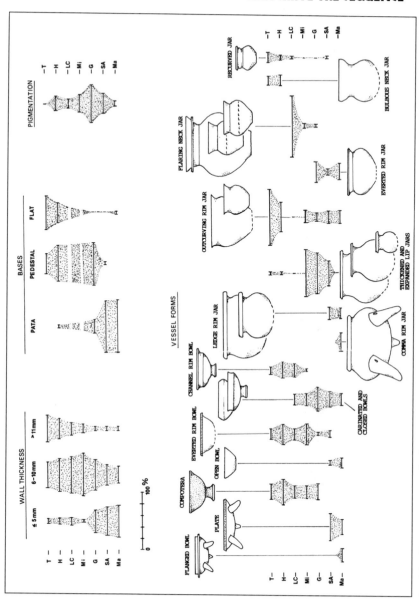

Fig. 3.2 Frequency seriation of wall thickness, base form, pigmentation, and vessel form. Phases abbreviated as in fig. 3.1.

Table 3.1 *Distribution of annular bases and patas.*

	PROVENIENCE	ANNULAR BASE	PATA Hollow Oversize	Hollow Conical	Hollow Mammiform	Hollow Elaborated	Solid Perforated	Solid Simple
TUMBAVIRO	C6	–	–	–	–	–	–	–
	C20	–	–	–	–	–	–	–
	C30	–	–	–	–	–	–	–
	C48	–	–	–	–	–	–	–
	C55-III	–	–	–	–	–	–	–
	C101	–	–	–	–	–	–	–
	C108	–	–	–	–	–	–	–
	C121	–	–	–	–	–	–	–
	C131	–	–	–	–	–	–	–
	C133	–	–	–	–	–	–	–
	C136	–	–	–	–	–	–	–
	C41	–	–	–	–	–	–	–
	C29	–	–	–	–	–	–	–
	C7	–	–	–	–	–	–	–
	C5	–	–	–	–	–	–	–
	C102	–	–	–	–	–	–	–
	C110	–	–	–	–	–	–	–
	C137	–	–	–	–	–	–	–
	C82	–	–	–	–	–	–	–
	C4	–	–	–	–	–	–	–
	C2-3	–	–	–	–	–	–	–
	C25	–	–	–	–	–	–	–
	C28	–	–	–	–	–	–	–
	C32	–	–	–	–	–	–	–
	C53	–	–	–	–	–	–	–
	C96	–	–	–	–	–	–	–
	C34	–	–	–	–	–	–	–
	C39	1	–	–	–	–	–	–
HERRADURA	C139	–	–	–	–	–	–	–
	C49-50	–	–	1	–	–	–	–
	C55-II	–	–	–	–	–	1	1
	C57	1	–	–	–	–	–	–
	C130	–	–	–	–	–	–	–
	C138	–	–	–	–	–	–	–
	R28	–	–	1	–	–	–	–
	C45	–	–	–	–	–	–	–
	C56	–	–	–	–	–	–	–
	C129	–	–	–	–	–	–	–
	C10	–	–	1	–	–	–	–
LAS CRUCES	R60	–	–	–	–	–	1	–
	R61	–	–	–	–	–	–	–
	R19	–	–	–	–	–	–	–
	R43	–	–	–	–	–	–	–
	R30-II	–	–	1	–	1	–	–
MINA	R47	–	–	–	–	–	–	–
	R49	–	–	2	–	1	–	1
	R55	–	–	–	–	–	–	–
	R57	–	–	–	–	–	–	–
	R62	–	–	1	–	–	–	–
	R63	–	–	–	–	–	–	–
	R66	1	–	2	1	–	–	–

	PROVENIENCE	ANNULAR BASE	PATA					
			Hollow Oversize	Hollow Conical	Hollow Mammiform	Hollow Elaborated	Solid Perforated	Solid Simple
GUADUAL	C62	–	–	–	–	–	–	–
	C63	–	–	2	–	–	–	–
	C51	–	–	–	–	–	–	–
	C55–I	–	–	–	1	–	2	1
	C69–III	1	–	1	–	–	–	1
	C36–II	1	–	5	–	–	–	1
	R10–II	–	–	4	–	–	–	–
	R2	–	–	2	–	–	1	–
	C54	–	–	–	–	–	–	–
	C68	–	–	–	–	–	–	–
	C98	–	–	–	–	1	–	–
SELVA ALEGRE	R3	–	–	–	–	–	–	–
	R10–I	–	–	3	1	–	–	–
	C61	–	–	6	2	–	–	4
	R9	–	–	2	1	–	–	–
	R46	–	–	1	–	–	–	1
	C73	–	–	2	–	–	–	–
	R24	–	–	9	6	–	–	2
	R27	–	–	1	–	–	–	–
	R35	–	–	1	–	–	–	–
	R36–I	1	–	15	–	–	–	1
	R37	–	–	1	–	–	–	–
	R41	–	–	–	2	–	–	–
	C69–II	–	–	5	–	–	–	1
	C81	–	–	1	–	–	–	–
	C90	–	–	2	1	–	–	–
	C141	–	–	1	–	–	–	–
	C36–I	–	–	2	–	–	–	–
	R25	–	1	5	–	–	–	–
MAFA	R6	–	–	1	–	–	–	–
	R16	–	–	1	–	–	–	–
	C11–18	–	6	6	–	–	–	7
	C116	–	–	1	–	–	–	1
	C123	–	–	1	–	1	–	2
	C69–I	–	1	1	–	–	–	3
	C33	–	3	–	–	–	–	1
	R38	–	5	5	1	–	–	2
	C76B	–	1	–	–	–	–	–
	C89	–	16	13	1	–	–	–
TOTAL BY PHASE								
	TUMBAVIRO	1	–	–	–	–	–	–
	HERRADURA	1	–	3	–	–	1	1
	LAS CRUCES	–	–	1	–	1	1	–
	MINA	1	–	5	1	1	–	1
	GUADUAL	2	–	14	1	1	3	3
	SELVA ALEGRE	1	1	57	13	–	–	9
	MAFA	–	32	29	2	1	–	16

Table 3.2   *Distribution of pedestal, round, and flat bases.*

| | | PEDESTAL | | | | ROUND BASE | FLAT BASE |
PROVENIENCE	Hollow Simple	Cande-labrum	Indented Bottom	Concave Bottom	Solid Flat		
TUMBAVIRO							
C6	–	–	–	–	–	–	1
C20	–	–	–	–	–	–	1
C30	–	–	–	–	–	–	1
C48	–	–	–	–	–	–	1
C55-III	–	–	–	–	–	–	1
C101	–	–	–	–	–	–	1
C108	–	–	–	–	–	–	1
C121	–	–	–	–	–	–	1
C131	–	–	–	–	–	–	1
C133	–	–	–	–	–	–	1
C136	–	–	–	–	–	–	1
C41	–	–	–	–	1	–	2
C29	–	–	–	–	1	–	3
C7	–	–	–	–	1	–	3
C5	–	–	–	–	2	–	2
C102	–	–	–	–	2	–	3
C110	–	–	–	–	1	–	3
C137	–	–	–	–	2	–	1
C82	–	–	–	–	–	2	12
C4	–	–	–	3	6	–	5
C2-3	–	–	–	1	1	–	4
C25	–	–	–	2	–	–	1
C28	–	–	–	3	1	–	2
C32	–	–	–	1	–	–	3
C53	1	–	–	–	1	–	6
C96	1	–	–	–	–	–	1
C34	1	–	–	1	2	–	2
C39	1	–	–	–	–	–	–
HERRADURA							
C139	–	–	–	–	–	–	1
C49-50	2	–	–	4	2	1	10
C55-II	17	1	–	16	9	–	17
C57	–	–	–	–	–	–	1
C130	1	–	–	–	1	–	–
C138	–	–	–	1	–	–	**1**
R28	–	–	–	1	–	–	–
C45	1	–	–	–	–	–	–
C56	1	–	–	–	–	–	–
C129	1	–	–	–	–	–	–
C10	1	–	–	–	–	–	–
LAS CRUCES							
R60	–	–	–	–	–	–	–
R61	–	–	–	2	–	–	–
R19	2	–	–	–	–	–	–
R43	2	–	–	–	–	–	–
R30-II	2	–	–	–	–	–	–
MINA							
R47	1	–	–	–	–	–	–
R49	3	–	–	–	–	–	–
R55	–	1	–	–	–	–	–
R57	1	–	–	–	–	–	–
R62	1	–	5	–	–	–	–
R63	1	–	–	–	–	–	–
R66	3	–	–	–	–	–	–

	PROVENIENCE	PEDESTAL Hollow Simple	Cande-labrum	Indented Bottom	Concave Bottom	Solid Flat	ROUND BASE	FLAT BASE
GUADUAL	C62	1	1	-	-	-	-	-
	C63	-	1	-	-	-	-	-
	C51	1	2	-	-	-	-	-
	C55-I	-	4	-	-	-	-	-
	C69-III	2	4	4	-	-	-	1
	C36-II	11	6	9	3	-	4	-
	R10-II	12	1	2	-	-	2	-
	R2	1	-	-	-	-	-	-
	C54	2	-	-	-	-	-	-
	C68	1	-	-	-	-	-	-
	C98	-	-	-	-	-	-	-
SELVA ALEGRE	R3	1	-	-	-	-	-	-
	R10-I	-	-	-	-	-	-	-
	C61	-	-	-	-	-	-	-
	R9	-	-	-	-	-	-	-
	R46	2	-	-	-	-	-	-
	C73	1	-	-	-	-	-	-
	R24	-	-	-	-	-	-	-
	R27	-	-	-	-	-	-	-
	R35	-	-	-	-	-	-	-
	R36-I	-	-	-	-	-	-	-
	R37	-	-	-	-	-	-	-
	R41	-	-	-	-	-	-	-
	C69-II	-	-	-	-	-	-	-
	C81	-	-	-	-	-	-	-
	C90	-	-	-	-	-	-	-
	C141	-	-	-	-	-	-	1
	C36-I	-	-	-	-	-	-	1
	R25	-	-	-	-	-	-	-
MAFA	R6	-	-	-	-	-	-	-
	R16	-	-	-	-	-	-	-
	C11-18	-	-	-	-	-	-	2
	C116	-	-	-	-	-	-	-
	C123	-	-	-	-	-	-	-
	C69-I	-	-	-	-	-	-	-
	C33	-	-	-	-	-	-	1
	R38	-	-	-	-	-	-	-
	C76B	-	-	-	-	-	-	-
	C89	-	-	-	-	-	-	-

TOTAL BY PHASE

	Hollow Simple	Cande-labrum	Indented Bottom	Concave Bottom	Solid Flat	ROUND BASE	FLAT BASE
TUMBAVIRO	4	-	-	11	21	2	64
HERRADURA	24	1	-	22	12	1	30
LAS CRUCES	6	-	-	2	-	-	-
MINA	10	1	-	-	-	-	-
GUADUAL	31	19	15	3	-	7	1
SELVA ALEGRE	4	-	-	-	-	-	2
MAFA	-	-	-	-	-	-	3

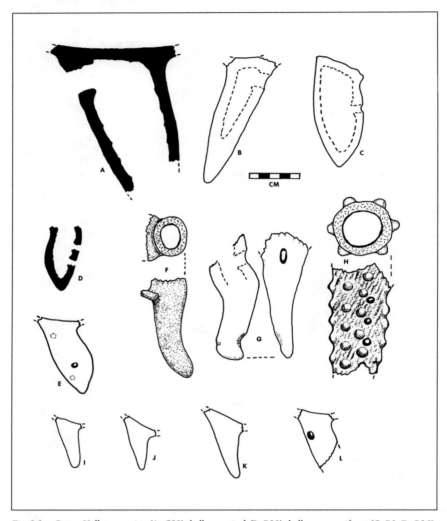

Fig. 3.3   *Patas. Hollow oversize (A, C89); hollow conical (B, R28); hollow mammiform (C, R9; D, R36I; E, C89); hollow elaborated (F, R30II; G, R38; H, C123); solid simple (I, R36I; J, C61; K, C123); solid perforated (L, C55II). H has a brushed surface embellished with perforations and nubbins.*

3. pedestal: the great range in form and decorative treatment of pedestal bases is shown in fig. 3.4;
4. round base;
5. flat base.

Of these general categories, only patas, pedestals, and flat bases are sufficiently common to lend themselves to a frequency analysis. As portrayed in fig. 3.2, the frequency shifts in these three forms are clear enough. Patas dominate in Mafa

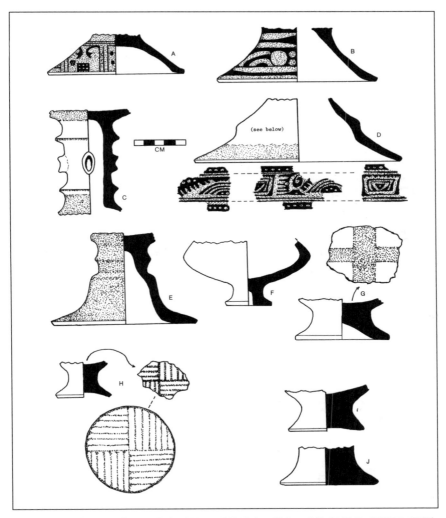

Fig. 3.4 Pedestal bases. Hollow simple (A, C36II; B, C69III); "candelabrum" (C, R10II; D, C69III; E, C36II); indented bottom (F, C36II); concave bottom (G, C55II; H, C55II); solid flat (I, C4; J, C34). Here and elsewhere, stippling indicates a red paint or slip; the black designs in A, B, and D indicate resist decoration. The reconstructed design in H is not to scale.

and Selva Alegre and subsequently decline. Pedestals proliferate in Guadual and continue through Tumbaviro, whereas flat bases, although present in most phases, are common only in Herradura and Tumbaviro. Not only do these general base categories seriate quite well, but specific varieties within these categories also make seriational sense. For instance, the "hollow oversized" pata (fig. 3.3A) is a Mafa hallmark. Hollow pedestals, including the so-called candelabrum (fig. 3.4C–E), are salient Guadual characteristics, whereas later pedestals tend to be solid with concave or flat bottoms (fig. 3.4G–J).

Table 3.3   Distribution of vessel forms by phase.

VESSEL FORM	MAFA	SELVA ALEGRE	GUADUAL	MINA	LAS CRUCES	HERRA-DURA	TUMBA-VIRO
Ladle	-	5	-	-	-	-	-
Double Spout and Bridge	2	1	8	1	-	-	-
Miniature Pinch Pot	-	-	3	-	1	7	-
Griddle	1	1	2	1	-	1	-
Biglobular Vessel	-	-	-	-	1	1	-
Square Vessel	-	1	-	1	-	-	-
Plate Direct Rim	5	9	-	-	-	-	-
Plate T-shape Rim	10	16	-	-	-	-	-
Plate Cornice Rim	-	53	-	-	-	-	-
Plate Everted Rim	-	7	-	-	-	-	-
Open Bowl Flanged	13	-	-	-	-	-	-
Open Bowl Direct Rim	10	14	-	(-)	(-)	(-)	(-)
Open Bowl Carinated	5	11	-	-	1	-	-
Open Bowl Everted Rim	-	19	14	27	12	35	10
Open Bowl Thickened Lip	-	-	-	-	-	18	7
Compotera Direct Rim	-	-	56	(18)	(13)	(63)	(26)
Compotera Beveled Rim	-	-	44	-	-	-	-
Closed Bowl Direct Rim	4	19	55	6	4	-	-
Closed Bowl Carinated	4	15	71	-	-	-	-
Closed Bowl Buttress Rim	-	-	24	-	10	1	-
Bowl Channel Rim	-	-	1	4	16	38	13
Bowl Trellis Decoration	-	-	-	10	-	-	-
Comma Rim Basin	5	24	2	3	-	2	4
Rampiral Cup	-	-	-	-	1	6	2
Jar Ledge Rim	12	37	-	-	-	-	-
Jar Comma Rim	18	-	-	-	-	-	-
Jar Cambered Rim	4	3	1	6	1	-	-
Jar Outcurving Rim	14	37	50	17	-	73	93
Jar Expanded Lip	-	42	178	63	-	7	6
Jar Everted Rim	17	18	133	-	-	1	-
Jar Thickened Lip	3	22	-	-	-	-	-
Small Thick Wall Jar	-	7	4	-	-	-	-
Jar Tall Flaring Neck	-	-	1	3	34	-	-
Jar Short Flaring Neck	-	-	-	3	34	-	-
Jar Wedge Rim (I)	-	10	73	2	-	-	-
Jar Wedge Rim (II)	-	-	11	-	-	-	-
Jar Cornice Rim	-	1	-	-	-	-	-
R49 Jar	-	-	-	3	-	-	-
C69 Jar	-	-	13	-	-	-	-
San José Jar	-	-	2	3	3	-	-
Jar Recurved Rim	-	5	4	-	2	12	16
Jar Bulbous Neck	-	-	-	-	-	26	14
Jar Convergent Neck	-	-	-	2	1	-	2
Total	127	377	750	173	134	291	193

Grand Total: 2045

Entries in parentheses indicate the occasional ambiguity in distinguishing compoteras from open bowls.

Vessel Forms

More than two thousand rim sherds, including several complete or totally reconstructible vessels, were recovered during survey and excavations. These data will carry a heavy burden when ceramic phases are formally described in later chapters. Here this evidence is only sketched. Table 3.3 presents the phase distribution of forty-three recognized vessel forms. Fig. 3.2 plots the relative fre-

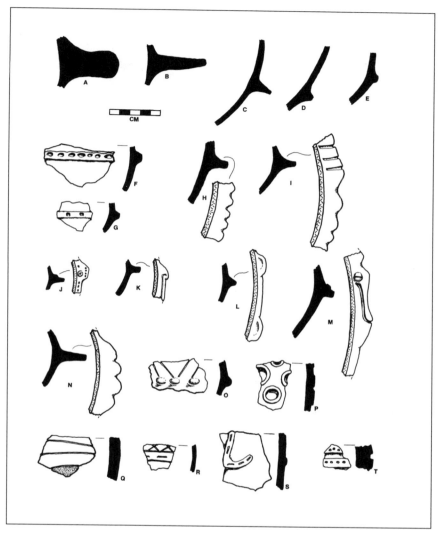

Fig. 3.5   Flanges and other miscellaneous features. Continuous massive (A, C123); continuous extended (B, C123); continuous medium (C, C33); diminutive plain (D, R3; E, C55II); diminutive punctate (F, C14; G, C36I); continuous scalloped (H, R36I; I, C90); discontinuous modeled (J, R10I; K, C61; L, C89; M, C97); discontinuous scalloped (N, C69II); nubbins (O, R10I); stamping (P, C36I); fine-line incision (Q, C61; R, C69I); curved fillet (S, R19); deep punctation (T, C36I).

quency of fifteen of the more common of these forms. Although not an ideal plot in that a few forms (e.g., everted rim bowls) fluctuate in frequency over time, overall the vessel evidence paints a rather coherent seriational picture.

Flanges and Other Odds and Ends

Flanges, handles, and a variety of decorative techniques comprise a lingering

Table 3.4   *Distribution of flanges.*

PROVENIENCE		Continuous Massive	Continuous Extended	Continuous Medium	Diminutive Plain	Diminutive Punctate	Continuous Scalloped	Discontinuous Modeled	Discontinuous Scalloped	Impressed Fillet
TUMBA-VIRO	C4	–	–	–	–	–	–	–	–	–
	C34	–	–	–	–	–	–	–	–	–
	C38	–	–	1	–	–	–	–	–	–
	C53	–	–	–	–	–	–	–	–	1
HERRA-DURA	C10	–	–	2	–	–	–	–	–	–
	C49–50	–	–	–	–	–	–	–	–	–
	C55–II	–	–	4	2	–	–	1	1	1
	R28	–	–	1	–	–	1	1	–	–
LAS CRUCES	C93	–	–	–	–	–	–	–	–	2
	R19	–	–	–	–	–	–	–	–	5
	R30–II	–	–	2	–	–	1	–	1	6
	R43	–	–	–	–	–	–	–	–	3
	R60	–	–	–	–	–	–	–	–	4
	R61	–	–	–	–	–	–	–	–	2
MINA	R12	–	–	–	–	–	–	–	–	–
	R36–II	–	–	–	–	–	–	–	–	–
	R47	–	–	–	–	–	–	–	–	–
	R48	–	–	–	–	–	–	–	–	–
	R49	–	1	–	–	–	–	–	–	–
	R50	–	–	–	–	–	–	–	–	–
	R55	1	1	–	–	–	–	–	–	–
	R62	–	–	–	–	–	1	–	–	–
	R63	–	–	1	–	–	–	–	–	1
	R64	–	1	1	–	–	–	–	–	–
	R65	–	–	–	–	–	–	–	–	1
	R66	–	–	4	1	–	2	–	–	1
GUADUAL	R2	–	–	1	–	–	–	–	–	–
	R10–II	–	–	4	3	2	–	2	1	2
	C36–II	–	1	7	1	2	–	3	–	–
	C51	–	1	–	1	–	–	–	–	–
	C54	–	–	–	–	–	–	–	–	1
	C55–I	–	–	–	–	–	1	–	–	4
	C62	–	–	–	–	–	–	–	–	–
	C68	–	1	–	–	–	–	–	–	–
	C69–III	1	1	1	–	–	–	–	–	16
	C91	–	–	–	–	–	–	–	–	–
SELVA ALEGRE	R3	–	–	–	1	–	–	–	–	–
	R4	–	–	1	–	–	–	–	–	–
	R9	–	1	1	–	–	–	–	–	–
	R10–I	1	–	5	1	–	–	1	1	–
	R24	–	–	1	3	–	1	–	–	–
	R25	–	–	4	2	–	2	1	–	–
	R27	–	–	–	–	–	1	–	–	–
	R35	–	–	2	–	–	1	1	–	–
	R36–I	–	–	–	1	1	1	4	1	–
	R37	–	–	1	–	–	–	–	–	–
	R41	–	1	–	–	–	1	–	–	–
	R46	–	–	–	–	–	–	–	–	–
	C36–I	1	3	5	3	2	1	3	–	–
	C61	–	1	–	1	–	–	1	–	–
	C69–II	1	6	–	–	–	–	–	1	–
	C73	–	–	18	–	–	1	–	2	–
	C74	–	–	–	1	–	–	–	–	–
	C90	–	–	2	–	–	2	–	–	–
	C97	–	–	1	–	–	–	1	–	–
	C141	–	–	1	–	–	–	–	–	–

PROVENIENCE	Continuous Massive	Continuous Extended	Continuous Medium	Diminutive Plain	Diminutive Punctate	Continuous Scalloped	Discontinuous Modeled	Discontinuous Scalloped	Impressed Fillet
R6	-	1	2	-	-	-	-	-	-
R16	1	-	-	-	-	-	-	-	-
R18	-	-	-	1	-	-	-	-	-
R20	-	1	-	-	-	-	-	-	-
R21	-	-	-	-	-	-	-	-	-
R38	1	-	-	1	-	-	2	-	-
C11-18	5	2	2	-	3	-	-	-	-
C33	1	-	1	-	1	-	-	-	-
C69-I	-	-	-	-	-	-	-	-	-
C89	1	-	-	-	1	1	1	-	-
C92	-	-	1	-	-	-	-	-	-
C107	1	-	-	-	-	-	-	-	-
C123	1	1	-	-	-	-	-	-	-

(MAFA)

TOTAL BY PHASE

	Continuous Massive	Continuous Extended	Continuous Medium	Diminutive Plain	Diminutive Punctate	Continuous Scalloped	Discontinuous Modeled	Discontinuous Scalloped	Impressed Fillet
TUMBAVIRO	-	-	1	-	-	-	-	-	1
HERRADURA	-	-	7	2	-	1	2	1	1
LAS CRUCES	-	-	2	-	-	1	-	1	22
MINA	1	3	6	1	-	3	-	-	3
GUADUAL	1	4	13	5	4	1	5	1	23
SELVA ALEGRE	3	12	42	13	3	11	12	5	-
MAFA	11	5	6	2	5	1	3	-	-

Table 3.5   *Distribution of decorative techniques and handles.*

| | PAINT | | | TEXTURING/APPLIQUE | | | | HANDLE | |
PROVENIENCE	White and Red	Resist	Brushing	Nubbin	Fine Line Incision	Curved Fillet	Deep Punctation	Loop	Strap
TUMBAVIRO									
C4	–	–	–	–	1	–	–	–	–
C34	–	–	–	–	–	–	–	1	–
C38	–	–	–	–	–	–	–	–	–
C53	–	–	–	–	–	–	–	–	–
HERRADURA									
C10	–	–	–	–	–	–	–	–	–
C49–50	–	–	–	–	2	–	–	–	–
C55–II	–	–	–	–	1	1	–	–	–
R28	–	–	–	–	–	–	–	–	–
LAS CRUCES									
C93	–	–	–	–	–	–	–	–	–
R19	–	–	–	1	–	1	–	1	–
R30–II	–	–	–	1	–	–	–	–	–
R43	–	–	–	1	–	–	–	1	–
R60	–	–	–	–	–	–	–	–	–
R61	–	–	–	–	–	–	–	1	–
MINA									
R12	–	–	–	–	1	–	–	–	–
R36–II	–	–	–	–	4	–	–	–	–
R47	–	–	–	–	4	–	–	–	–
R48	–	–	–	–	1	–	–	–	–
R49	–	–	–	–	1	1	–	–	–
R50	–	–	–	–	5	–	–	–	–
R55	–	–	–	–	1	–	–	–	–
R62	2	–	–	–	2	1	–	–	–
R63	–	–	–	–	2	–	–	–	–
R64	–	–	–	–	–	–	–	–	–
R65	–	–	–	–	1	–	–	–	–
R66	1	–	–	–	–	–	–	–	–
GUADUAL									
R2	–	–	–	–	1	–	–	–	–
R10–II	2	1	3	5	–	–	–	–	–
C36–II	1	20	1	1	–	–	–	1	1
C51	–	–	–	–	–	–	–	–	–
C54	–	–	–	–	–	–	–	–	–
C55–I	1	–	2	–	1	1	–	–	–
C62	–	1	–	1	–	–	–	–	–
C68	–	–	–	–	1	–	–	–	–
C69–III	1	10	–	1	–	–	–	–	1
C91	–	–	–	–	–	1	–	–	–
SELVA ALEGRE									
R3	–	–	–	1	–	–	–	–	–
R4	–	–	–	–	–	–	–	–	–
R9	–	–	–	–	1	–	–	–	–
R10–I	1	–	14	5	3	1	4	–	–
R24	1	–	–	–	1	–	–	–	–
R25	–	–	–	–	1	–	–	–	–
R27	–	–	–	–	–	–	–	–	–
R35	–	–	–	–	–	–	–	–	–
R36–I	7	–	–	3	2	–	–	–	–
R37	–	–	–	–	–	–	–	–	–
R41	–	–	–	–	–	–	–	–	–
R46	–	–	–	–	1	–	–	–	–
C36–I	2	–	11	5	4	–	–	–	–
C61	–	–	6	–	4	1	1	–	–
C69–II	1	1	8	–	–	–	–	–	1
C73	–	–	–	1	–	–	–	–	–
C74	–	–	–	–	–	–	–	–	–
C90	–	–	–	–	–	–	–	–	–
C97	–	–	–	2	–	–	–	–	–
C141	–	–	–	–	1	–	–	–	–

		PAINT			TEXTURING/APPLIQUE				HANDLE	
PROVENIENCE		White and Red	Resist	Brushing	Nubbin	Fine Line Incision	Curved Fillet	Deep Punctation	Loop	Strap
	R6	–	–	2	–	1	–	–	–	–
	R16	–	–	1	–	–	–	–	–	–
	R18	–	–	–	–	–	–	–	–	–
	R20	–	–	1	–	–	–	–	–	–
	R21	–	–	1	–	–	–	–	–	–
	R38	–	–	1	–	3	–	–	–	–
MAFA	C11–18	–	–	23	–	–	–	–	–	–
	C33	–	–	12	3	1	–	–	–	–
	C69–I	–	–	3	–	1	–	–	–	–
	C89	–	–	–	–	–	–	–	–	–
	C92	–	–	–	–	–	–	–	–	–
	C107	–	–	–	–	–	–	–	–	–
	C123	–	–	7	1	–	–	1	–	1

TOTAL BY PHASE

	White and Red	Resist	Brushing	Nubbin	Fine Line Incision	Curved Fillet	Deep Punctation	Loop	Strap
TUMBAVIRO	–	–	–	–	1	–	–	1	–
HERRADURA	–	–	–	–	3	1	–	–	–
LAS CRUCES	–	–	–	2	–	1	–	2	–
MINA	3	–	–	–	22	2	–	–	–
GUADUAL	5	32	6	8	3	2	–	1	2
SELVA ALEGRE	12	1	39	17	17	2	5	–	1
MAFA	–	–	51	4	6	–	1	–	1

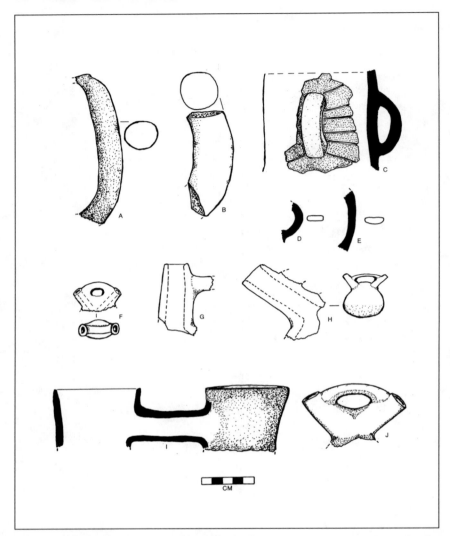

Fig. 3.6   *Handles and double-spout-and-bridge bottles. Loop handles (A, R19; B, R43); strap handles (C, C69III; D, C36II; E, C123); double-spout-and-bridge bottles (F, C36II; G, C55I; H, C55I; I, C55I; J, C69III).*

group of attributes often numerous enough to lend themselves to "chronology by counting." These attributes are "disembodied" in the sense that they usually cannot be situated accurately in the whole vessels from which they come; therefore, they are considered here rather than in the later detailed descriptions of vessel assemblages. The frequency of these attributes is listed in tables 3.4 and 3.5.

Flanges are numerous and come in the diversity of forms illustrated in fig. 3.5. As a group, flanges are early with the exception of a finger-impressed fillet that

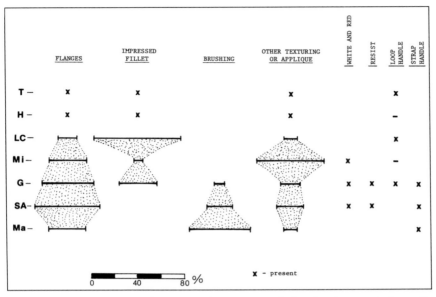

Fig. 3.7   *Composite frequency and presence-or-absence seriation of selected attributes. T, Tumbaviro; H, Herradura; LC, Las Cruces; Mi, Mina; G, Guadual; SA, Selva Alegre; Ma, Mafa.*

predominates in Las Cruces. Of the two painted decorative techniques, the bichrome white-and-red is a Selva Alegre specialty, whereas a black resist (*always* applied over a red slip) is a virtual monopoly of Guadual. Among textured decorative techniques, brushing is most common in Mafa, and incision (fig. 3.5Q–R) and nubbins (fig. 3.5O) become more popular in subsequent phases. Handles are rare, but the few examples suggest that the strap variety (fig. 3.6C–E) precedes the loop handle (fig. 3.6A–B). Figure 3.6 also illustrates several of the more complete specimens of double-spout-and-bridge bottles. This form, to be treated in later chapters, is uncommon except in Guadual.

A partial summary of the above observations is presented in fig. 3.7. Given that some attributes are too rare to be rendered as percentages, this figure combines presence-and-absence with frequency observations. Although the result resembles a reasonable seriation, the hourglass distribution of impressed fillets with a waist centered on Mina is bothersome. As will be seen on other occasions, Mina can be an "ill-behaving" phase whose seriational placement is problematic.

Despite problems, the above survey blocks out a fairly convincing seriation in which several classes of abundant evidence—wall thickness, base and vessel forms, and so on—are largely concordant with stratigraphy and with each other in terms of their chronological implications. There remains a residual body of information to which we now turn.

This additional evidence consists of those relatively rare but conspicuous items and "oddballs" that, regardless of occasional disclaimers, still furnish much of the emotional appeal of the archaeological enterprise. Furthermore, by embed-

Table 3.6   *Distribution of spindle whorls, figurines, and daub.*

PROVENIENCE	SPINDLE WHORL			Mold	FIGURINE			DAUB
	Simple Conical	Complex Conical	Oval		Hollow	Solid Plaque	Solid in Round	
TUMBAVIRO								
C34	2	–	–	–	–	–	–	–
C39	–	–	–	–	–	–	–	–
C55-III	2	–	–	–	–	–	–	–
C96	–	–	–	–	–	–	1	–
HERRADURA								
C10	1	–	–	–	–	–	–	–
C45	1	–	–	–	–	–	–	–
C49-50	1	1	–	–	–	–	1	–
C55-II	6	2	–	–	3	–	3	–
C57	–	–	–	–	–	–	1	–
LC								
R19	–	–	–	–	–	–	1	–
R30-II	–	–	–	–	–	–	6	1
R61	–	1	–	–	–	–	–	–
MINA								
R47	–	–	–	–	–	–	–	–
R49	–	–	–	–	–	–	–	–
R62	–	–	–	–	–	–	1	–
R63	–	–	–	–	–	–	–	–
R66	–	–	–	–	–	–	–	–
GUADUAL								
C36-II	–	–	–	–	2	–	10	–
C54	–	–	–	–	–	–	–	–
C55-I	–	–	–	–	2	–	1	–
C69-III	–	–	–	–	–	–	6	–
R10-II	–	–	–	–	1	2	2	–
SELVA ALEGRE								
C36-I	–	–	–	–	–	–	2	–
C61	–	–	–	–	–	2	–	–
C69-II	–	–	–	1	–	–	1	–
C73	1	–	1	–	–	1	–	1
C80	–	–	–	–	–	–	–	–
C81	–	–	–	–	–	–	–	–
C97	–	–	–	–	–	–	–	–
C141	–	–	–	–	–	–	–	–
R9	–	–	–	–	–	–	–	–
R10-I	–	–	–	–	–	–	1	–
R24	–	–	–	1	–	1	3	1
R25	–	–	–	–	–	–	2	1
R30-I	–	–	–	–	–	1	–	–
R31	–	–	–	–	–	–	–	–
R34	–	–	–	–	–	–	–	–
R35	–	–	–	–	–	1	1	–
R36-I	–	–	–	–	–	1	2	100
R46	–	–	–	–	–	–	–	–
MAFA								
C15	–	–	–	–	–	–	–	–
C89	–	–	–	–	–	–	–	1
R16	–	–	–	–	–	–	–	–
TOTAL BY PHASE								
TUMBAVIRO	4	–	–	–	–	–	1	–
HERRADURA	9	3	–	–	3	–	5	–
LAS CRUCES	–	1	–	–	–	–	7	1
MINA	–	–	–	–	–	–	1	–
GUADUAL	–	–	–	–	5	2	19	–
SELVA ALEGRE	1	–	1	2	–	7	12	103
MAFA	–	–	–	–	–	–	–	1

Table 3.7   *Distribution of graters.*

PROVENIENCE		Geometric Punctate	Linear Impressed	Uniface Impressed	Biface Impressed	Stone Studded
TUMBA-VIRO	C34	-	-	-	-	-
	C39	-	-	-	1	-
	C55-III	-	-	-	-	-
	C96	-	-	-	-	-
HERRA-DURA	C10	-	-	1	1	1
	C45	-	-	-	-	-
	C49-50	-	-	-	-	-
	C55-II	-	-	4	3	-
	C57	-	-	-	-	-
LC	R19	-	-	-	-	1
	R30-II	-	2	10	-	-
	R61	-	-	1	-	-
MINA	R47	-	1	-	-	-
	R49	-	-	2	1	-
	R62	-	-	-	-	-
	R63	-	-	1	-	-
	R66	-	1	-	-	-
GUADUAL	C36-II	-	-	2	-	1
	C54	-	-	1	-	-
	C55-I	-	-	3	-	-
	C69-III	1	-	9	1	2
	R10-II	2	-	5	-	-
SELVA ALEGRE	C36-I	-	-	-	-	-
	C61	-	-	1	-	3
	C69-II	-	-	-	-	-
	C73	-	-	-	-	-
	C80	-	-	-	-	1
	C81	-	1	-	-	-
	C97	1	-	-	-	-
	C141	-	-	1	-	-
	R9	-	-	1	-	-
	R10-I	-	-	-	-	-
	R24	-	-	-	-	1
	R25	-	-	-	-	1
	R30-I	-	-	-	-	-
	R31	-	-	1	-	-
	R34	-	1	-	-	-
	R35	-	-	1	-	-
	R36-I	3	2	7	-	-
	R46	-	-	2	-	1
MAFA	C15	-	-	-	-	1
	C89	-	-	-	-	-
	R16	-	-	1	-	-
TOTAL BY PHASE						
	TUMBAVIRO	-	-	-	1	-
	HERRADURA	-	-	5	4	1
	LAS CRUCES	-	2	11	-	1
	MINA	-	2	3	1	-
	GUADUAL	3	-	20	1	3
	SELVA ALEGRE	4	4	14	-	7
	MAFA	-	-	1	-	1

Table 3.8   Distribution of axes, adzes, and net sinkers.

	PROVENIENCE	T-shaped Axe	Adze	Celt	Butt of Axe or Adze	NET SINKER
			AXE/ADZE			
TUMBAVIRO	C2-3	–	–	–	–	–
	C4	–	–	1	–	–
	C5	–	1	–	–	–
	C7	–	–	–	1	–
	C22	–	–	–	1	–
	C29	–	1	–	–	–
	C30	–	–	–	–	–
	C32	–	–	–	–	–
	C34	–	–	1	–	–
	C41	–	1	–	–	–
	C44	–	–	1	–	–
	C113	–	–	–	–	–
	C126	–	–	1	1	–
	C6	–	–	–	–	–
	C38	–	1	–	–	1
	C55-III	–	–	1	–	–
HERRADURA	C130	–	–	2	–	–
	R28	–	–	–	1	1
	C40	–	–	–	–	–
	C49-50	–	1	–	–	–
	C55-II	–	6	–	9	10
	C57	–	–	–	–	1
LAS CRUCES	R19	–	1	1	2	–
	R43	–	–	–	–	–
	R30-II	–	–	–	–	–
MINA	R49	2	–	–	–	–
GUADUAL	R2	–	1	–	–	–
	R10-II	1	–	–	–	–
	C36-II	4	–	–	–	–
	C51	–	–	–	–	–
	C54	–	–	–	–	–
	C55-I	4	–	–	1	6
	C68	1	–	–	–	–
	C69-III	1	–	–	–	2
SELVA ALEGRE	R10-I	–	–	–	–	–
	R24	–	–	–	–	–
	R27	–	1	–	–	–
	R35	–	–	–	–	–
	R36-I	1	–	–	1	1
	R46	2	–	–	–	–
	C36-I	–	–	–	–	–
	C61	1	–	–	–	3
	C69-II	–	–	–	–	–
	C74A	–	1	–	–	–
	C141	–	1	–	–	1
TOTAL BY PHASE						
	TUMBAVIRO	–	4	5	3	1
	HERRADURA	–	7	2	10	12
	LAS CRUCES	–	1	1	2	–
	MINA	2	–	–	–	–
	GUADUAL	11	1	–	1	8
	SELVA ALEGRE	4	3	–	1	5
	MAFA	–	–	–	–	–

Table 3.9   Distribution of assorted ground stone artifacts and obsidian.

	PROVENIENCE	PESTLE	HAMMERSTONE	MEALING STONE			POLISHED DISC	POLISHED GREEN STONE	OBSIDIAN CHIP
				Mano	Metate	Piedra de Bala			
TUMBAVIRO	C2-3	-	-	-	-	2	-	-	-
	C4	-	-	-	-	1	-	-	-
	C5	-	-	-	-	-	-	-	-
	C7	-	-	-	-	-	-	-	-
	C22	-	-	-	-	-	-	-	-
	C29	-	-	-	-	-	-	-	-
	C30	-	-	-	-	1	-	-	-
	C32	-	-	-	-	1	-	-	-
	C34	-	-	-	-	1	-	-	-
	C41	-	-	-	-	-	-	-	-
	C44	-	-	-	-	1	-	-	-
	C113	-	-	-	-	1	-	-	-
	C126	-	-	-	-	-	-	-	-
	C6	-	-	-	-	-	1	-	-
	C38	1	1	-	-	-	-	-	1
	C55-III	1	-	-	-	2	-	-	-
HERRADURA	C130	-	-	1	-	-	-	-	-
	R28	-	-	-	-	-	1	1	-
	C40	-	-	1	-	-	-	-	-
	C49-50	-	-	1	-	-	-	-	-
	C55-II	1	1	2	-	-	-	2	2
	C57	-	-	-	-	-	-	-	-
LC	R19	-	-	1	-	-	-	1	-
	R43	1	-	-	-	-	-	-	-
	R30-II	-	-	-	1	-	-	-	1
MINA	R49	-	-	-	-	-	-	-	-
GUADUAL	R2	-	-	-	-	-	-	-	-
	R10-II	2	-	6	1	-	-	-	-
	C36-II	1	-	1	-	-	-	3	4
	C51	-	-	-	-	-	-	-	1
	C54	-	-	1	-	-	-	-	-
	C55-I	-	-	4	-	-	-	-	-
	C68	-	-	-	-	-	-	-	-
	C69-III	1	-	2	-	-	-	-	8
SELVA ALEGRE	R10-I	-	-	-	-	-	-	-	1
	R24	-	-	-	1	-	-	-	-
	R27	-	-	-	-	-	-	-	-
	R35	-	-	1	-	-	-	-	-
	R36-I	-	-	-	-	-	-	-	2
	R46	-	-	-	1	-	-	-	-
	C36-I	-	1	-	-	-	-	-	1
	C61	-	-	-	-	-	-	-	2
	C69-II	-	-	-	-	-	-	-	20
	C74A	-	-	-	-	-	-	-	-
	C141	-	-	-	-	-	-	-	1
TOTAL BY PHASE									
	TUMBAVIRO	2	1	-	-	10	1	-	1
	HERRADURA	1	1	5	-	-	1	3	2
	LAS CRUCES	1	-	1	1	-	-	1	1
	MINA	-	-	-	-	-	-	-	-
	GUADUAL	4	-	14	1	-	-	3	13
	SELVA ALEGRE	-	1	1	2	-	-	-	27
	MAFA	-	-	-	-	-	-	-	-

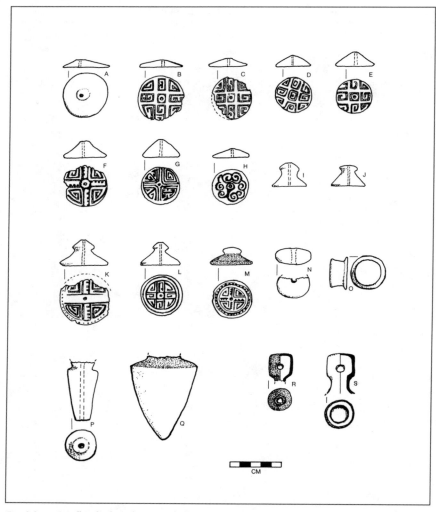

Fig. 3.8   Spindle whorls and more miscellanea. Simple conical (A, C55II; B, C10; C, C50; D, C55II; E, unprovenienced; F, C45; G, C55II; H, C55II); complex conical (I, unprovenienced; J, C55II; K, C45; L, C55II; M, R61); oval (N, C73); earspool (O, C36II); cone-shaped objects (P, C55II; Q, C55II); hollow perforated appendages (R, C55II; S, C55II).

ding treatment of ceramic figurines, spindle whorls, and the lapidary arts in a chapter devoted to chronology, I obviate the necessity of later text to "mop up" the interstitial miscellanea found in any archaeological collection. The distribution of these various items is given in tables 3.6 through 3.9.

Spindle Whorls

Of nineteen ceramic spindle whorls, seventeen pertain to the Herradura or

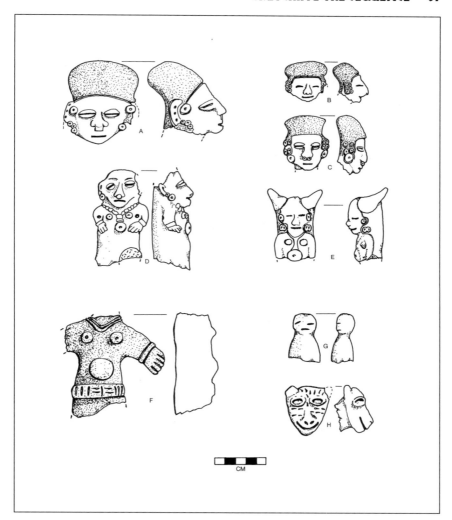

Fig. 3.9   Figurines (A–D, C36II; E–F, C69III; G, C55II; H, C96).

Tumbaviro segments of our developing chronology. These whorls have either a simple conical (fig. 3.8A–E) or complex conical (fig. 3.8I–M) shape. Some are plain, but most have bottoms stamped with geometric designs arranged in quadrant fashion around the spindle perforation. Two whorls from Selva Alegre contexts are plain and have an oval shape that is completely distinct from these Herradura and Tumbaviro examples (fig. 3.8N). Notably, the presence or absence of these durable ceramic whorls need not be a reliable guide to the importance of weaving (appendix 1). The Chachi, for instance, fashion their whorls from coconut shell or hardwood (Barrett 1925: 253).

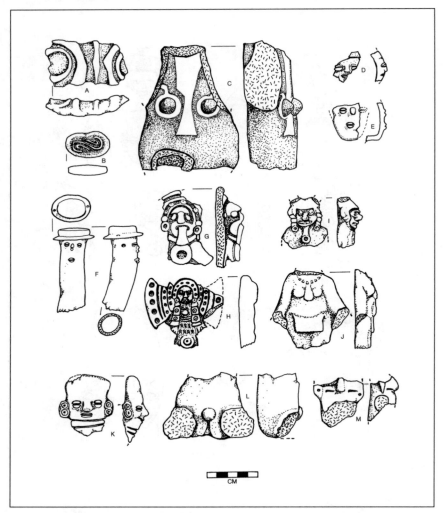

Fig. 3.10   *Molds or stamps (A, R24; B, C69II) and figurines (C–D, C36II; E–F, C55I; G, R24; H, R35; I–J, R36I; K, R10II; L, R24; M, R30II).*

More Ceramic Odds and Ends

A ceramic ear spool (fig. 3.8O), not dissimilar to those portrayed on figurines, was encountered in the Guadual deposits at C36. The Herradura midden at C55 produced several "mystery objects." These include two cone-shaped objects (fig. 3.8P–Q) and the hollow perforated appendages, conceivably parts of whistles, shown in fig. 3.8R–S.

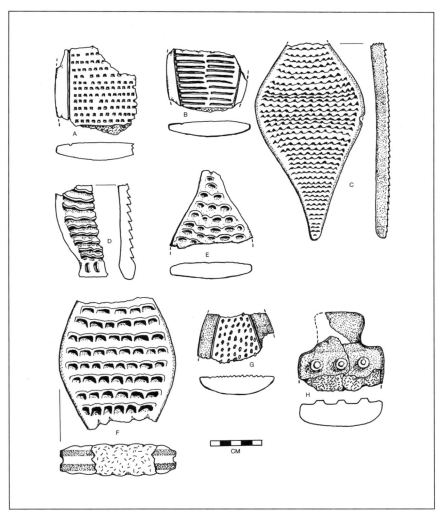

Fig. 3.11 "Graters." Geometric punctate (A, R36I); linear impressed (B, R36I); uniface impressed (C, R10II; D, R36I; E, C55I); biface impressed (F, C69III); stone-studded (G, C61); unique specimen (H, C36II).

Figurines

Although the Santiago-Cayapas region, especially the site of La Tolita, is renowned for its ceramic figurines (Uhle 1927, Ferdon 1945, Raddatz 1977, Sánchez Montañés 1981), such remains are relatively rare in common middens. Our sample is limited to sixty-four fragmentary specimens of which the more complete are shown in figs. 3.9 and 3.10. This array displays a bewildering variety that does not reduce readily to categorization. Perhaps the only obvious grouping is *A–C* of fig. 3.9; this trio of heads is clearly of classic La Tolita style (Valdez 1987: 60) and comes from the buried Guadual deposits at C36. In fact, almost all of the flamboyant and often iconographically rich figurines, whether solid (figs. 3.9*D–F*, 3.10*G–L*) or hollow (fig. 3.10*D–F*), are found in Selva Alegre or Guadual contexts. In addition, the two cases of figurine molds or stamps (fig. 3.10*A–B*) are of Selva Alegre provenience. In contrast, later phases display a decline and simplification of the figurine art. Examples include an elemental specimen assigned to Herradura (fig. 3.9*G*), a broken head from the Las Cruces deposits at R30 (fig. 3.10*M*), and a "smiling cat" adorno (fig. 3.9*H*). The latter, the only recovered Tumbaviro figurine, is significant in that it resembles a specimen attributed to the late prehistoric Atacames phase to the south (Alcina Franch 1979: lám. [plate] 26e).

It is worth mentioning that the "curing kit" (or *arte* in the local idiom) of a Chachi shaman typically includes ceramic figurines and ground stone axes. This recycling of the archaeological record for current purposes also includes utilitarian implements such as mealing stones (Barrett 1925:163).

Ceramic "Graters"

So-called graters, particularly the fish-shaped specimens of La Tolita (e.g., Labbé 1986: 66, Valdez 1987: 68), are virtually a motif of Esmeraldas archaeology. Yet, in fact, the actual use of these implements remains uncertain. Although often likened to the well-known manioc graters of greater Amazonia, most of these objects hardly seem well-suited to the shredding of manioc tubers. Most specimens are textured either unifacially (fig. 3.11*A–E*) or bifacially (fig. 3.11*F*). More rarely one surface is studded with small, sharp splinters of stone (fig. 3.11*G*). The latter stone-studded examples may indeed have been graters, but the more common textured variety probably had a different function. On one occasion in the field, our workmen suggested that these implements would be excellent fish-scaling devices and proceeded to demonstrate their point by scaling the catch of the day. Although this cannot be regarded as a critical experiment, I would wager that the local contemporary suggestion is more informed than the conventional archaeological interpretation. After all, the ichthyomorphy of these artifacts might suggest that they have something to do with fish. Scalers or graters are absent in Tumbaviro, exceedingly rare in Mafa, but reasonably common in other phases (table 3.7).

Adzes and Axes

Polished stone adzes and axes, the classical wood-working and tree-felling implements of the tropical forest, comprise a highly salient class of artifacts. Of fifty-eight recovered examples, a sample of complete specimens is illustrated in fig. 3.12. Adzes (fig. 3.12*D–H*) are distinguished from axes or celts by their asymmetrically worn bits, a wear pattern indicating that these implements were mounted and used normal to the plane of the haft. Axes may be T-shaped or

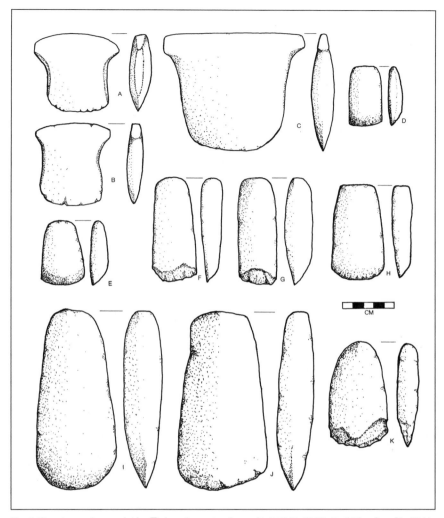

Fig. 3.12   Axes, adzes, and celts. **T**-shaped or waisted axes (A, R46; B, C36II; C, C61); adzes (D, C74A; E, C50; F, R19; G, C5; H, C29); celts (I, C4; J, C55III; K, C130).

waisted (fig. 3.12A–C) or, in the case of celts, lack any obvious hafting modification (fig. 3.12I–K). As shown in table 3.8, **T**-shaped axes have clear chronological precedence over celts, whereas the functionally distinct adzes occur throughout the sequence.

Net Sinkers

Twenty-six flat pebbles, notched on opposing edges, are identified tentatively as net sinkers (fig. 3.13A–G). This identification receives support from Chachi

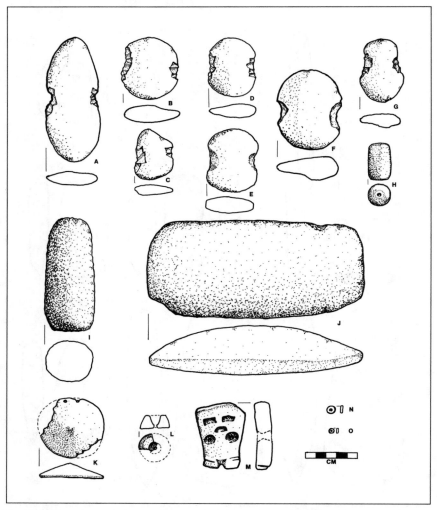

Fig. 3.13   *Net sinkers and other miscellanea. Sinkers (A, C55II; B–D, C55I; E, C69III; F, C61; G, C141);
possible ceramic sinker (H, R36I); pestle (I, C38); mano (J, C55I); polished pendant (K, C6); green stone
ear spool? (L, C36II); unidentified green stone object (M, C36II); green stone beads (N, C55I; O, C36II).*

ethnography where sinkers (*co poka*) consist of water-worn pebbles that are occasionally notched and tied to nets (Barrett 1925: 158). These nets are most commonly strung across the lower or middle reaches of esteros when shad-rich
floodwaters recede to the main channel. In this regard, it is probably significant
that twenty of the twenty-six recovered specimens come from the site of C55 (the
village of Herradura) where such net fishing is performed today. A perforated
ceramic cylinder (fig. 3.13H) seems somewhat large and heavy for a bead and
may represent a different style of sinker. As simple and utilitarian tools found in
most phases, net sinkers are not effective chronological markers.

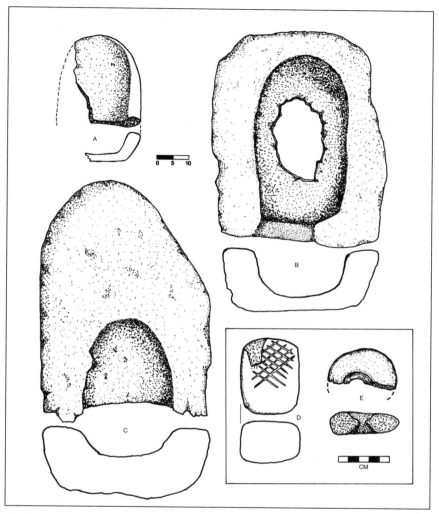

Fig. 3.14   Metates (A, R10I); piedras de bala (B, C4; C, C55III); bark-beater? (D, C4); perforated disc
(E, C55I).

Mealing Stones

Although found in most phases, mealing stones, food-processing implements, are relatively rare. They include manos (fig. 3.13J), metates (fig. 3.14A), cylindrical pestles (fig. 3.13I—matching mortars are not found), and gigantic grinding stones (fig. 3.14B–C). As heavy "furniture" unlikely to be casually moved, the latter constitute a virtual signature of Tumbaviro sites. Although immediately identified as *piedras de bala* by the Chachi, these large nether stones cannot be associated securely with the processing of any specific foods. *Bala* (a plantain-based mash and a staple of the Chachi) is an unlikely candidate given that plantains are presumably a post-Columbian introduction and that Tumbaviro sites almost certainly extend well back into prehistory.

Polished Discs

Herradura and Tumbaviro each produce a single example of a polished disc (fig. 3.13K). Both are perforated, as if worn as pendants, and are of highly polished, dark-colored stone.

Lithic Odds and Ends

Several items carved from a distinctive green stone occur in Guadual and subsequent phases (fig. 3.13L–O). Two of these objects are beads, whereas one may be an ear spool or pendant (fig. 3.13L). The green stone remains mineralogically unidentified.

One ground stone implement from C4, a Tumbaviro site, displays a diagonal mesh of engraved lines on one surface (fig. 3.14D). It could be a bark-beater, but this is a guess. The specimen does not resemble in any detail the alleged bark-beaters from Bahía (Estrada 1962: 200), nor is it similar to the wooden mallets still occasionally used by the Chachi and blacks to make their bark cloth sleeping mats. A remaining ground stone object is a perforated disc of unknown use (fig. 3.14E). Similar specimens are known from the Esmeraldas valley to the south (Rivera, et al. 1984: fig. 111a).

Finally, to end this catalogue, there is obsidian. Given the abundance of obsidian at La Tolita (Francisco Valdez, personal communication), the relative paucity of this material in sites of the Santiago and Cayapas basins is perhaps surprising. The sample is limited to forty-four pieces, forty of which are associated with Selva Alegre or Guadual. Twelve of these specimens were submitted to John Isaacson who, on the basis of neutron activation analyses, tentatively derives them from the Mullumica source located near the volcano of Antisana (Isaacson and Tolstoy, personal communications). None of the obsidian recovered from the Santiago-Cayapas includes clearly fashioned artifacts; rather it consists of debitage or unmodified flakes used as expedient tools. In this respect, obsidian does not differ from the chert and other siliceous flakes that are common at sites such as C36 and that appear to have been knapped ("bashed" is perhaps a better word) from water-worn nodules. These nodules are common on the present-day beaches of both the upper Santiago and Cayapas and presumably were so in the past. This informal flaked stone industry is currently being studied by Line Rigazio of the University of Montreal and will not be considered further here.

It is now time to stand back and attempt to summarize the seriational implications of this potpourri of sherds and stones: all the variously scaled attributes considered so far (tables 3.1–3.9) sum to 102. If daub and the ambiguous "axe or adze butt" are excluded, the total is an even hundred, a pleasant sum for calculation purposes. Of these, thirty-three or one third are particularly "well-behaved"

Table 3.10 Distribution of thirty-three selected attributes by phase.

	MAFA	SELVA ALEGRE	GUADUAL	MINA	LAS CRUCES	HERRADURA	TUMBAVIRO
Jar Comma Rim	X						
Open Bowl Flanged	X						
Pata Hollow Oversized	X	X					
Deep Punctation	X	X					
Plates	X	X					
Ledge Rim Jar	X	X					
Brushing	X	X	r				
Flange Diminutive Punctate	X	X	X				
Closed Carinated Bowl	X	X	X				
Strap Handle	X	X	X	X			
Flange Continuous Massive	X	X	X	X			
Flange Continuous Extended	X	X	X	X			
Pata Hollow Mammiform	X	X	X	X			
Double Spout and Bridge	X	X	X	X			
Cambered Jar	X	X	X	X			
Ladle	X	X	X		X		
Small Thick Wall Jar		X	X				
Wedge Rim Jar I		r	X				
Resist Decoration		r	X				
Red and White Painting		X	X				
T-Shaped Axe		X	X				
Pedestal Base		r	X				
Tall Flaring Neck Jar			X	X	X	X	X
San José Jar			X	X	X		
Loop Handle			X	X	X		
Channel Rim Bowl			r		X		
Impressed Fillet			r	X	X	X	X
Short Flaring Neck Jar			X	X	X	X	r
Celt					X		X
Complex Conical Whorl					X	X	X
Rampiral Cup					X	X	X
Simple Conical Whorl						X	X
Bulbous Jar						X	X

X, present; r, present but rare.

Table 3.11   Comparison of phases by shared attributes.

	Ma	SA	G	H	Mi	LC	T	
Ma	/	.51	.35	.20	.26	.16	.08	.26
SA	.51	/	.52	.35	.35	.25	.19	.36
G	.35	.52	/	.52	.44	.42	.27	.42
H	.20	.35	.52	/	.30	.44	.54	.38
Mi	.26	.35	.44	.30	/	.31	.23	.32
LC	.16	.25	.42	.44	.31	/	.30	.31
T	.08	.19	.27	.54	.23	.30	/	.26

	Ma	SA	G	H	Mi	LC	T	
Ma	/	.45	.27	.16	.26	.26	.08	.23
SA	.45	/	.37	.29	.27	.32	.20	.32
G	.27	.37	/	.37	.33	.31	.22	.32
H	.16	.29	.37	/	.44	.26	.54	.34
LC	.16	.29	.33	.44	/	.31	.30	.30
Mi	.26	.32	.31	.26	.31	/	.23	.28
T	.08	.20	.22	.54	.30	.23	/	.26

Top, matrix of Jaccard similarity coefficients based on entire sample of attributes; *bottom,* matrix of Jaccard similarity coefficients with each phase represented by 225 randomly drawn attributes.

Ma, Mafa; *SA,* Selva Alegre; *G,* Guadual; *H,* Herradura; *Mi,* Mina; *LC,* Las Cruces; *T,* Tumbaviro.

in that their presence-or-absence distributions can be arranged to form a nearly perfect seriation (table 3.10). Although there is no reason to expect all traits to be chronologically sensitive, I am not happy with a seriational solution that excludes two out of three attributes. A more convincing, if messier, solution would encompass *all* the evidence. The following is a simple attempt to do this.

Imagine a "megamatrix," a composite of all preceding tables in this chapter, consisting of seven rows for the phases and one hundred columns for the attributes. Cell entries are coded as either present or absent, ignoring the frequen-

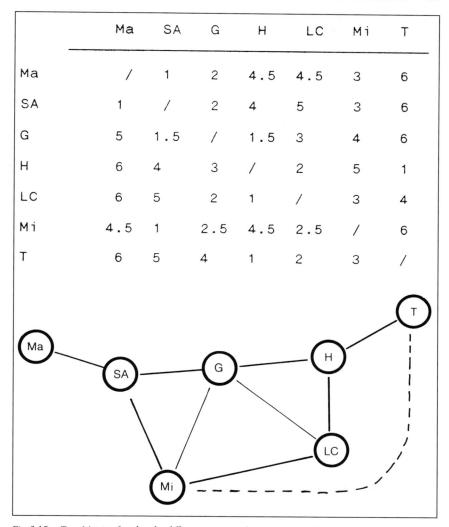

	Ma	SA	G	H	LC	Mi	T
Ma	/	1	2	4.5	4.5	3	6
SA	1	/	2	4	5	3	6
G	5	1.5	/	1.5	3	4	6
H	6	4	3	/	2	5	1
LC	6	5	2	1	/	3	4
Mi	4.5	1	2.5	4.5	2.5	/	6
T	6	5	4	1	2	3	/

Fig. 3.15   Top, *Matrix of rank order differences among phases; entries ending in .5 indicate ties.* Bottom, *Two-dimensional representation of relationships among phases; dashed line indicates that Mi–T does not fit the diagram.*

cies treated earlier. This unwieldy matrix can be reduced readily to a more manageable 7 x 7 matrix in which phases are compared with each other in terms of the number of shared attributes. An appropriate cell entry in this reduced matrix is the Jaccard similarity coefficient, simply defined as shared attributes over unshared attributes where the denominator excludes shared absences (Shennan 1988: 203). My aversion to the complex when the simple will do and the fact that, once the tables are prepared, the entire exercise can be completed with a hand calculator in twenty minutes prompt this primitive approach.

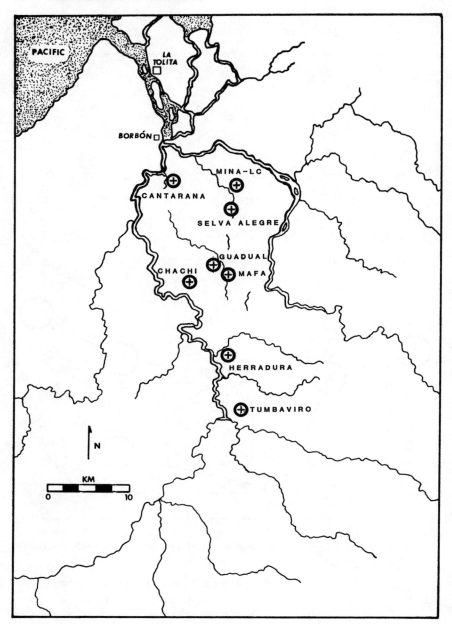

Fig. 3.16   *Median centers for sites of each phase.*

Table 3.12   Uncalibrated radiocarbon dates for Santiago and Cayapas basins.

Beta Laboratory #	Provenience	C-14 Age Years BP
33778	R36: TP1,160-180 cm (Selva Alegre)	3580 ± 210
33782	R36: TP5,100-120 cm (Selva Alegre)	2390 ± 80
20647	C61: 20-40 cm (late Selva Alegre)	1640 ± 110
25521	C61: 20-40 cm (late Selva Alegre)	1805 ± 70
20645	R10: 1A-Dark Layer (SA or Guadual)	1520 ± 70
20646	R10: 1A-Brown Fill (SA or Guadual)	1670 ± 70
25519	R10: 1A-Brown Fill (SA or Guadual)	3200 ± 150
25520	R10: 1A-Dark Layer (SA or Guadual)	3120 ± 160
25514	C36: C2-L4 (SA or Guadual)	1740 ± 80
20637	C36: C2-L4 (SA or Guadual)	1790 ± 300
20636	C36: C2-L4 (SA or Guadual)	1540 ± 80
25513	C36: C2-L3 (Guadual)	1460 ± 90
20635	C36: C2-L2 (Guadual)	1570 ± 60
28150	C69: Ashy Midden (Guadual)	1660 ± 60
25514	C55: J7,30-90 cm (Guadual)	1840 ± 140
33781	C55: Feature 1 (Guadual)	1660 ± 120
20642	C55: Q,10 cm (Herradura)	1590 ± 140
33779	C55: C12,35-50 cm (Herradura)	1450 ± 90
33780	C55: C12,50-70 cm (Herradura)	1300 ± 120
20640	C55: J7,0-30 cm (Herradura)	560 ± 60
28148	R30: Deposit 2 (Las Cruces)	1030 ± 80
28149	R30: Deposit 3 (Las Cruces)	1390 ± 60
25518	R19: TP2,60 cm (Las Cruces)	1720 ± 80
20638	C52: TP2 (Chachi)	modern
20643	C37: TP1 (Chachi)	150 ± 70

All samples are charcoal.

The first-run matrix shown at the top of table 3.11 is promising in that terminal members (Ma and T) have the lowest mean similarity to all other phases while more central members have higher mean values, expected results in an ideal seriational matrix. One problem with this solution, however, is that mean similarity is also detectably correlated with sample size. This result, of course, is also expected and does not necessarily vitiate the seriational ordering, but it does suggest that sample size may be an influential determinant of that ordering. To evaluate this possibility, a random sample of 225 observations was drawn from the empirical distribution of attributes in each phase, and a new resultant matrix prepared (table 3.11, *bottom*). This solution (suspiciously derived by eliminating data!) does not alter the order of the more data-endowed matrix, although it does lower the value of the coefficients. Note, however, that in either solution, the placement of Herradura, Mina, and Las Cruces differs from that favored in earlier seriations (e.g., fig. 3.2).

As practiced above, seriation is fundamentally a unidimensional technique in which multiple sources of variability are flattened out onto the singular dimension of temporal change. That this is more an operational goal than a realistic premise can be illustrated in a simple way by converting the Jaccard coefficients of the preceding exercises into ordinal proximities (fig. 3.15, *top*). This new matrix, in which only the order of similarity is measured, can be readily portrayed as a map (fig. 3.15, *bottom*). This map, in which only the relationship between Mina and Tumbaviro cannot be accommodated to the constraints of a two-dimensional page, is instructive in that it shows that a "best-fit" seriation cannot be projected as a single time line. In addition, the shape of this map has an interesting analogue. The analogue is the spatial distribution of the phases themselves. In fig. 3.16, the median centers for sites assigned to each phase are plotted (Cantarana and Chachi are historic phases not treated in this chapter). Note that Mina and Las Cruces center in the Santiago basin, whereas Guadual, Herradura, and Tumbaviro center in the Cayapas basin. It is now necessary to entertain the possibility that part of our laboriously argued "sequence," in fact consists of contemporary phases localized in neighboring river drainages. Perhaps radiocarbon dating can help to assess this possibility.

Radiocarbon to the Rescue?

It is claimed by some archaeologists that, since Libby and radiocarbon dating, chronology construction is no longer the creative and challenging task that it once was (Renfrew and Bahn 1991: 34). This may be so, but the set of radiocarbon dates from the Santiago-Cayapas presents as much a chronological conundrum as a crutch. These dates, listed in table 3.12, require critical evaluation.

An initial problem is context. Originally it was thought that several of the artificial mounds bearing carbon samples had grown through the accretion of primary midden. Later study shows that these mounds were raised through the

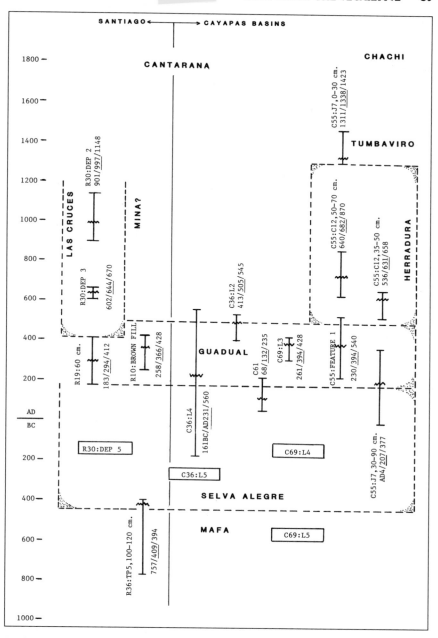

Fig. 3.17   Summary sequence for Santiago and Cayapas basins based on calibrated C-14 dates (Stuiver and Reimer 1986), stratigraphy, and seriation.

piling up of fill. As a secondary deposit, fill can (and often does) contain ceramics and carbon pertaining to any period *before* mound construction. Thus the third millennium B.C. dates from mound 1A at R10 and from the tola at R36 are not to be trusted. These samples are interesting in that they indicate probable human activity before three thousand years ago, but they do not date the Selva Alegre or Guadual ceramics with which they are fortuitously juxtaposed. Similar problems beset the suite of three dates from C36, C2-L4. In hindsight, it is a cruel irony that the one excavation unit (C2-L4) rich in charcoal should also turn out, on subsequent study, to be a mixed deposit of both Selva Alegre and Guadual ceramics. The "associated" dates, therefore, could apply to either phase.

These apologies aside, the calibrated C-14 evidence otherwise requires only a little bending and cajoling to conform to the independent testimony of stratigraphy and seriation. As sketched in fig. 3.17, this accommodative chronology can be summarized as follows:

Mafa: no associated C-14 dates but stratigraphically precedent to Selva Alegre;

Selva Alegre: 409 B.C. (#33782) is acceptable with A.D. 132 (#25521) marking the end of the phase;

Guadual: a series of dates ranging from A.D. 207 (#20640) to A.D. 505 (#20635); Guadual, of course, is superposed over Selva Alegre and by Herradura;

Herradura: although stratigraphically inverted, A.D. 631 (#33779) and A.D. 682 (#33780) are acceptable as they overlap at one sigma; although later than expected, A.D. 1338 (#20640) could conceivably mark the end of the phase;

Las Cruces: A.D. 644 (#28149) and A.D. 997 (#28148) date this phase at R30, indicating a substantial contemporaneity with Herradura; even the upper sigma of sample #25518 (A.D. 412) from R19 is seemingly too early, unless a considerable overlap with Guadual is postulated;

Mina: neither chronometric nor stratigraphic evidence is available, and the placement of this phase remains problematic; as will be argued later, a ca A.D. 1000 age is favored on the basis of stylistic similarities to the Bucheli phase in neighboring Colombia;

Tumbaviro: a rather convincing seriational argument derives the ceramics of this phase from Herradura antecedents; Tumbaviro probably extends into the historic period;

Chachi: historical evidence to be reviewed in a later chapter indicates that the Chachi were in the upper Santiago by the sixteenth century and had entered the Cayapas basin, their present homeland, by at least the eighteenth century; the poorly defined Cantarana materials are tentatively assigned a recent date on the basis of their co-occurrence with Chachi ceramics at a few sites.

Although uncertainties and inconsistencies remain, this chapter has indeed sketched the cultural sequence in broad outline. Contrary to predilections, I have not been able to confirm all initial hunches without alteration. Discoveries have been made along the way, and the emergent sequence for the Santiago-Cayapas presents a more complex and interesting scenario than one reducible to a single seriational dimension. It is now time to put this sequence to work.

4
VAGRANT VESTIGES
Valdivia and the Mafa Phase

For many archaeologists, the earlier the better. While the most elaborate pottery dating to a mere A.D. 500 may be described in a technical monograph or regional journal, even the scrappiest of sherds, if dated to several millennia B.C., warrant a press release. Participants in the Santiago-Cayapas Project are not immune to this common archaeological ailment of the "earlies"; we always hoped that truly ancient remains would be encountered. Alas, preceramic and early ceramic occupations in Esmeraldas continue to be elusive. Only one flaked projectile point has been reported for the province, but this specimen is probably of ceramic age (Valdez 1987: fig. 45a). Although lithic scatters have been recorded in our survey, the associated chips, flakes, and chunks of bashed stone are indistinguishable from those known from ceramic contexts. Such nonceramic sites, therefore, probably represent special activity loci of ceramic age. At present, the beginning of our sequence is fully ceramic and not all that early.

Valdivia, Where Are You?

One candidate for early ceramics would be, of course, Valdivia—that precocious pottery that continues to spawn a large and often contentious literature (Meggers et al. 1965; Lyon 1972–74; Lathrap et al. 1975; Damp 1988; Marcos 1988). In its heartland in southwestern Ecuador, Valdivia spans the entire third millennium and continues through the first half of the second millennium B.C. Its areal distribution encompasses El Oro province to the south and the Jama valley in Manabí to the north (Jadán 1986). In the latter locale, the Valdivia occupation is assigned to the terminal phase VIII of the refined chronology developed by Hill (1972–74), a dating that conforms to a time-transgressive distribution northward along the Ecuadorian coast. If there is a Valdivia presence in the Santiago-Cayapas area, therefore, one might expect it to be late within the Valdivia sequence. This expectation is in accord with certain ceramic features recorded in the area of the Esmeraldas valley that are said to be Valdivia related but, if such, are more likely to be Valdivia *derived* and of a later age (Guinea Bueno 1986). To the north, in the Tumaco region, the earliest discovered ceramics date to the latter half of the first millennium B.C. and do not evince any Valdivia vestiges (Bouchard 1985). The relevant evidence from the Santiago-Cayapas is exiguous at best, consisting as it does of two sherds from a mixed surface deposit. But the sherds would appear to be vintage Valdivia.

The sherds in question come from R53, a ca 0.2 ha surface deposit located about 100 m west of the Estero María (fig. 4.1). A 4 m high hillock is located at

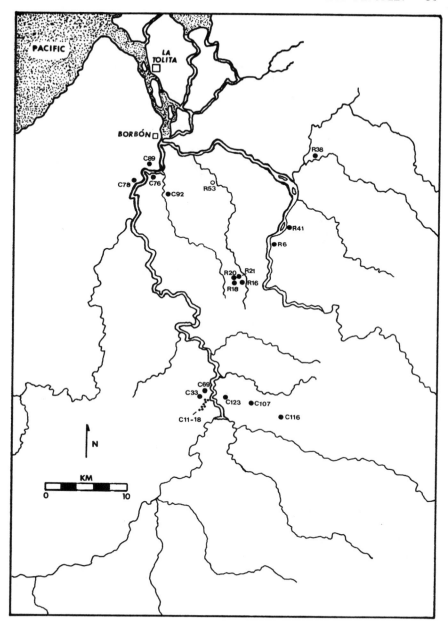

Fig. 4.1   Distribution of Mafa sites (solid circles). R53 is the site yielding possible Valdivia materials (open circle).

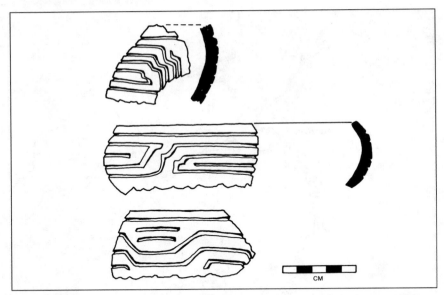

Fig. 4.2   *Valdivia sherds of the type Broad-line Incised.* Top, R53. Center: *Real Alto (Marcos 1988, II: fig. 458).* Bottom, *Meggers et al. (1965: plate 38j).*

the center of the site, but a shovel probe atop this elevation suggests that it is a natural formation. The surface collection from R53 is a mixture of Selva Alegre, Guadual, and other materials including the piece shown in fig. 4.2. This latter specimen has a dense, coffee-colored paste and well-smoothed surfaces. The exterior design consists of nested stepped figures executed in broad-line incision. A second sherd, probably from the same vessel, has an identical color and paste but lacks incision.

As seen in fig. 4.2, the similarity of the R53 specimen to the Valdivia type Broad-line Incised (Meggers et al. 1965: 47–51) is sufficiently specific to argue for this identification. Thus, however fugitive it might be, the R53 evidence tentatively supports a Valdivia presence in the Santiago-Cayapas, a presence almost missed in the survey and excavations carried out to date. Although the 3580 B.P. date from nearby R36 (table 3.12) is perfectly concordant with a late Valdivia time frame, the necessary association between sherds and dated carbon is lacking. Documentation of such an association should be a target of future fieldwork.

The Mafa Phase

The Mafa phase is named after a left-bank estero of the upper Cayapas where the distinctive ceramics of the phase were initially discovered by Paul Tolstoy in his reconnaissance of December 1985. The Mafa actually consists of two esteros locally called the Mafa Sucio and the Mafa Claro. These dual esteros, joined near

Table 4.1   *Characteristics of Mafa sites.*

SITE	ENVIRONMENTAL CODE	DRAINAGE	DEPOSITIONAL CONTEXT	SIZE (HA)	ARTIFACTS COLLECTED	COMMENTS
R6	CCGC	I	SE	?	44	
R16	EEIC	III	P	0.2	234	in platanal atop hill
R18	EEIC	III	SE	?	4	
R20	EEIC	III	P	0.1	39	probably Mafa
R21	EEIC	III	P	0.1	52	probably Mafa; in platanal
R38	CCGC	II	P	0.1	104	
R41	CCGC	I	P?	?	7	beneath modern community of La Peña
C11-18	HGDC	III	SE	?	434	some mixing with later materials
C33	HGDC	III	SS	0.3	392	
C69-I	HFDC	III	P	?	65	buried by later components
C76B	CCEB	I	SS	?	3	
C78B	CCFB	I	SE	?	14	mixed with recent Chachi sherds
C89	CCFB	I	P	0.02	121	
C92	DBEB	II	SE	?	5	in Estero Canchurí
C107	HGDC	III	P&SS	0.03	17	on ridge top
C116	HHDC	III	SE	?	3	
C123	HGHC	III	SE	?	33	in Estero Hijo de Chipero

Environmental code summarizes indices defined in figs. 2.6–2.7; for example, CCGC (code for site R6) means *C* coding for pedology, *C* for geology, *G* for agriculture, and *C* for bioclimate. For drainage, *I* means location along Santiago or Cayapas mainstream; *II*, location along navigable secondary tributary; and *III*, along unnavigable estero or in interfluves. Under depositional context, *P* means intact primary deposit; *SS*, secondary deposit found as slope wash or embedded in land-slump; and *SE*, secondary deposit found in bed of estero.

their mouths by a sluggish channel, are navigable by dugout for only a short distance inland, after which they become shallow creeks bordered by the high and steep ridges that characterize the interfluvial topography of the upper Cayapas.

The distribution of Mafa sites is plotted in fig. 4.1, and the characteristics of individual sites are given in table 4.1. On seriational grounds, Mafa antecedence to Selva Alegre was predicted previously (Tolstoy and DeBoer 1989). Subsequently this seriational argument has been supported by the cultural stratigraphy at C69. As seen in fig. 4.3, Mafa pottery at this site *tends* to be stratigraphically prior to

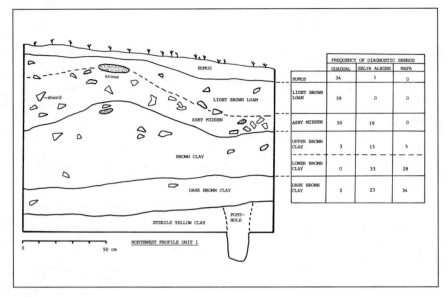

	FREQUENCY OF DIAGNOSTIC SHERDS		
	GUADUAL	SELVA ALEGRE	MAFA
HUMUS	34	1	0
LIGHT BROWN LOAM	59	0	0
ASHY MIDDEN	50	19	0
UPPER BROWN CLAY	3	15	3
LOWER BROWN CLAY	0	33	28
DARK BROWN CLAY	2	23	34

Fig. 4.3   *Profile of unit 1, C69.*

Selva Alegre ceramics. I do not believe, however, that this statistical tendency represents a gradual and in-place transition from Mafa to Selva Alegre. At C69, as elsewhere in the Santiago-Cayapas basins, abundant crawfish and other burrowing critters (including the deadly bushmaster) seem to be particularly fond of soft archaeological middens. These agents are potentially capable of scrambling archaeological deposits, thereby creating a vertical mix that mimics gradual change.

Mafa sites are indeed dominated by vagrant vestiges. Although one does not ordinarily think of sites as "moving," more than half of the twenty-four Mafa examples consist of bar or beach deposits in the beds of esteros. The sources of these transported sherds have not been successfully identified except in a few cases. At C123, a small relict of intact midden is preserved a short distance upstream from a concentration of Mafa sherds in the bed of the Estero Chipero. At R38, located off the Río Cachabí, this erosional process can be observed in action. Here an estero is actively slicing through a small (0.1 ha) Mafa midden, and sherds almost outnumber pebbles and cobbles in downstream deposits. At C33, the Mafa deposit is again disturbed, embedded as it is in a massive *derrumbe,* or land-slump, triggered by the headward undercutting of the bluff on which C33 was originally situated. The pre-derrumbe size of this blufftop community can be estimated at 0.3 ha. No other phase in our sequence is subjected to such taphonomic treachery. Following a "ravages of time" premise, this fact perhaps supports indirectly the relative antiquity of Mafa.

Mafa, however, is not totally devoid of primary archaeological context. Although several undisturbed sites produce small sherd samples with only a few Mafa diagnostics, others more securely anchor the reality of the phase. For in-

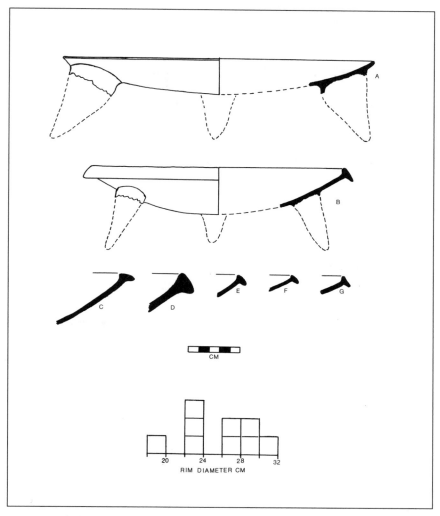

Fig. 4.4 *Mafa plates (A, R16; B–D, R38; E–F, C33; G, C69I). On histograms, each square represents a single vessel.*

stance, C89, a small but dense patch of *in situ* Mafa debris located off the lower Cayapas, isolates the phase with great fidelity. R16 is another example of an intact deposit. In terms of settlement pattern, Mafa sites tend to be small (0.02–0.3 ha) and located overwhelmingly in the interfluves, away from the major courses of the Santiago and Cayapas (table 4.1). Later phases display different distributional patterns, but now it is time to turn to the ceramics that actually define the Mafa phase.

Collectively Mafa ceramics tend to be thin-walled with well-smoothed surfaces when surfaces have not been worn away. A red slip is often preserved,

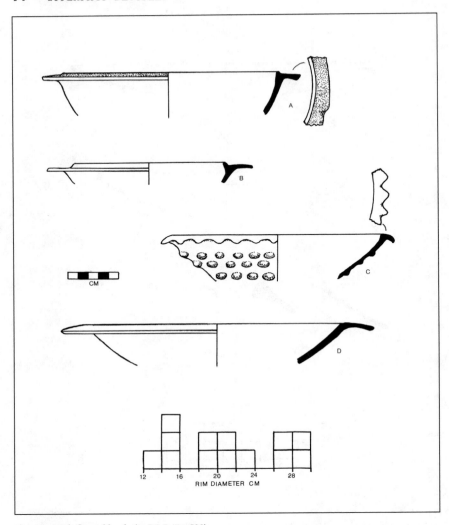

Fig. 4.5 Mafa flanged bowls (A, R6; B–D, C33).

although such texturing techniques as incision and brushing are more common than pigmentation. Both surface and core colors tend to be dark, ranging from black to gray or brown with only an occasional ruddy outlier. Paste is variable, ranging from a fine sand temper to a seemingly temperless and chalky fabric in serving vessels, whereas thicker-walled jars have a coarser paste often studded with white plagioclase fragments up to 2 mm in size. The latter ware has a speckled appearance and is a Mafa hallmark. A full account of Mafa paste characteristics should be forthcoming from the studies of Daniel Poulin of the University of

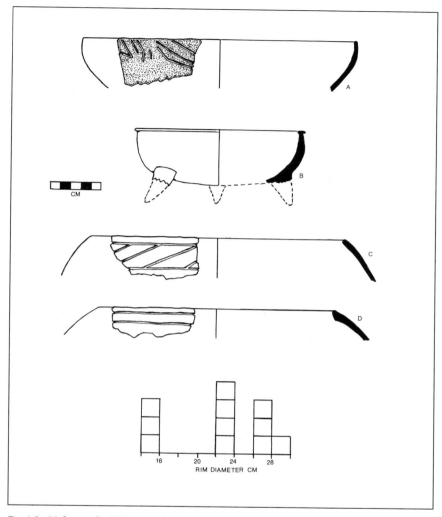

Fig. 4.6 *Mafa open (A, R38; B, C123) and closed (C, R38; D, C33) bowls.*

Montreal. Here the focus will be on Mafa vessel forms. The sample is small and the discussion accordingly brief.

Plates

Plates, supported by three or more (?) patas, were almost certainly used as serving vessels. They are too shallow to contain liquids effectively but would be perfectly good food dishes. Plates can be divided into two forms, one with a direct rim (fig. 4.4A) and a second, more common variety with a T-shaped rim

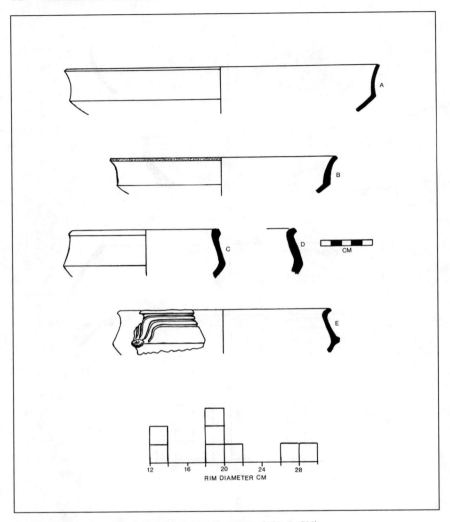

Fig. 4.7   *Mafa carinated bowls (A, C33; B, C89; C, C14; D, C78B; E, C33).*

(fig. 4.4B–G). One direct rim plate has a red-slipped exterior, but otherwise decorative elaboration is absent. Rim diameters range from 19 to 31 cm, but the sample is too small to specify size modes.

Flanged Open Bowls ·

The flanged open bowl is a Mafa specialty with the flange being either sublabial (fig. 4.5A–B) or labial (fig. 4.5C–D). Of thirteen examples, two have red-slipped flanges, whereas one fancy specimen has a modeled flange and a nubbin-studded exterior (fig. 4.5C).

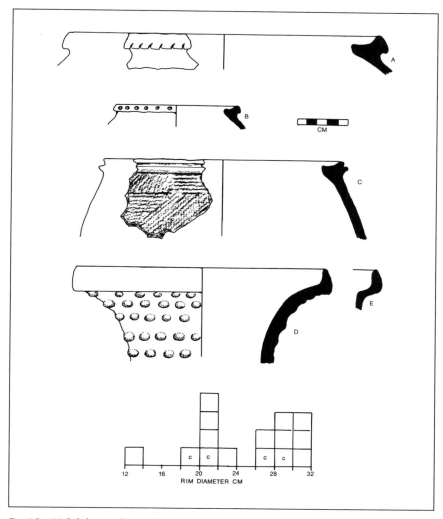

Fig. 4.8 *Mafa ledge rim (A–B, C89; C, C123) and cambered rim (D, C33; E, C15) jars. In histogram,* blank squares *refer to ledge rim jars, and* c *refers to cambered rim jars.*

Open Bowls

Except for the example shown in fig. 4.6B, open bowls have direct, unmodified rims. Decoration is restricted to the exterior surface and includes two cases of fingernail indentations, one of nubbins, and a single specimen with incision over a polished red slip (fig. 4.6A).

Closed Bowls

Of four examples of closed bowls, two bear incisions on the exterior (fig. 4.6C–D), whereas a third, unillustrated specimen has a red-slipped exterior.

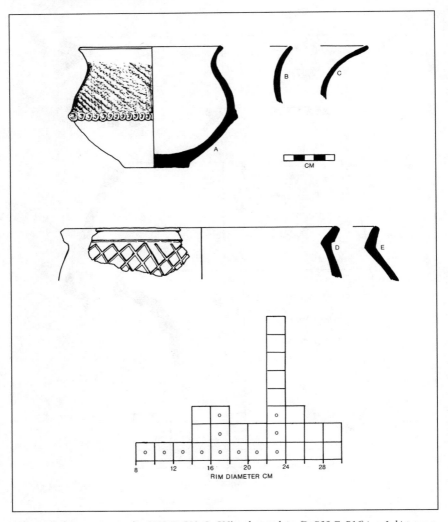

Fig. 4.9 Mafa outcurving rim (A, C123; B, C18; C, C33) and everted rim (D, R38; E, R16) jars. In histogram, blank squares refer to everted rim jars, and o refers to outcurving rim jars.

Carinated Bowls

Carinated bowls, gracefully contoured vessels, come in open (fig. 4.7A–B) and closed (fig. 4.7C–E) versions. Nearly half are decorated. Decorative treatment includes single cases of a red lip, a nicked lip, incision over a red-slipped exterior, and incision coupled with shoulder nubbins (fig. 4.7E). As a group, these bowls were probably food-serving or drinking vessels.

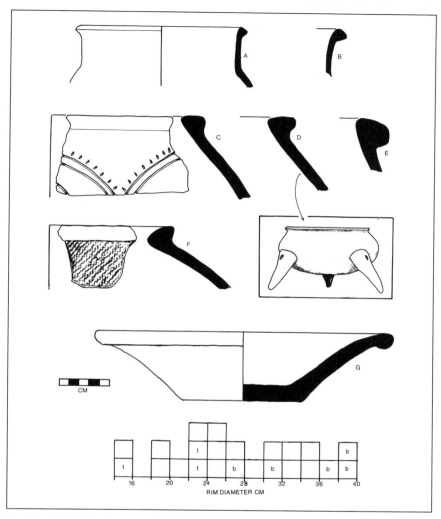

Fig. 4.10 *Mafa thickened lip jars (A, C13; B, C33), comma rim jars (C, R6; D, R38; E, C89; F, C123), and comma rim basins (G, C89). In* histogram, blank squares *refer to comma rim jars,* t *refers to thickened lip jars, and* b *refers to comma rim basins.*

Ledge Rim Jars

Ledge rim jars, named after a salient inward extension of the rim that creates a virtual ledge around the interior of the vessel mouth, are better seen than described (fig. 4.8A–C). Decorative embellishment includes single cases of an incised exterior, an incised lip, a nicked lip (fig. 4.8A), a punctate lip (fig. 4.8B), and a brushed exterior (fig. 4.8C). The absence of pigmentation may suggest that

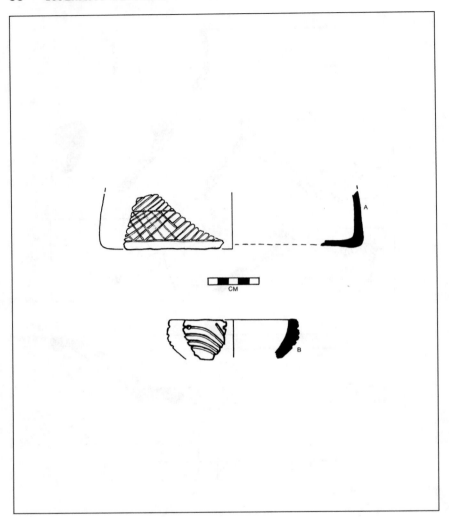

Fig. 4.11   Mafa miscellaneous vessels (A, R38; B, C123).

this form functioned as an *olla* or cooking pot. The limited sample suggests two modal rim diameters of 21 and 31 cm.

Cambered Rim Jars

Cambered rim jars are limited to four specimens, one with a nubbined exterior (fig. 4.8*D–E*). Similar cambered rim jars are popular late within the Valdivia sequence (Meggers et al. 1965: 92). Whether the Mafa form has an ultimate source in Valdivia or not, it continues as a minor category in subsequent phases of the Santiago-Cayapas sequence.

Outcurving Rim Jar

The outcurving rim jar is a common form in Mafa and subsequent phases. Its characteristic feature is a smoothly outcurving rim without a break separating neck from body (fig. 4.9A–C). Decoration consists of a red-slipped exterior (one), a red-slipped exterior and interior (one), punctate lips (two), and the brushed and shoulder-impressed specimen illustrated in fig. 4.9A. Modal rim diameters center at 17 and 23 cm.

Everted Rim Jars

The everted rim jar is distinguished by a sharply angled juncture between rim and body (fig. 4.9D–E). The single case of decoration consists of crisscross incisions on the exterior (fig. 4.9D). The modal diameter is 23 cm.

Thickened Lip Jars

A few specimens of thickened lip jars (fig. 4.10A–B) presage a more common Selva Alegre form. None is decorated.

Comma Rim Jars

Restricted to Mafa, the comma rim jar is a thick-walled form with a distinctive rim that in profile resembles a comma (fig. 4.10C–F). Three specimens have red-slipped exteriors, one is brushed, one is incised, and one bears the composite incised and punctate motif shown in fig. 4.10C. Along with ledge rim jars, these vessels typically have a dense, granular paste flecked with white plagioclase. Oversized patas (fig. 3.3A) and massive flanges (fig. 3.5A) have the same distinctive paste and are probably associated with these forms.

Comma Rim Basins

Although never abundant, comma rim basins are found in most phases of the sequence. Of the five Mafa examples, two are plain (fig. 4.10G), two have red lips, and one has its exterior indented with fingernail impressions.

Miscellaneous Vessels

The flat-based cylindrical vessel shown in fig. 4.11A is unique. Its paste is fine and chalky to the feel. The exterior surface bears paneled fine-line incision. A second unusual specimen is a miniature, thick-walled bowl decorated on the exterior with broad-line incision (fig. 4.11B). This vessel was perforated after firing, perhaps in an attempt to repair a crack in the wall (e.g., DeBoer and Lathrap 1979: 127).

This completes the roster of Mafa vessel forms. Spread over twenty-four sites or secondary "find spots," the 127 rim sherds that are sufficiently complete to intimate whole vessel shapes are not numerous enough to suggest an internal chronology of Mafa subphases. Because Mafa displays a great deal of continuity with the subsequent Selva Alegre phase, a discussion of the external relationships of both phases is deferred until the next chapter.

5
LA TOLITA'S HINTERLAND
The Selva Alegre Phase

As Lathrap et al. (1985: 68) wryly observe: "It seems almost an operative corollary of Murphy's Law that archaeological traditions are usually named after their least appropriate members." Selva Alegre, although a phase rather than a tradition, might comply with this complaint. The phase is named after the modern community of Selva Alegre, a town of about eight hundred inhabitants situated on a shallowly buried outcrop of bedrock on the left bank of the upper Santiago (R10, the type site, and other Selva Alegre sites are plotted in figs 5.1 and 5.2). The entire community is underlain by prehistoric refuse, and ancient mounds abound where not destroyed by modern construction. Most conspicuous is a group of mounds located at the eastern periphery of the town. This mound group consists of three parallel linear embankments with associated domed tumuli (fig. 5.3). A trench excavated through this mound group exposed fill containing quantities of Guadual ceramics mixed with a residuum of distinctive Selva Alegre pottery (fig. 5.4). Test pits scattered throughout the modern community reveal either pure Guadual deposits or a mix of Selva Alegre and Guadual materials. Clearly the most extensive occupation and the bulk of mound construction at Selva Alegre took place during the Guadual phase, with earlier midden being scooped up in the process of mound building. R10, the site of Selva Alegre, therefore is primarily a Guadual monument.

In an earlier report (Tolstoy and DeBoer 1989), Selva Alegre and Guadual, although recognized as sequent phases, were considered together, just as they are found together in the mixed secondary deposits at R10. In fact, the two phases are radically distinct, a point to be made evident in this and the following chapter. The notations R10I and R10II refer to the Selva Alegre and Guadual components respectively. Although not as extensive as the Guadual component, R10I covers an area estimated at more than 5 hectares and is the largest Selva Alegre settlement recorded in the survey. In size, its only rival is R36, a ca 5 ha site located beneath the modern village of Colón Eloy on the lower Estero María. Like R10, R36 contains a number of domed tumuli; however, a distinctive feature of the R36 earthworks is a pair of elevated causeways connecting several of the mounds (fig. 5.5). Because these causeways parallel a recently constructed road, it was suspected that they might be the berms resulting from the bulldozing of the road. This suspicion, however, is unfounded because one of the causeways extends beneath modern houses built before the road arrived in Colón Eloy.

Unlike R10, R36 is almost a pure Selva Alegre occupation. The qualifier "almost" is required because a small sample of highly distinctive, non–Selva Alegre ceramics also occurs at R36. This distinctive pottery, always mixed with Selva

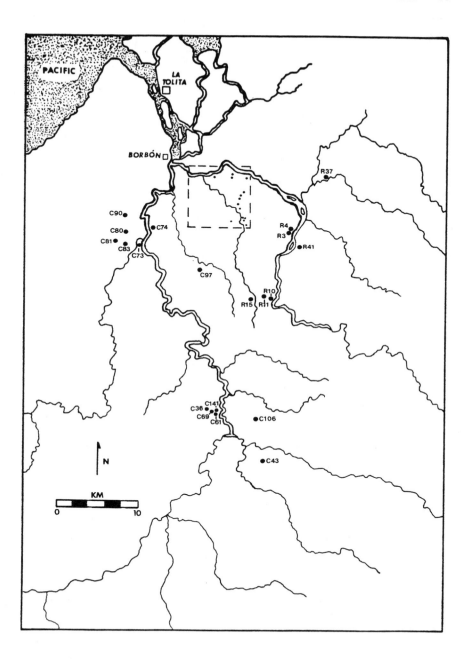

Fig. 5.1   Distribution of Selva Alegre sites. See fig. 5.2 for amplification of the area enclosed by dashed rectangle.

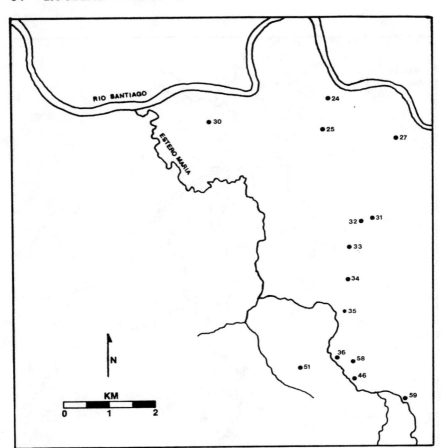

Fig. 5.2   *Distribution of Selva Alegre sites within the inset of fig. 5.1.*

Alegre materials, is found on the surface, exposed in drip-lines of modern houses, and in the surficial deposit of test pit 1. These ceramics, so sparsely represented at R36, are assigned to the problematic Mina phase and will be considered in a later chapter. Following the same notational system employed at R10, R36I refers to the major Selva Alegre occupation, whereas R36II designates the poorly defined Mina component at Colón Eloy.

Natural hillocks are common in the Santiago and Cayapas basins, and distinguishing these natural formations from artificial mounds is not always an easy task, especially as natural elevations are often favored spots for human occupation today and were so in the past. This ambiguity is further complicated by the current (and perhaps ancient) practice of scooping up soil (archaeological middens seem to be preferred) to form elevated garden beds. To evaluate the nature of the mounds at R36, test pits were excavated atop two of the more prominent tolas (1 and 2 in fig. 5.5). The profile of the "telephone booth" sunk into tola 1 is shown

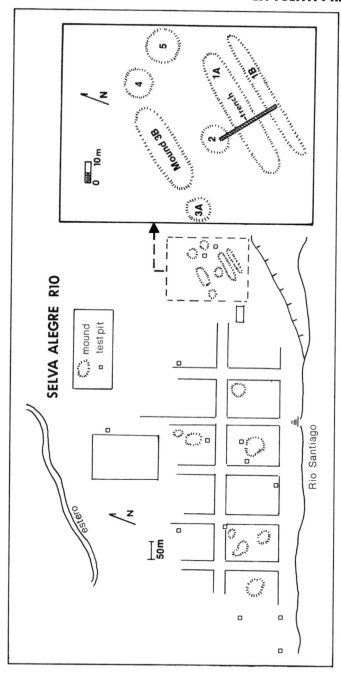

Fig. 5.3 Plan of the Selva Alegre site.

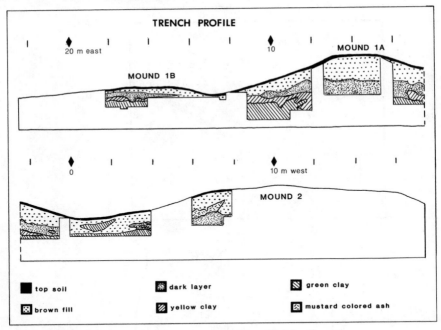

Fig. 5.4 *Profile of trench excavation across mounds 1B, 1A, and 2, Selva Alegre site.*

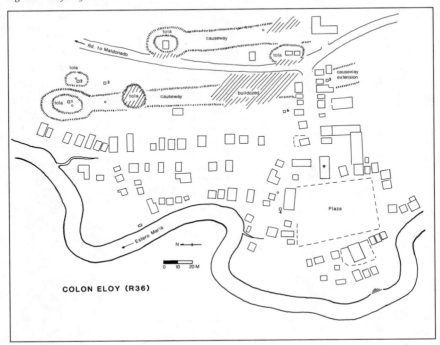

Fig. 5.5 *Plan of modern community of Colón Eloy and associated archaeological monuments.* Small numbered squares indicate test pits.

ceramic comparisons; however, such comparisons must await fuller published description of the La Tolita pottery sequence.

As lamented earlier, the surface survey of the Santiago and Cayapas basins hardly approaches complete coverage, and the obtained sample of sites need not be representative. Under these conditions, most spatial analytic techniques are inappropriate. Yet the imperfect data at hand do permit a glimpse of the Selva Alegre settlement pattern (fig. 5.8). As a multiple-mound site covering as much as 100 ha and yielding an abundance of ceramic and gold finery, La Tolita stands alone as an unrivaled paramount center. Secondary centers with multiple mounds include R36 at the upstream limit of canoe navigation on the Estero María and R10 on the upper Santiago, gateway to the placer gold deposits still mined at the aptly named Playa de Oro. In this regard, it is significant that the *only* gold encountered in our survey is a small (ca 12 mm) leaf found in the fill of mound 1A at R10. This gold piece could pertain to either the Selva Alegre or Guadual occupations. Furthermore, our designation of R10I as a Selva Alegre secondary center is based primarily on the size (5+ ha) of the site; the extent of mound construction during this phase remains uncertain.

The Selva Alegre presence on the Cayapas is less conspicuous, although an extensive settlement (C73), now largely destroyed and reduced to a remnant 0.2 ha, was once perched atop a high knoll overlooking the mouth of the Onzole. On the upper Cayapas, two buried Selva Alegre components (C36I, C69II) are located near the esteros Mafa, tributaries historically known to be gold producing (Wolf 1975: 364). It is unfortunate that our survey could not pay more attention to the Estero Zapallito, a right bank tributary of the Cayapas that is still panned for gold; however, a major task throughout fieldwork was to convince the local inhabitants that archaeologists are *not* gold-seekers.

By momentarily emphasizing gold, I do not mean to suggest that this valuable was a major determinant of the Selva Alegre settlement pattern. Such an inference would clearly exceed the hard evidence of one unassociated gold fragment. It is known, however, that La Tolita is a virtual gold mine and, in fact, has been treated as such throughout historic times (Valdez 1987: 44–48). Much of this gold was presumably extracted from the auriferous deposits of the Santiago-Cayapas hinterland. In return, La Tolita may have been the hub for the local distribution of obsidian, a material imported from the sierra. Isaacson's analysis of Santiago-Cayapas obsidian specimens indicates a Mullumica source, although the exact route by which this obsidian reached the Esmeraldas coast remains unknown (see discussion in Alcina Franch et al. 1987). In this context, the recent finds from Jardín del Este, a site near Quito, are of relevance (Buys and Domínguez 1988). Jardín del Este produces a number of artifacts of clear La Tolita affiliation including figurines and ceramic "graters"; the associated date of 130 B.C. ± 65 indicates a temporal cross-tie with the Selva Alegre phase. It is quite reasonable to suppose that La Tolita material in the Quito basin and Mullumica obsidian in Esmeraldas are manifestations of the same exchange network linking coast and sierra.

As an import from the sierra, obsidian has an interesting distribution in the Santiago-Cayapas. According to Valdez (personal communication), it is abundant at La Tolita, in some areas of the site literally peppering the surface. Obsidian is never this abundant in the hinterland. The entire collection from the Santiago-Cayapas survey consists of forty-four pieces, of which twenty-seven pertain to the Selva Alegre phase (table 3.9). Of this small sample, twenty pieces come from the modestly sized site of C69, and even the small site of C61 yields as much as the large secondary centers of R10 and R36. Thus, although La Tolita can be accused of hoarding or at least reluctantly releasing its imported obsidian and locally extracted gold, there is no evidence that secondary centers such as Selva Alegre or Colón Eloy had greater access to obsidian than did the most ordinary of settlements. In this light, one might reduce the site "hierarchy" displayed in fig. 5.8 to the following: La Tolita—big with lots of exotica; all other sites—smaller with scant exotica. Some archaeologists might consider this pattern to be diagnostic of a "simple chiefdom," as if the waving of an appellative wand actually sheds light on the processes involved. We shall return to Selva Alegre and the nature of its settlement pattern after the comparative and contrasting data for later phases have been presented.

While it is true that people do not live by bread alone, they do not live at all without it. Some meager evidence is available concerning Selva Alegre subsistence. The indirect evidence consists of manos and metates—classical maize-processing implements, net sinkers, and what we have reinterpreted to be fish scalers (see chapter 3). Ceramic griddles occur as a rare form in several phases, including Selva Alegre, but whether they figured in the preparation of maize tortillas, manioc cakes, or some other product is unknown. Despite flotation of soil samples from C36 and fine-mesh screening at R10 and C36, no macrobotanical or faunal remains were recovered (except for decidedly fresh rootlets and, on one occasion, a very much alive and annoyed Conga ant!). The phytolith picture is somewhat better. As tabulated in appendix 2, large cross-shaped phytoliths believed to be diagnostic of maize have been identified in Selva Alegre, Guadual, Las Cruces, and Herradura phase soil samples. The case for the genera *Canna* and *Maranta* is also good, although the likely presence of the corresponding cultivated species—achira and arrowroot respectively—cannot be certified. Various palms, bamboos, and sedges are also attested. Textile impressions on sherds leave little doubt that cotton was cultivated by Selva Alegre times (appendix 1). In general, these data paint an unsurprising picture. Sites consist of clearings in a humid tropical forest setting. Maize, palm fruits, and tuber crops coupled with proteinaceous fish and an as yet undetected terrestrial fauna comprise a typical tropical forest dietary base.

Selva Alegre Ceramics

Even in the form of weathered sherds, Selva Alegre pottery intimates a ceramic art that is well made, that encompasses a number of generally gracile

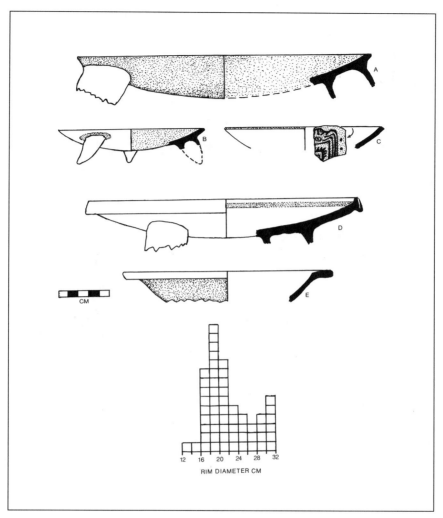

Fig. 5.9   Selva Alegre plates (A, R10I; B, R36I; C, C69II; D–E, R36I).

vessel forms, and that bears a variety of decorative elaborations. The word "art" is preferable to the widely used "craft" (as in "craft production") of archaeological discourse. The Selva Alegre potter is an artist who creatively and aesthetically engages and explores the bounds of cultural prescription, not a craftsperson producing for externally defined or purely utilitarian standards. This potter is a bit of a show-off and dilettante.

Selva Alegre wares generally have a fine paste. In serving vessels such as plates and most bowls, the ceramic fabric is seemingly temperless and has a chalky, even silky, feel and a distinctive pinkish cast to both surface and core. Larger and thicker-walled storage or cooking vessels have a coarser sand-tempered paste

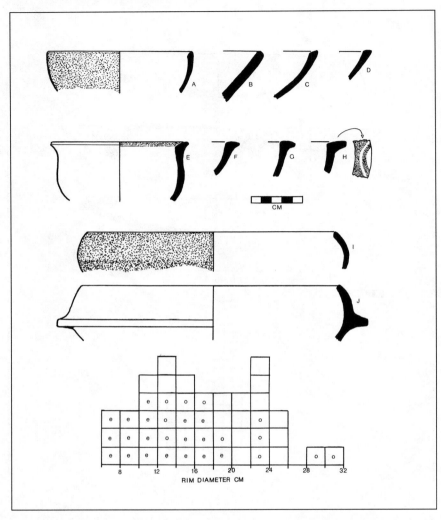

Fig. 5.10　*Selva Alegre open bowls with direct rims (A, R10I; B, R36I; C, R46; D, C69II), open bowls with everted rims (E, R36I; F, R10I; G, C61; H, C69II), and closed bowls (I, R36I; J, C83). In histogram, open squares are closed bowls, and e and o are everted rim and direct rim open bowls, respectively.*

with colors ranging from oranges and maroons to browns and blacks. The plagioclase-studded ware of Mafa is absent, but the Mafa techniques of modeling, incision, and brushing continue as part of the decorative repertoire, although pigmentation assumes a more important role in Selva Alegre. Most common is a red pigment applied as an all-over or zoned slip. White and red bichromes also characterize the phase, although the kaolin-based white pigment is extremely fugitive and the rarity of this color scheme probably represents a preservational bias. A singular specimen with resist decoration from C69II is arguably Selva

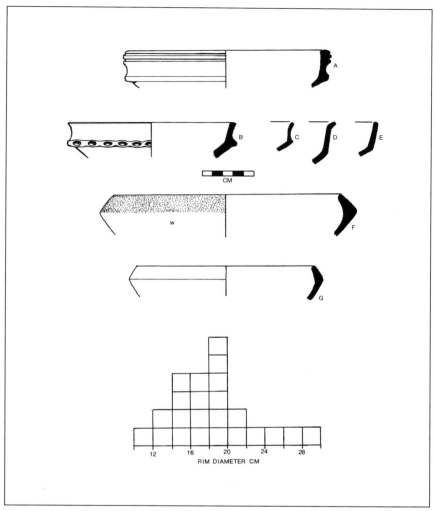

Fig. 5.11   *Selva Alegre open carinated (A, R101; B–D, R361; E, C61) and closed carinated bowls (F, R361; G, C73).*

Alegre as this distinctive technique is abundant in superposed Guadual levels and considerable vertical mixing characterizes this site (see fig. 4.3).

The major descriptive thrust of this chapter, however, depends on the reconstructed pots themselves. The following survey parallels that of Mafa, although a few vessel forms do not carry over from Mafa whereas others are Selva Alegre innovations.

Plates

As common serving vessels, plates come with a variety of rim modifications. Direct (fig. 5.9A–C) and T-shaped rims (fig. 5.9D) continue from Mafa; corniced and everted rims (fig. 5.9E) are distinctive of Selva Alegre. More than half of the eighty-five plates are decorated with a red pigment. The most frequent treatment (twenty-five) is a red-painted lip; red-slipped exterior or interior surfaces are also common (nineteen). As seen in fig. 5.9, plate diameters have a bimodal distribution, one mode centering at 19 cm, the other at 31 cm. It is tempting to regard the smaller plates as everyday eating vessels with the larger examples reserved for feasts. One might pursue this reasoning to argue that feasting is more likely to take place at large centers such as R10 or R36 (e.g., Blitz 1993). Alas for this hypothesis, however, large plates are proportionally more abundant at small sites.

Open Bowls with Direct Rims

The simple form of open bowls with direct rims (fig. 5.10A–D) comes in two size modes of 13 and 23 cm. Half of the fourteen examples have red-slipped surfaces, and one specimen bears traces of white and red pigments on the exterior.

Open Bowls with Everted Rims

Open bowls with everted rims are a Selva Alegre innovation. They appear to come in two size modes (11 and 16 cm, respectively) and are frequently decorated. In the most common decorative treatment, the everted rim is painted red (fig. 5.10E) or white and red (fig. 5.10H).

Closed Bowls

Seven of nineteen closed bowls bear a shoulder flange (fig. 5.10J) or punctated shoulder fillet. In contrast to other bowls, this form is only occasionally slipped (fig. 5.10I). The modal diameter is 21 cm.

Carinated Bowls

Carinated bowls include open (fig. 5.11A–E) and closed (fig. 5.11F–G) varieties. The carination is often accentuated by a plain (fig. 5.11A) or impressed (fig. 5.11B) flange. When present, a red slip is limited to the exterior surface above the carination. In one case, both red and white slips occur (fig. 5.11F). The modal diameter is 19 cm.

Ledge Rim Jars

Ledge rim jars, a common Mafa form, continue to be popular in Selva Alegre. In eight cases, the ledge and lip of the vessel are painted red (fig. 5.12A). Other decorative embellishments include a nicked or impressed lip (fig. 5.12B–C) and a zoned exterior slip (fig. 5.12C). As in Mafa, there appear to be two size modes centering at 20 and 28 cm.

Cambered Rim Jars

The distinctive cambered rim jar continues as a rare form (fig. 5.12E–F). One unillustrated specimen has a red-slipped exterior.

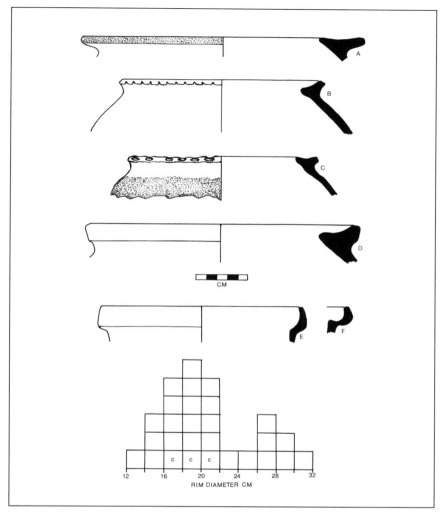

Fig. 5.12   Selva Alegre ledge rim (A–B, R10I; C, R35; D, C61) and cambered rim jars (E, C69II; F, C36I). In histogram, blank squares *represent ledge rim jars, and* c *marks cambered rim jars.*

Outcurving Rim Jars

Of thirty-seven examples of outcurving rim jars, eleven preserve traces of a red pigment applied as an exterior slip and on the rim interior (fig. 5.13B). Incision is limited to the single piece illustrated in fig. 5.13A. In two cases, the exterior surface below the shoulder is carbon crusted, suggesting that this form was occasionally used over a fire. Diameters range widely from 11 to 33 cm with a mode at 19 cm.

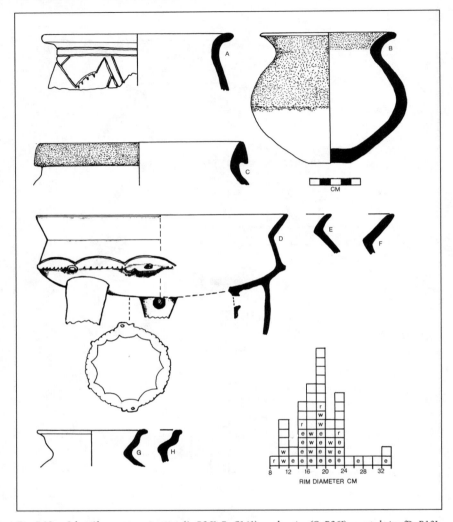

Fig. 5.13   *Selva Alegre outcurving rim (A, R36I; B, C141), wedge rim (C, R36I), everted rim (D, R10I; E, R24; F, R36I), and recurved rim jars (G, C90; H, R10I). In histogram,* blank squares *are outcurving rim jars, and* e, w, *and* r *stand for everted rim, wedge rim, and recurved rim jars, respectively.*

Everted Rim Jars

As in Mafa, the everted rim jar is defined by an angular juncture separating neck from body (fig. 5.13D–F). Most vessels are plain, but decoration can be elaborate as in the modeled and incised piece shown in fig. 5.13D. In five cases, the interior of the rim eversion is painted red.

Wedge Rim Jars

New to Selva Alegre, the wedge rim jar (fig. 5.13C) becomes one of the more common vessels in the subsequent Guadual phase.

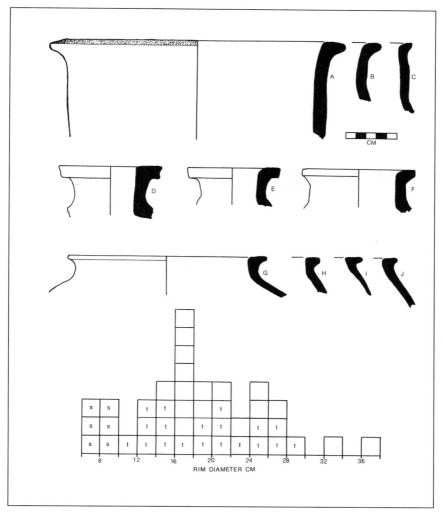

Fig. 5.14 *Selva Alegre thickened lip (A, R10I; B, R24; C, R36I), small thick wall (D, R35; E, R36I; F, C83), and expanded lip jars (G,R10I; H, R24; I, R36I; J, C80). In histogram,* blank squares *indicate expanded lip jars;* t *and* s *mark thickened lip and small thick wall jars, respectively.*

Recurved Rim Jars

Another Selva Alegre innovation, the distinctively shaped recurved rim jar (fig. 5.13G–H) has a long subsequent history in the Santiago and Cayapas basins, peaking in popularity during the Herradura and Tumbaviro phases (table 3.3).

Thickened Lip Jars

Presaged in Mafa, thickened lip jars gain modest popularity in Selva Alegre (fig. 5.14A–B). Of twenty-two specimens, four have a red lip (fig. 5.14A), and two have red-slipped exteriors.

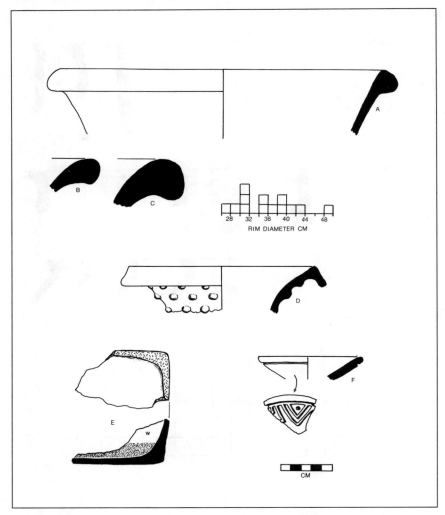

Fig. 5.15   Selva Alegre comma rim basins (A, R27; B–C, R24) and miscellaneous vessels (D–F, R36I). Histogram pertains to comma rim basins only.

Small Thick Wall Jars

So-named for obvious reasons (fig. 5.14D–F), the small thick wall jar is new to Selva Alegre.

Expanded Lip Jars

Although the descriptive terminology is perhaps approaching exhaustion with the label "expanded lip," nonetheless, this form is readily distinct from other vessel categories (fig. 5.14G–J). It is new to Selva Alegre and reaches maximum

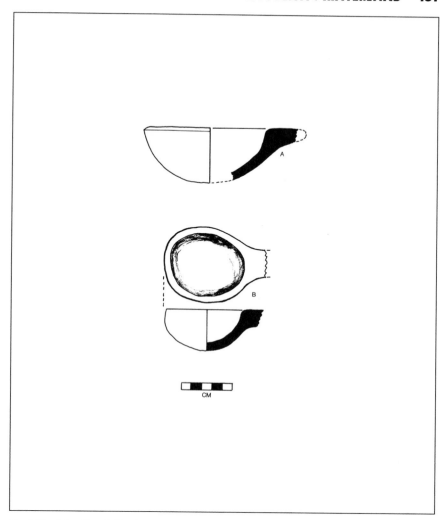

Fig. 5.16   Selva Alegre ladles (A, R361; B, R46).

popularity in the following Guadual phase. Of forty-two Selva Alegre examples, eighteen have a red lip. Although the diameter range is great, there is a clear mode at 17 cm.

Comma Rim Basins

Although present throughout the sequence, the large comma rim basin vessel is relatively common only in the Selva Alegre phase. Of twenty-four specimens, none is decorated (fig. 5.15A–C).

Table 5.2   Distribution of selected Selva Alegre vessel forms.

vessels

	Site	1	2	3	4	5	6	7	8	9	10
a	R36I	2	16	3	3	–	1	3	5	2	3
	R35	–	6	2	–	–	–	–	3	1	–
	R51	–	1	–	–	–	–	–	–	–	–
	R58	–	1	–	–	–	–	–	–	–	–
	C73	–	3	–	–	–	–	–	1	–	–
	C80	–	1	–	–	–	–	–	–	–	–
	C83	–	–	1	1	–	–	–	1	–	–
	C90	–	–	–	–	2	–	–	–	–	–
b	R10I	10	5	1	2	3	7	4	13	11	8
	R24	–	4	–	–	–	–	3	2	2	–
	R27	–	1	–	–	–	–	–	1	1	–
	R46	–	2	–	–	–	1	–	–	1	–
	C36I	2	–	–	–	–	2	–	1	1	4
	C61	3	1	–	3	–	2	1	5	–	5
	C69II	1	–	–	–	–	1	–	1	–	3
	C81	–	–	–	1	–	–	–	–	1	1
	C97	–	1	–	–	–	–	–	–	1	–
	C141	1	–	–	–	–	–	–	1	–	–
	R3	–	–	–	–	–	–	–	1	–	–
	R25	–	–	–	–	–	–	–	1	1	–
	R30I	–	–	–	–	–	–	–	1	–	–
	R37	–	–	–	–	–	–	–	–	–	1

Vessel key: *1*, open bowl with everted rim; *2*, expanded lip jar; *3*, small thick wall jar; *4*, wedge rim jar; *5*, recurved rim jar; *6*, open bowl with direct rim; *7*, open carinated bowl; *8*, ledge rim jar; *9*, thickened lip jar; *10*, plates with direct or T-shaped rim.

[a] Sites where vessels shared with Guadual (1–5) predominate.

[b] Sites where vessels shared with Mafa (6–10) predominate.

Miscellaneous Vessels

The corniced rim jar shown in fig. 5.15D is unique; its nubbined exterior recalls a Mafa decorative treatment (fig. 4.8D). Two other unusual specimens include a square vessel with a red and white exterior (fig. 5.15E) and a small excised bowl (fig. 5.15F); the latter may have a Mafa counterpart (fig. 4.11B). Ladles—all five of them—are peculiar to Selva Alegre (fig. 5.16). All are undecorated and made of a dense, sandy paste that otherwise characterizes Selva Alegre storage and cooking vessels.

It should be evident from the above survey that Selva Alegre continues a number of Mafa vessel forms and also anticipates several forms that become more common in Guadual. On seriational grounds, such a pattern is expectable and raises the possibility that Selva Alegre can be broken down into early and late subphases, the former displaying greater continuity with Mafa antecedents, the latter with Guadual successors. The site-by-site distribution of ten "sensitive" vessel forms is plotted in table 5.2 to evaluate this possibility. These sensitive forms include vessels shared by Selva Alegre and Guadual but absent in Mafa or, alternatively, vessels shared by Selva Alegre and Mafa but absent in Guadual. As can be seen in table 5.2, it is easy to generate a pattern from these data by simply separating site collections into those where vessels shared with Mafa predominate from those where vessels shared with Guadual predominate. This procedure, however, is of doubtful validity for several reasons. First is the impressive fact that most collections contain forms shared with *both* Mafa and Guadual. Second, those few sites that share forms with only Mafa or Guadual are characterized by woefully small samples. Third, if we were to accept table 5.2 as a genuine seriation, then the two C-14 dates used to bracket the Selva Alegre phase fall in inverted order! All in all, this is not a happy diagnosis and suggests that the present evidence is insufficient for subdividing the Selva Alegre phase in a convincing manner.

External Similarities

I have purposely chosen the word "similarity" rather than the more often used "connection" or "relation(ship)." Undoubtedly, the Selva Alegre phase, as any cultural entity, had external connections or relations—witness the obsidian imported from the sierra or the possible La Tolita colony at Jardín del Este. Although of great interest and importance, these connections need not map onto the humdrum, everyday debris of local archaeological records. Here my focus is precisely the everyday ceramic debris of the Selva Alegre phase and the specific similarities it displays to the pottery of neighboring regions. This task is greatly handicapped by the fact that adequately reported ceramic assemblages with which to compare the Selva Alegre material are rare.

The crucial La Tolita ceramic sequence is the subject of several ongoing but still unpublished studies. On two separate occasions, however, Francisco Valdez kindly permitted us to look at the recently excavated La Tolita collections housed in the archaeological laboratory of the Banco Central in Quito. The following comments are based on notes taken during these visits. Temprano phase material (the Terminal Formative at La Tolita) resembles Mafa in a number of features. Both share thin-walled carinated bowls (fig. 4.7A–B), an emphasis on modeling and incision including the specific rendition shown in fig. 4.7E, a variety of flange forms, and extra-large patas that are often brushed (fig. 3.3A). Tentatively then, Temprano and Mafa can be viewed as contemporary phases or even manifestations of the same phase. As argued earlier, chronometric evidence indicates contemporaneity between Selva Alegre and the Clásico phase at La Tolita. The case for this contemporaneity is supported by some shared ceramic features such as double-spout-and-bridge bottles, ceramic "graters," and a plethora of figurines. Tripod plates and small thick wall jars (fig. 5.14D–F) are also common to both phases. Other alleged Clásico features, such as resist painting and compoteras, however, are rare or absent in Selva Alegre, although they are typical of the following Guadual phase. At present, no further comparisons are justified. Undoubtedly, completion of the La Tolita ceramic analyses will shed new light on the Santiago-Cayapas sequence, just as we hope that our studies prove useful to the investigators at La Tolita.

To the south, Alcina Franch has directed a long-term project on the prehistory of the Esmeraldas valley and vicinity. Although producing several handsome volumes containing much useful information, members of this project, the Misión Arqueológica Española, are dedicated to the most hypertrophied of type-variety approaches to pottery classification and seem adverse to reconstructing vessel forms (Alcina Franch 1979; Sánchez Montañés 1981; Guinea Bueno 1984; Rivera et al. 1984). Regrettably, therefore, these potentially critical data are of limited comparative value. Farther south in Manabí, the ceramic sequence for the Jama valley has been outlined in a preliminary paper (Sutliff and Zeidler 1991), and a brief report on the Tarqui excavations near Manta is available (Stirling and Stirling 1963). Similarities between these Manabí materials and Selva Alegre or any other Santiago-Cayapas phase are either absent or too highly general to emphasize.

To the north in the Tumaco area, Bouchard (1985) has detailed a long ceramic sequence beginning in the later half of the first millennium B.C. The earliest phase in this sequence, Inguapí (the formal difference between Inguapí I and II is unclear), displays numerous and specific similarities to both Mafa and Selva Alegre. In fact, one could recognize a Mafa or Selva Alegre counterpart for almost every Inguapí vessel illustrated by Bouchard. The most salient similarity is a tripodal and often red painted or slipped plate. Every rim modification found in the Santiago-Cayapas specimens—direct, T-shaped, corniced, everted—is also recorded in Inguapí (Bouchard 1985: figs. 12.5–8; 13.8–13; 14.17). The same range of carinated bowls characterizes both areas; in particular compare figs. 16.12 and 17.1 in Bouchard with the Mafa piece shown in fig. 4.7E of the present volume. Oddly, jars appear to be rare in Inguapí, or at least few are illustrated. Everted, outcurving, and thickened lip jars, however, are present (Bouchard 1985: figs. 16.11; 28.13–14), although the conspicuous ledge rim form of Mafa and Selva Alegre is apparently absent. In the Tumaco sequence, Inguapí is followed by the El Balsal phase dated to A.D. 50 ± 70. This date suggests contemporaneity with at least the later part of the Selva Alegre phase, a suggestion conformable with the presence of tripod plates and cambered rim jars in the small El Balsal assemblage (Bouchard 1985: fig. 25).

Farther northward along the Colombian coast, Patiño (1988) has developed a ceramic chronology for the Guapi and Timbiquí drainages in which the largely coeval Las Delicias and El Tamarindo phases (with respective dates of 190 B.C. ± 90 and 140 B.C. ± 60) display a number of similarities to Selva Alegre including red-slipped or red-and-white plates supported by hollow tripods.

As discussed in following chapters, close similarities between Santiago-Cayapas and Chocó ceramics to the north continue in later periods. From Inguapí on, both regions, today separated by the border between Ecuador and Colombia, participate in the same enduring cultural tradition.

6
FROM PATAS TO PEDESTALS
The Guadual Phase

The Guadual phase begins with a bang. There is a major shift from polypod patas to tall, often flamboyantly shaped or decorated pedestals. There is a sudden and related transformation in serving vessels: plates with chalky pastes are replaced by compoteras with fine sandy pastes. Although several vessel forms persist from Selva Alegre, two of these increase dramatically in frequency, and a suite of seven new forms appears for the first time in Guadual. Black resist decoration, always executed as a postfire addition to a red-slipped background, becomes common. This series of innovations lends Guadual pottery a novel cast and suggests a major shift in Santiago-Cayapas "foodways." Moreover, this new culinary technology, however fancy in its elaboration of ceramic form and design, intimates a standardized aspect that departs from the more playful artistry of Selva Alegre (one happy consequence of this impression is that Guadual ceramics are fairly easy to recognize). It is as if the "happy forest" of Selva Alegre were supplanted by the repetitive nodes of a stalk of bamboo (*guadúa* means bamboo in Cayapas Spanish). Perhaps these phase names are not so inappropriate after all.

The most salient difference between Selva Alegre and Guadual, however, is the change in vessel supports. Although continuing in reduced numbers, patas are on the way out. A requiem for the passing of the pata and a respite from the tedium of humorless pottery description are both in order.

A Digression into Base Symbolism

The following vignette, one dared by amused or even alarmed colleagues, begins with several anecdotes. One night in 1986, perched on the elevated floor of Jesusito's house with the Cayapas rushing below, Elka Weinstein, Paul Tolstoy, and I chatted after a dinner of beans, *bala,* and slices of papaya. Just that day, Elka had returned from the Boca Onzole with news of a pata shaped like a draconic crocodilian. This was not totally remarkable because dragon-cayman representations are relatively common in La Tolita art. Responsible for drawing all the artifacts coming in from the field, I knew about the mammiform patas characterizing the still nascent Selva Alegre phase. Furthermore, I had seen and sketched an obviously phallic pata in the collection of a local North American expatriate. As a cooling breeze picked up to promise rain, seemingly unrelated thoughts fleetingly came together. Trained by Don Lathrap, I remembered his obsession with the cayman (specifically the monstrous black cayman, *Melanosuchus niger*) and his argument that this beast is the primordial nexus of Neotropical cosmology—

the androgynous monster mediating between night and day, earth and sky, and female and male. With a vague sense of discovery and levity, I suggested to Elka and Paul that we coauthor an article to be called "The Tit, the Prick, and the Croc." Immediately Paul replied that this was a bad idea as many readers would assume that the title referred to the authors. Elka found the idea completely silly. The rain began to pound, the candles went out, and the coauthors of a stillborn article retired to their hammocks.

Anecdote two—spring semester, 1991. Lynda Carroll and Kimberly Pierce pick away at the soil matrix filling several hollow Selva Alegre patas. They discover water-rolled quartz pebbles embedded in the matrix of one. Their discovery is important—it demonstrates that patas were occasionally rattling vessel supports. I remember the rattle-base beer mug used in recent Shipibo-Conibo female puberty ceremonies. An identical vessel form is attested in the millennium old Cumancaya ceramics of the Peruvian Amazon. As a more general observation, it should be recalled that semen-associated quartz crystals and shamans go together throughout Amazonia and that quartz is the preferred rattler for the shamanic gourd rattle, the focal instrument, simultaneously phallus and womb, linking the multiple tiers of the cosmos (Lathrap 1977; Reichel-Dolmatoff 1979).

Anecdote three—June vacation in Oaxaca, 1991. Tripod vessels on exhibit at the Frissell Museum at Mitla include patas faithfully modeled in crocodilian, mammiform, and phallic representations. A vessel realistically modeled as a human foot is also on display. Back in Oaxaca City, I buy a copy of *Pueblos de la Sierra Madre* and read of the important role that beings with a missing foot play in Otomí folklore. According to Galinier (1987: 437–38), the Otomí liken the foot to the phallus, whereas both (or perhaps better stated, all three) are symbolically equated with the triad of stone pot-rests found in every hearth. The Desana of the Colombian Amazon make precisely the same connections—a "culinary triangle" indeed!

Anecdote four—a sweltering July in New York City, 1991. While writing the previous chapter, I return to Buys's description of the Jardín del Este ceramics. One pot attracts particular attention: a tripod vessel with one shortened foot. Fortuitously I come across Ginzburg's (1991) marvelous study of the monopedal motif in Eurasian and American folklore and world view. Cinderella's missing slipper, the goat-footed Satan, Achilles' heel, Oedipus as "swollen foot," and all of the above anecdotes begin to converge ("to resonate," as the postmodernists would say).

This convergence is pictured in fig. 6.1. The vessel at the top of this figure is a plate from R36 with a cornice rim and one preserved mammiform pata; the crocodilian pata recorded by Elka Weinstein and the phallic pata from a private collection have been added to complete the composite tripod. Critics might complain that my composition is purely chimerical, and I must admit that the pictured reconstruction is, in part, my creation. This criticism, however, is largely beside the point. Most patas are of a simple conical sort, but when patas are elaborated

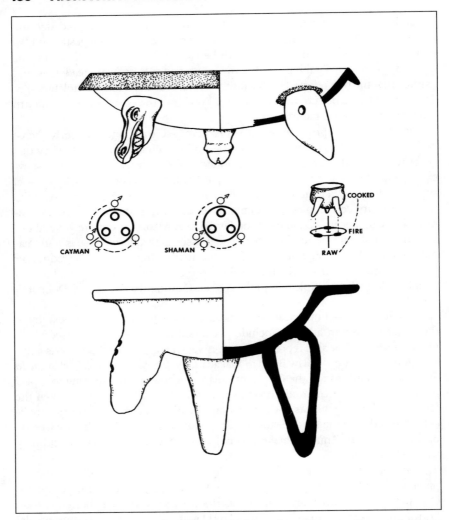

Fig. 6.1   Top, *Tripod plate from R361 with added phalliform and crocodilian patas.* Bottom, *tripod plate with shortened pata from Jardín del Este (Buys and Domínguez 1988: fig. 61).* Center, *Schema for interpreting these two vessels.*

they *do* assume crocodilian, mammary, and phallic forms. I would argue, therefore, that the composite tripod of fig. 6.1 is a plausible portrayal of the underlying system of meanings that only occasionally surface in ceramic form.

The short-footed tripod vessel from Jardín del Este needs no creative amplification to convey its message (fig. 6.1, *bottom*). It stands on its own by not being able to stand at all. It is obviously a specific manifestation of the witch- and shaman-associated monopedal syndrome as universally diagnosed by Ginzburg. These multiple observations, disparate alone but coherent together, can be condensed to the schematic diagrams shown in the center of fig. 6.1. It is hardly surprising that the androgynous cayman maintains its central place in tripod imagery as mediator between female and male principles. Similarly, it requires little imagination to see the short-footed, shaman-associated pata as the equally androgynous and liminal link between the genders. Rotate these trisected circles 90°, and they become the plane of the Otomí or Desana hearth with the three pot-rests rimming the fire that transforms the raw into the cooked. I always wondered why Shipibo-Conibo *topia* (pot-supports) and the functionally equivalent "stump-ware" of Cahokia (Titterington 1938: figs. 44–45) are occasionally modeled as "feet."

With the passing of the pata, a widespread symbolic system that sporadically surfaces throughout the Old and New Worlds is suspended in the Santiago and Cayapas basins. This suspension further highlights the gulf separating the Selva Alegre and Guadual phases. But this digression has become lengthy, and so much footwork remains to be done.

Back to Basics

Guadual sites are plotted in fig. 6.2, and individual site characteristics are listed in table 6.1. Although the number of Guadual sites is about half that of Selva Alegre, this reduction is not meaningful when other factors are considered. First, according to the radiocarbon chronology developed in previous chapters, the Selva Alegre phase has a greater duration than Guadual, so more Selva Alegre sites could be expected on temporal grounds alone. Second, total site *area* in the Guadual phase is greater than in Selva Alegre, although this increase is due solely to the 15 ha extent of R10II. Thus, when phase duration is controlled, there appears to be a major increase in total site area during the Guadual phase (table 6.2). I am skeptical, however, about attaching much demographic significance to this result. Large and salient sites such as R10 are less likely to be missed in archaeological reconnaissance than are small sherd patches. Thus a population dispersed in single house settlements would appear to be smaller than the same population aggregated in larger, more visible sites, an effect that may account for the evident correlation between mean site size and total site area in the phases of the Santiago-Cayapas sequence.

If the matter of estimating relative population size remains problematical, it is nonetheless possible to detect a major change in the distribution of Guadual sites. Whereas only 20% of Selva Alegre sites occur along the Santiago or Cayapas mainstream, this figure doubles to 40% in the case of Guadual. In comparison to precedent and subsequent phases, Guadual is decidedly mainstream in orientation. It is tempting to attribute this shift to the increasing importance of La Tolita as a determinant of regional settlement pattern. Today and in the past, the Santiago and Cayapas are the main highways linking the interior and the coast. As the Tardío phase at La Tolita is contemporary with at least the early half of the Guadual

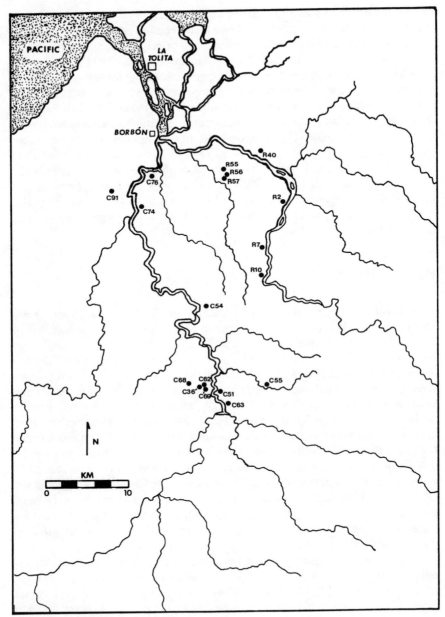

Fig. 6.2   Distribution of Guadual sites.

Table 6.1   Characteristics of Guadual sites.

SITE	ENVIRONMENTAL CODE	DRAINAGE	DEPOSITIONAL CONTEXT	SIZE(HA)	ARTIFACTS COLLECTED	COMMENTS
R2	CCGC	I	P	1.6	627	in modern community of San José de Tagua
R7	EDHC	III	P	0.1	71	site centers on tola, ca 30 m diameter, 3-4 m high
R10-II	C/D-E/FC	I	P	15	3661+	several associated mounds
R40	CCCC	I	P	0.02	25	
R55	DDFC	II	P	0.1	123	site centers on tola, ca 30 m diameter, 0.5 m high
R56	DDFC	II	P	0.01	19	
R57	DDFC	II	P	0.04	33	
C36-II	HFDC	III	P	1	9002	in cafetal
C51	HGHC	I	P&SS	0.5	313	
C54	CEHC	III	P&SS	0.03	385	on steep slope in platanal
C55-I	C/G-H/FC	II	P	?	122+	buried by Herradura component
C62	H/F-G/DC	III	P	0.03	30+	
C63	C-H/G/F-H/C	I	P&SS	0.1+	none	atop Loma Linda
C68	HFDC	III	P	1.5	89	in cafetal
C69-III	HFDC	III	P	0.04	700+	single house mound
C74C	CCFB	I	SS	?	4	
C76C	CCEB	I	SS	?	4	
C91	EDIB	III	SS	?	56	washing down steep slope in pasture

Environmental code summarizes indices defined in figs. 2.6–2.7; for example, CCGC means *C* coding for pedology, *C* for geology, *G* for agriculture, and *C* for bioclimate. For drainage, *I* means location along Santiago or Cayapas mainstream; *II*, location along navigable secondary tributary; and *III*, along unnavigable estero or in interfluves. Under depositional context, *P* means intact primary deposit; *SS*, secondary deposit found as slope wash or embedded in land-slump; and *SE*, secondary deposit found in bed of estero. Note: cafetal is a field planted in coffee.

Table 6.2   Selected phase characteristics.

Phase	Number of Sites	Total Ha[a]	Total Ha / Number of Sites	Estimated Phase Duration	Total Ha (100) / Duration
Cantarana–Chachi	30	1.82	.06	150 yrs	1.21
Tumbaviro	49	6.56	.13	400	1.64
Las Cruces	7	2.32			
Mina	13	4.83			
Herradura	16	4.79			
Total	36	12.14	.34	700	1.73
Guadual	18	20.15	1.12	300	6.71
Selva Alegre	34	14.30	.42	500	2.86

[a] Sites of unknown size are coded as .02 ha, the modal size of measurable sites.

phase (fig. 5.7), such an account is chronologically plausible but remains unconvincing for other reasons. One reason is that what really needs to be explained is why people live in the interfluves at all. The main rivers are richer in fish, are flanked by generally better agricultural soils, and are the main avenues for canoe travel, so there is nothing particularly problematic about a riverine settlement preferendum. A second reason is that if La Tolita were attracting the regional population onto the mainstream then it is odd that this resettlement should concentrate on the upper reaches of the Santiago and Cayapas, more than a day's canoe trip upstream from La Tolita. In contrast, the Colón Eloy area, only a few hours from La Tolita by canoe and the site of a major Selva Alegre settlement (R36), seemingly experiences a population decline during the Guadual phase. Third, there is no evidence that the exchange of imported commodities such as obsidian increases during Guadual times. If anything, obsidian is less abundant in the Guadual phase (table 3.9). Overall then, the nature of the linkages between La Tolita and its Santiago-Cayapas hinterland remains poorly understood.

As in Selva Alegre, R10 continues to be the largest settlement, now covering 15 ha and boasting a minimum of fifteen domestic or public mounds (fig. 5.3). Other sites include 1.0 to 1.6 ha middens without mounds (R2, C36II, C68), whereas the more common Guadual site is a small sherd scatter occasionally associated with a single house mound (table 6.1). Of these modestly sized sites, C36 deserves special comment because it produced the initial stratigraphic evidence for the precedence of Selva Alegre to Guadual. As seen in fig. 6.3, C36 consists of a sherd scatter covering about 1 ha. A series of augers was sunk in the central part of the site where surface sherds were most common. A 4 x 4 m excavation unit was then opened in the area where augers indicated the greatest abundance of subsurface ceramics. It should be remembered that this excavation took place in 1986 when Guadual ceramics were yet to be defined; our purpose therefore was to acquire a large sample of pottery. This goal was achieved. The details of the excavation are diagrammed in fig. 6.4. A sherd-rich Guadual midden, yellow-brown in color, is superposed over a friable yellow clay in which Selva Alegre materials predominate. Although the vertical distribution of diagnostic Selva Alegre and Guadual ceramics as plotted in fig. 6.5 might suggest an *in situ* transition between the styles, such an interpretation is unlikely for several reasons. First, we were slow to recognize and track properly a sloping lens of dark midden in square C2; this lapse on our part mixed dark Guadual midden with the underlying Selva Alegre deposit. Second, crawfish burrows provide additional opportunities for vertical mixture. In addition, the Selva Alegre pottery from C36 does not appear "transitional" in any sense—that is, it is as different from Guadual as is the pottery from single-component Selva Alegre sites. This latter point prompts a fuller description of Guadual ceramics.

Guadual Ceramics

The following survey is keyed to major vessel forms and, when feasible, parallels the earlier descriptions of Mafa and Selva Alegre ceramics.

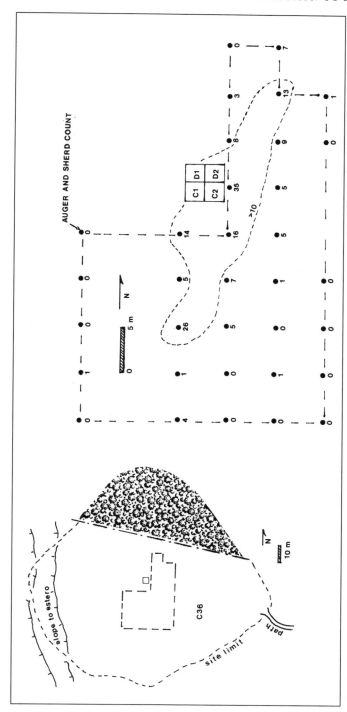

Fig. 6.3 Plan of C36 (left) with inset shown at expanded scale (right).

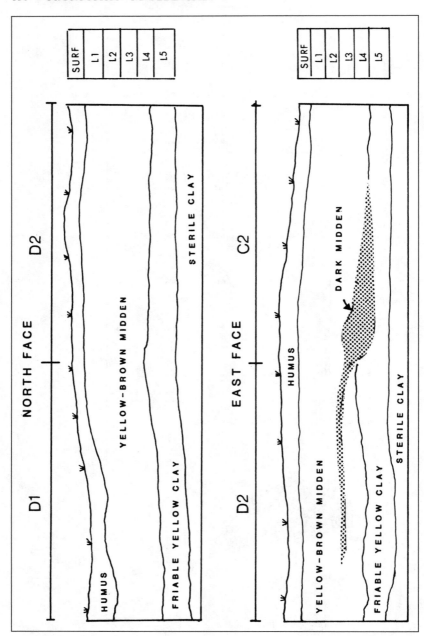

Fig. 6.4 Profiles of excavation units at C36.

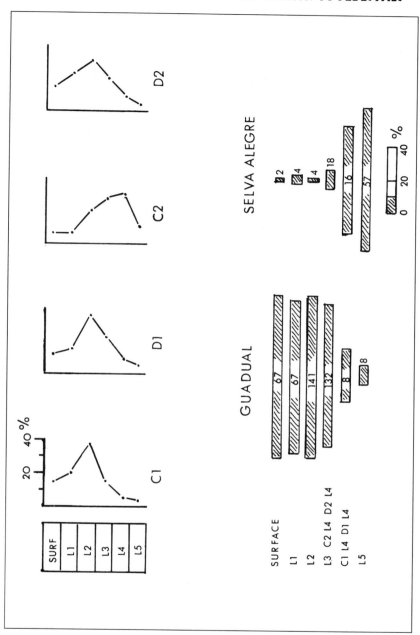

Fig. 6.5 Top, *Vertical distribution of all sherds by percentage within cuts, C36. Bottom, Vertical distribution of diagnostic Selva Alegre and Guadual sherds within levels, C36.*

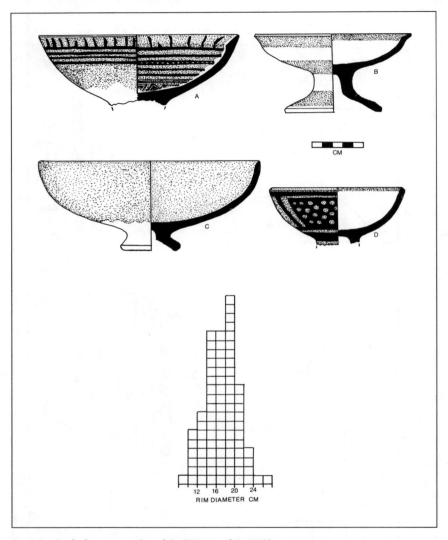

Fig. 6.6   Guadual compoteras (A and C, C36II; B and D, R10II).

Compoteras

Compoteras are a new and highly distinctive form with a modal rim diameter of 19 cm. The sample of one hundred vessels is about evenly divided between those with an unmodified or direct rim (fig. 6.6C–D) and those with a sharply beveled rim (fig. 6.6A–B). Compoteras are usually decorated, with only eighteen specimens being plain. Decorative treatments include an all-over red slip on both exterior and interior surfaces (forty-nine), red bands painted on the vessel exterior (twenty-four), and a black resist over a red slip (nine). Two of the more complete designs executed in resist-over-red are shown in fig. 6.6.

Table 6.3   *Distribution of major vessel groups by site size and phase.*

	Phase	Compoteras or Plates	Bowls	Jars	Total
Selva Alegre	Large Sites (≥ 5 ha)	26 (17%)	39 (26%)	85 (57%)	150
	Medium Sites (0.2 - 0.4 ha)	12 (26%)	9 (20%)	25 (54%)	46
	Small Sites (<0.1 ha)	47 (32%)	30 (20%)	72 (48%)	149
	Total	85 (25%)	78 (22%)	182 (53%)	345
Guadual	Large Sites (R10II=15 ha)	26 (23%)	16 (15%)	69 (62%)	111
	Medium Sites (0.5 - 1.6 ha)	55 (14%)	84 (21%)	254 (65%)	393
	Small Sites (<0.1 ha)	19 (8%)	67 (29%)	147 (63%)	233
	Total	100 (14%)	167 (23%)	470 (63%)	737
Herradura	Medium Sites (0.2 - 1.0 ha)	58 (25%)	74 (31%)	102 (44%)	234
	Small Sites (<0.1 ha)	5 (11%)	25 (53%)	17 (36%)	47
	Total	63 (22%)	99 (35%)	119 (43%)	281

As emphasized earlier, the seemingly sudden and total replacement of plates by compoteras marks the onset of the Guadual phase. Although it is likely that both forms were food-serving vessels, there is contextual evidence that the two may have played different roles in their respective societies. In the Selva Alegre phase, plates are more common at small or medium-sized sites than at large centers such as R10I or R36I (table 6.3). In contrast, Guadual compoteras are most common at the large center of R10II and become progressively less abundant at medium-sized and small sites. This contrast suggests a fundamental change in either the social function of fancy serving vessels or in the nature of activities

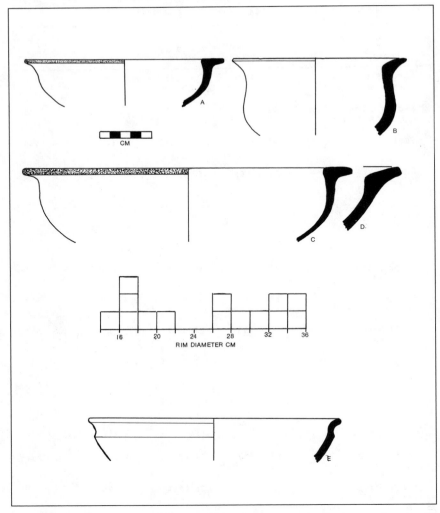

Fig. 6.7   *Guadual open bowls with everted rims (A–B, C55I; C–D, C69III) and with recurved rim (E, R2). Histogram refers to open bowls with everted rims.*

carried out at differently sized sites. For example, it could be that a Guadual elite residing at a center such as R10 had preferential access to compoteras and furthermore viewed the compotera as an appropriate medium for expressing elite status. Alternatively, whether such an imagined elite actually existed, it could be that during the Guadual phase the size and frequency of feasts varied according to settlement size, with larger settlements hosting bigger and more *fiestas* in which "good parties" required decoratively ostentatious compoteras. Although plausible, these speculations cannot be pursued further with the evidence at hand.

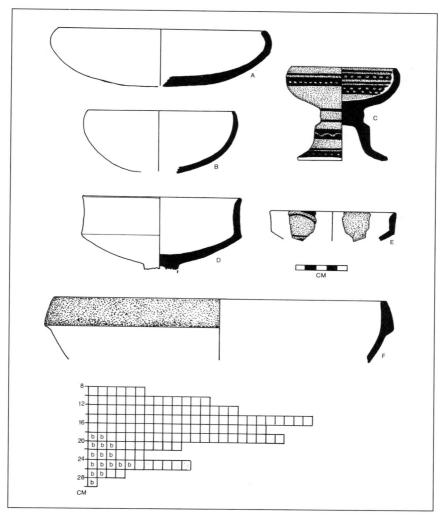

Fig. 6.8   Guadual closed bowls (A–B, C36II; C, C69III), carinated bowls (D–E, C36II), and buttress rim bowls (F, R2). In histogram, b refers to buttress rim bowls, and blank squares refer to closed or carinated bowls.

Open Bowls with Everted Rims

Also present in Selva Alegre, the open bowls with everted rims display a wide range in size but a standardized decorative treatment: in ten of fourteen cases, the rim eversion is painted red (fig. 6.7A, C).

Channel Rim Bowl

The distinctive form of the channel rim bowl makes its first appearance with a single specimen from R2 (fig. 6.7E). It becomes more common in later phases.

Closed Bowls with Direct Rims

Having their greatest frequency in Guadual, closed bowls with direct rims come in two size modes (15 and 25 cm, respectively), and more than half of the examples bear a red-slipped or painted exterior. One unique specimen, mounted on a pedestal, is decorated with resist on both surfaces (fig. 6.8C). Of twenty-six undecorated vessels within this category, fifteen are sooted below the shoulder, indicating that this form subsumed both serving and cooking functions.

Carinated Bowls

The carinated bowl is an abundant vessel and is ordinarily indistinguishable from the closed carinated bowls of Selva Alegre (fig. 5.11F–G). More rarely, the upper vessel walls are vertical above the carination (fig. 6.8D–E). Of seventy-one examples, fifty have red-slipped exteriors above the carination, and three bear resist decoration (fig. 6.8E). A few plain specimens are carbon sooted on their exteriors below the carination.

Buttress Rim Bowls

As a relatively large bowl with a modal rim diameter of 25 cm, the buttress rim bowl has its upper walls thickened or buttressed (fig. 6.8F). Almost all of the twenty-four examples have red-slipped buttresses; in six cases the base of the buttress is accentuated with a finger-impressed fillet. This latter embellishment anticipates a common Las Cruces treatment.

Cambered Rim Jars

One specimen of a cambered rim jar was found in Guadual deposits at C36.

Outcurving Rim Jars

The outcurving rim jar assumes the variety of shapes shown in fig. 6.9. Just over half of the fifty examples have decorated exteriors. The most common treatment is a red slip applied above the shoulder (eighteen), followed by painted red bands (six), whereas two instances of resist decoration are present. The modal orifice diameter is 10 cm for the numerous specimens from C36II. For unknown reasons, the few measurable examples from other sites dominate the upper reaches of the form's diameter range (see fig. 6.9 histogram).

Everted Rim Jars

The everted rim jar is an abundant form, with modal diameters centering at 13 cm and between 21 to 25 cm. Following the Guadual penchant for pigment, more than 75% of the 133 examples are slipped or painted. The interior of the rim eversion is usually painted red (fig. 6.10A, D), whereas the vessel exterior is commonly slipped or painted with horizontal bands. One unillustrated specimen bears traces of resist decoration on the interior of the rim eversion.

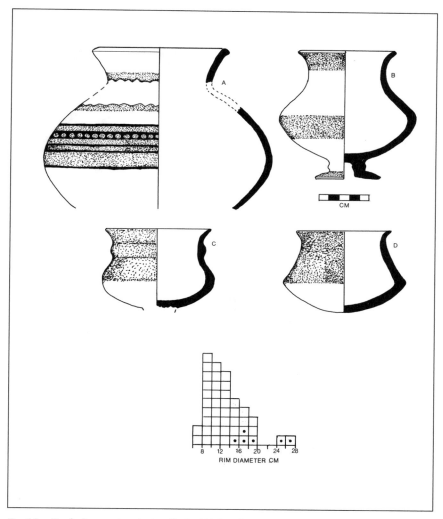

Fig. 6.9   Guadual outcurving rim jars (A–D, C36II). In histogram, dotted squares are vessels **not** from C36II.

Wedge Rim Jars

Presaged in Selva Alegre, the wedge rim jar gains its maximum popularity in the Guadual phase. Two formal variants can be recognized depending on the presence (fig. 6.11D–F) or absence (fig. 6.11A–C) of a concavity on the rim interior. This concavity (defining variant II) is restricted to the Guadual phase. Wedge rim jars are decorated in a highly standardized way: of eighty-four examples, sixty-nine have red-painted rims that contrast with a plain vessel body. Orifice diameters vary considerably, with two tentative modes at 13 and 27 cm.

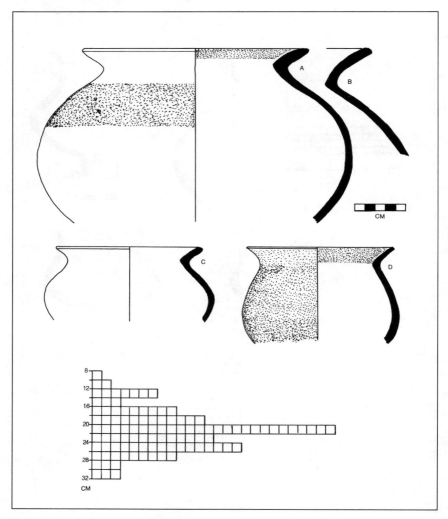

Fig. 6.10   *Guadual everted rim jars (A–C, C36II; D, R10II).*

Recurved Rim Jars

The recurved rim jar, a distinctive and infrequent jar, continues from Selva Alegre. Two of the four vessels are painted with horizontal red bands (fig. 6.12A).

Small Thick Wall Jars

Another holdover from Selva Alegre, the small thick wall jar is represented by four specimens, all decorated in the manner shown in fig. 6.12G–H.

Expanded Lip Jars

As the most frequent vessel form, the expanded lip jar is the "generic jar" of the Guadual phase (fig. 6.12C–F). It comes in three size modes centering at 15,

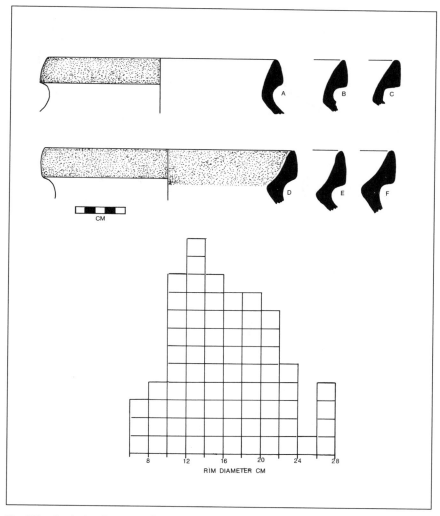

Fig. 6.11   Guadual wedge rim jars from C36II: variety I (A–C); variety II (D–F).

21, and 27 cm. Of 178 examples, 110 have red-painted lips as their only decoration. Rarer is the application of sloppily executed red bands to the exterior surface (fig. 6.12D). Carbon sooting of the subshoulder region of three specimens indicates that this form was occasionally used in a cooking capacity. In a unique case, the bottom of the vessel was perforated before firing to form a colander (fig. 6.12C).

C69 Jars

The C69 jar is so named because seven of the thirteen examples come from the Guadual component at C69. As seen in fig. 6.13A–B, it is a wide-mouthed jar with a flaring neck embellished by an indented fillet. The lip and upper interior

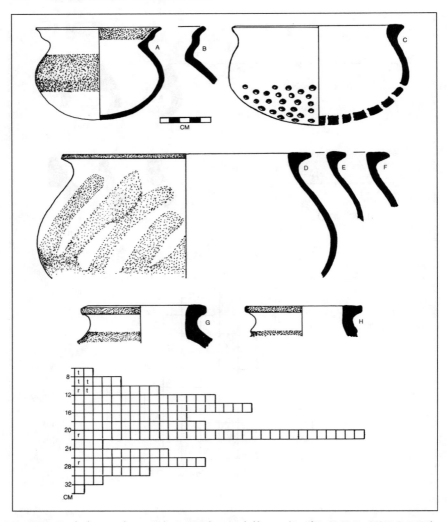

Fig. 6.12 *Guadual recurved rim jars (A–B, R10II), expanded lip jars (C and F, C36II; D, C69III; E, R10II), and small thick wall jars (G, C36II; H, C55I). In histogram, r is recurved rim jar, t is small thick wall jar, and blank squares are expanded lip jars.*

rim are customarily painted red. Similar filleted jars are known in Las Cruces assemblages.

San José Jars

Perhaps due to a tiring descriptive terminology, the San José jar is named after the place where it was first identified, San José de Tagua (R2) on the Santiago. It is characterized by a gently outcurving rim that thickens toward the lip. The two recovered specimens are illustrated in fig. 6.13C–D.

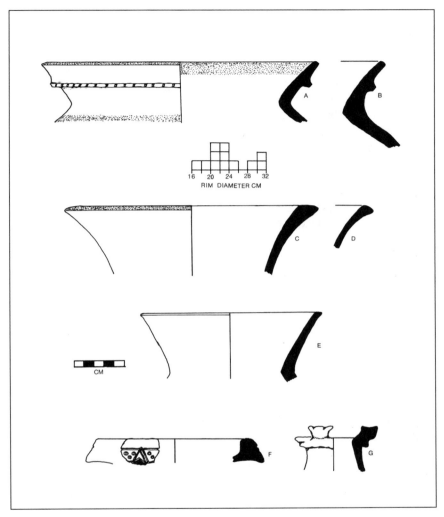

Fig. 6.13 Guadual C69 jars (A, C69III; B, C55I), San José jars (C, C55I; D, R2), tall flaring neck jar (E,C91), and miscellaneous vessels (F, C62; G, C69III). Histogram refers to C69 jars only.

Tall Flaring Neck Jar

To become common in the subsequent Las Cruces phase, the tall flaring neck jar is represented by a single example from C91 (fig. 6.13E).

Comma Rim Basins

Although greatly diminished in frequency, the comma rim basin continues from the Selva Alegre phase.

Miscellaneous Vessels

Both the incised and the reed-stamped vessel of fig. 6.13F and the small jar with an appended adorno shown in fig. 6.13G are unique. One remaining form, alluded to in chapter 3, is the double-spout-and-bridge bottle. Eight of the twelve specimens recovered from the Santiago-Cayapas come from Guadual contexts. These include a miniature (fig. 3.6F), two medium-sized examples with flaring spouts and solid bridge (fig. 3.6H, J), and the awkwardly shaped grotesquery pictured in fig. 3.6I. In the case of isolated spouts, it is possible that a single-spout-and-handle is represented (fig. 3.6G), although no independent evidence for this form is found.

The above survey indicates that Guadual pottery, although highly distinctive, shares many features with the ceramics of both preceding and following phases. These continuities suggest that an internal seriation of the phase may be possible. Following the same format used in the preceding chapter, table 6.4 arranges Guadual assemblages according to the distribution of eight vessel forms that are uniquely shared with either the earlier Selva Alegre phase or the later Las Cruces and Herradura phases. This arrangement is promising, although several assemblages are represented by vanishingly small samples. R2, San José de Tagua, is a good candidate for a late Guadual assemblage. C36II is an equally good candidate for an early assemblage within the phase. The sizable collections from R10II, C55I, and C69III would appear to be intermediate to these postulated early and late poles.

If additional evidence establishes that table 6.4 indeed represents a seriation, then the implications of this chronology are considerable. The largest Guadual site, R10II, would completely postdate C36II. This dating, in turn, would raise the possibility that R10II, rather than being a secondary center to La Tolita, actually postdates the latter's abandonment. As always, the issue of contemporaneity is a fundamental one.

External Similarities

In seeking comparative material, it is necessary to revisit the same terrain covered in the preceding chapter: nearby La Tolita, the Esmeraldas valley to the south, and Tumaco to the north.

It is premature to compare Guadual ceramics with those of the partially contemporary Tardío phase at La Tolita because full descriptions of the latter are still in preparation. Red-slipped and painted compoteras with elaborate hollow pedestals—a Guadual hallmark—are certainly found in the Tardío phase, as are wedge rim and expanded lip jars (Valdez 1987: fig. 25), but it is not presently possible to specify other shared features. Compoteras are also characteristic of the Tiaone phase of the Esmeraldas valley (Rivera et al. 1984: fig. 29a), but other similarities are difficult to detect in the descriptively thin account of this phase.

Table 6.4   Distribution of selected Guadual vessel forms.

| Site | Vessels Shared with Las Cruces or Herradura | | | | Vessels Shared with Selva Alegre | | | |
	1	2	3	4	5	6	7	8
R40[a]	1	–	–	–	–	–	–	–
R2[a]	6	1	1	1	–	–	–	3
R10II[b]	10	–	–	–	3	21	–	6
C55I[b]	2	–	5	1	17	11	1	6
C69III[b]	5	–	7	–	15	17	2	11
C91[b]	–	–	1	–	2	1	–	–
R7[c]	–	–	–	–	–	–	–	1
C36II[c]	–	–	–	–	32	74	1	41
C51[c]	–	–	–	–	–	1	–	–
C54[c]	–	–	–	–	–	3	–	–
C62[c]	–	–	–	–	2	4	–	3

Vessel key: *1,* buttress rim bowl; *2,* channel rim bowl; *3,* C69 jar *and* tall flaring neck jar; *4,* San José jar; *5,* closed carinated bowl; *6,* everted rim jars; *7,* small thick wall jar; *8,* wedge rim jar I.

[a] Sites where vessels shared with Las Cruces or Herradura predominate.

[b] Sites where vessels shared with Las Cruces or Herradura, although present, are in minority.

[c] Sites where Las Cruces or Herradura vessels are absent.

Neither Valdez (personal communication) for La Tolita nor Heras y Martinez (1991) for the Esmeraldas valley recognize the sharp break between tripod plates and compoteras that so effectively separates the Selva Alegre and Guadual phases. I would prefer to believe that future work will identify this break in these neighboring areas. Alternatively, it is conceivable (although unlikely) that the shift from plates to compoteras was localized in the Santiago and Cayapas basins. (I will not consider a third possibility—namely that the Santiago-Cayapas sequence is wrong.)

Guadual ceramics most convincingly resemble the El Morro style documented by Bouchard in the Tumaco area. Both share similar, if not identical, compoteras decorated with the same range of red-slipped or painted surfaces (Bouchard 1985: fig. 30). A number of other Guadual forms including San José and C69 jars are also present in El Morro. In his summary of the Tumaco sequence, Bouchard (1985: 317) emphasizes the seemingly unprecedented nature of the El Morro assemblage and argues that it represents the intrusion of a new population into the Tumaco region. From the perspective of the Santiago-Cayapas, this argument must be qualified. As outlined earlier, a number of features derived from Selva Alegre endure during the Guadual phase. Nonetheless, such continuities do not necessarily undermine the case for the introduction of radically new elements (notably the compotera) into the La Tolita–Tumaco region during the time frame encompassed by the Guadual, La Tolita Tardío, and El Morro phases. About 40 km northward from Tumaco, a similar story unfolds in the Patía drainage. Here Patiño (1993) has defined a Buena Vista phase in which compoteras, similar if not identical to El Morro and Guadual examples, are conspicuous.

The source of these new elements, however, is unknown. During the inappropriately titled "Regional Developmental Period," the northern Ecuadorian sierra is loaded with flamboyantly modeled compoteras bearing elaborate decorative schemes including resist (Francisco 1969; Doyon 1991). The local highland chronologies, however, remain too undeveloped for specifying *a* source (if such a singularity ever existed) for the "compotera revolution" that sweeps the northern Esmeraldas coast during the early first millennium A.D.

Guadual and Gradualism

The spelling check on my word processor always balked at the entry "Guadual" and urged its replacement with the more acceptable "gradual," inadvertently raising an interesting question. As argued above, my impression is that Guadual ceramics are structured in a new way even though they carry on numerous Selva Alegre attributes. This new way suggests a major change in culinary etiquette in which compoteras are the favored serving vessels, particularly at large centers such as R10II. The new "foodway" is apparently social in nature for the ecofactual evidence, as exiguous as it might be (appendix 2), does not indicate a correlative change in diet. Nor do subsistence-associated artifacts such as manos, net sinkers, or fish scalers change in any remarkable way. Francisco Valdez (personal communication) notes that what appear to be ridged fields—customary symptoms of agricultural intensification—have been spotted in aerial reconnaissance of the coastal marshes to the southwest of La Tolita (an area that today is provocatively called Laguna de la Ciudad), and archaeological validation of this intriguing report is now under way (Montaño 1991).

So, at present, our views of the La Tolita hinterland must lean heavily on ceramic evidence. As indicated, Guadual comes in with a bang. Further work suggested that temporal change within the Guadual phase could be detected with perhaps as many as three subphases being intimated. Contrast the failed attempt to identify temporal subdivisions within Selva Alegre, a phase that lasts about twice as long as Guadual. These observations indicate that not only was the beginning of Guadual a sudden or saltational event but that throughout its duration, ceramics witnessed a speeded up tempo of change in comparison to prior or, as we shall see, to subsequent periods. There was nothing gradual about Guadual.

7
LA TOLITA'S AFTERMATH
Herradura, Las Cruces, and Mysterious Mina

To understand a sequel is difficult if what it follows is very incompletely known. Yet that is the task here. To preface, let me review what is known and not known about what came before.

We do know that La Tolita was a large site with impressive mounds, some of which had a mortuary function. Despite centuries of systematic looting, La Tolita continues to yield goldwork, imported obsidian, fancy pottery, and a riot of iconographically rich figurines. Thanks to the efforts of Valdez and his associates, La Tolita's heyday can now be dated to the period from about 100 B.C. to A.D. 300. This period spans the Selva Alegre phase and at least the early part of the Guadual phase in La Tolita's upstream hinterland. During this time, we know that settlements shifted to the Santiago and Cayapas mainstreams, but whether this shift was related to the magnetlike effect of La Tolita or to other processes is unclear.

We know that major changes in ceramics took place while La Tolita reigned as the premier regional center. Whether viewed as replacements intruding or welcomed from elsewhere or as local innovations, these changes suggest that the Santiago-Cayapas landscape during La Tolita's heyday was a mercurial and experimental place in which nascent or partially achieved rearrangements of the traditional social fabric fostered new material expressions. One such expression was the compotera that redesigned that most basic of activities—the serving of food.

What is not known is more impressive. We do not know the nature of La Tolita itself. Was it indeed a metropolis with a sizable resident population? Or was it a ceremonial center where population aggregations were but periodic and short-lived? Was it the entrepôt linking a dependent and provincial Santiago-Cayapas hinterland with the wonders of the outside Pacific world? Or was it primarily a meganecropolis where regional elites from Tumaco and the Santiago-Cayapas were hurried to be buried (Bouchard 1991)? Was R10II an integral part of the La Tolita settlement system, or did its rise relate to the demise of La Tolita? With the present evidence, it is impossible to select from these not totally contradictory scenarios. This interpretive impasse is likely to persist until we learn more about the nature and internal history of La Tolita.

Whatever the workings of the La Tolita world, we can go on to observe that its sequel in the Santiago and Cayapas basins was structured in a markedly different way, in terms of both ceramic and settlement patterns. In contrast to Selva Alegre and Guadual ceramics, which are relatively uniform across both basins, the derivative ceramics of the following period tend to become balkanized with one phase (Herradura) centering in the Cayapas basin, another (Las Cruces) in the

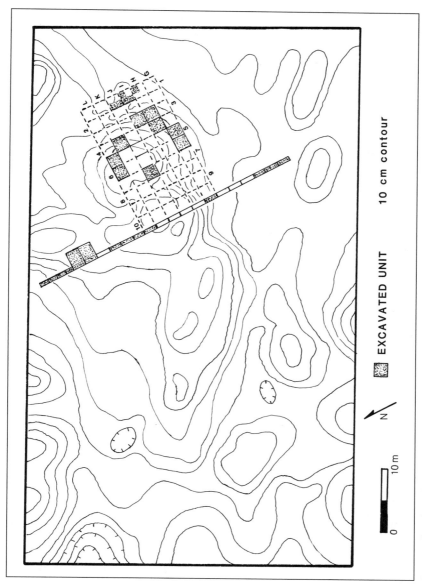

Fig. 7.1 *Plan of C55 showing extent of excavations.*

EXCAVATED UNIT

10 cm contour

N

0   10 m

Santiago basin. In contrast to the Guadual penchant for the mainstream, both Herradura and Las Cruces settlements withdraw to navigable secondary drainages and to the interfluves. Obsidian decreases in abundance, and there is a general decline in the ceramic arts. To document these changes, we begin in the Cayapas basin.

The Herradura Phase

The Herradura phase is named after the Chachi community of Herradura located on a peninsula of high ground defined by a horseshoe bend in the Zapallo Grande. Much of the modern community is underlain by an archaeological midden in which excavations first identified the distinctive ceramics of the phase. These excavations center on the *cancha,* or soccer field, and include a trench and a number of 2 x 2 m units (fig. 7.1). These units were placed to intersect several of the low mounds that give the *cancha* an undulating surface. In fact, the Herradura community agreed to our dig only on the condition that we redistribute the backfill to level out the playing field (at R36, Judy Kreid was asked *not* to backfill one of her deep cuts because it formed an excellent latrine—archaeology as public service indeed!). Before excavation proceeded, Paul Tolstoy and his team made a topographic map of the soccer field, a plan that intimates a structure in the size and distribution of the low undulations (fig. 7.2). With a little imagination, one can see this plan as consisting of generally paired mounds with each pair including a large primary mound and a smaller, secondary neighbor. Also with a little vision, one can arrange these dyads around a level and empty plaza. The plausibility of paired mounds of unequal size is increased when one recalls the plan of La Tolita where, albeit on a more monumental scale, such dyads are readily detected (fig. 1.3). The same tendency toward pairing also shows up in some of the Selva Alegre tumuli (fig. 5.3).

But do the undulations in the Herradura soccer field (subsequently designated by the more technical label C55) truly represent cultural deposits? On the basis of the long north-south trench, the answer is in the affirmative. As shown in fig. 7.3, the mounded elevations are totally attributable to midden deposits (*BCL* and *DM* in the profile), which feather out to extinction away from the mounds. If the mounds are middens, then where are the houses? It seems reasonable to presume that the Herradura folk lived in houses.

Full house plans were never identified, but we did outline a small shedlike structure underneath one of the secondary mounds, and a posthole for a large timber was encountered at the perimeter of the adjacent primary mound. This latter feature almost certainly represents an upright for a substantial residential structure. The evidence for the shedlike structure is given in fig. 7.4. The cardinally oriented grid, of course, hit the structure on the diagonal, and I mutilated some of the evidence before the context was properly diagnosed. Nonetheless, a small rectangular structure consisting of an elevated gray clay floor with postholes

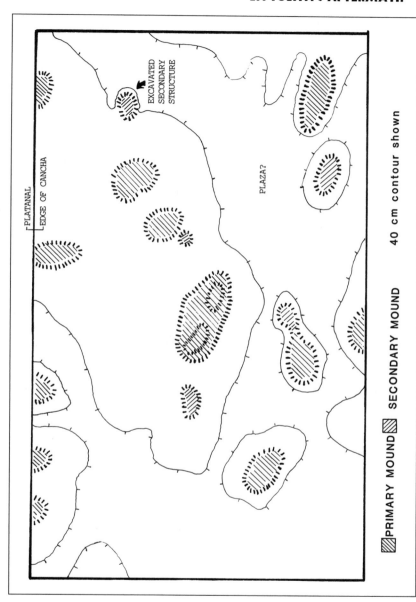

PLATANAL
EDGE OF CANCHA

EXCAVATED SECONDARY STRUCTURE

PLAZA?

PRIMARY MOUND   SECONDARY MOUND

40 cm contour shown

Fig. 7.2 Plan of C55 with topographic lines highlighted to show distribution of mounds.

preserved at three corners and with a well-defined dripline perimeter can be identified with confidence. The central floor encased a pit housing a large olla with the rim broken off; this vessel bears a set of subshoulder incisions resembling tally marks and was found capped by the basal portion of a broken compotera. The floor surface, easy to track once identified, was clear of debris except for a patch of nonconjoinable sherds.

In 1989, three years after the above excavation, Joe Jimenez, John Blitz, and I returned to Herradura and cleared the perimeter of the nearby primary mound. Our purpose was to remove quickly the undifferentiated overburden and to seek underlying traces of a structure to accompany the shed discovered in the 1986 work. This effort was successful, but not in the intended way. A wide and deep posthole, one fully adequate to support a timber for a major structure, was encountered in unit I3 (feature 1 in fig. 7.5). One posthole of this kind, however indicative of a house, does little to define its size and nature. While attempting to find a second posthole, we exposed a small pit in unit G5 (feature 2 in fig. 7.5). This pit was chock-full of Guadual ceramics and also contained a cluster of net sinkers (as if buried while still attached to a now decomposed net). This feature, sealed by Herradura overburden, defines a Guadual occupation (C55I) and, as indicated earlier, was a confirming piece of evidence in establishing the temporal priority of Guadual to Herradura. This sequence, however, was already strongly supported on solid seriational grounds, and we would gladly have traded in feature 2 for a second posthole of the Herradura house. Yes, the Herradura folk lived in houses, but we still don't know what they were like.

Figure 7.6 plots the distribution of Herradura sites, and the characteristics of individual sites are listed in table 7.1. Sites center on the tributaries of the upper Cayapas, although outliers are found on the Estero María (R17, R44) and at the confluence of the Santiago and Bogotá (R28). The ceramics of the Herradura phase are readily derived from Guadual antecedents. Major changes include coarser sandy pastes, surfaces that are generally less well smoothed, thicker vessel walls, and the dropping out of resist decoration and white pigmentation. The Guadual compotera tradition continues, but the typically hollow pedestals of Guadual are now solidified to a simple basal concavity. In an aesthetic and technical sense, Herradura can be viewed as a rustic descendent of Guadual. One exception to this downturn, however, is the proliferation of basally stamped spindle whorls, and one wishes to be able to see Herradura textiles (DeBoer 1991a).

Red painting, most commonly manifest in exterior horizontal bands in Guadual, continues, although the Herradura rendering of vertical bands arranged in quadrants on the interior of bowls (fig. 3.4H) is a departure that no Guadual artist would consider. In Guadual, decoration tends to emphasize the exterior of the vessel—the view from *outside*. In contrast, Herradura decoration is more likely to highlight the vessel interior—the view with the vessel tipped to one's lips. It is tempting to take this observation as a metaphor in keeping with the increasingly inward-turning and provincial cast of Herradura, but I will resist the temptation.

Herradura ceramics are described below in the manner to which the reader is now accustomed.

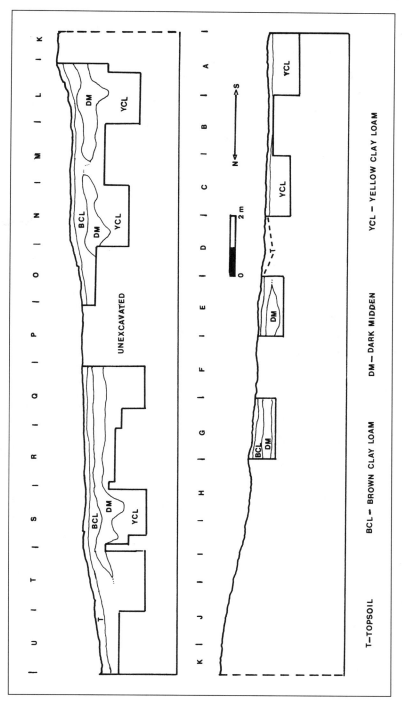

Fig. 7.3 Profile of trench at C55. A–U pertain to excavation units.

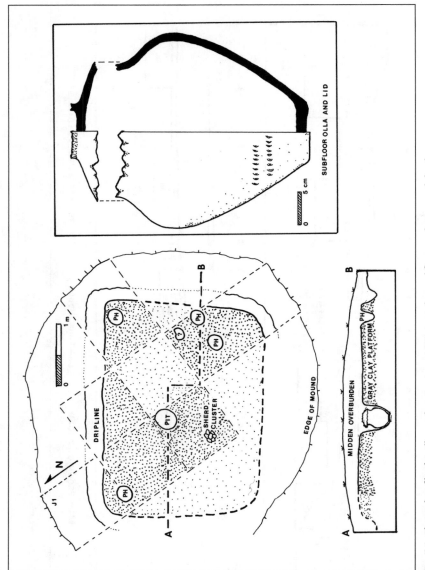

Fig. 7.4 Plan and profile of small secondary structure at C55; inset shows subfloor vessels at expanded scale.

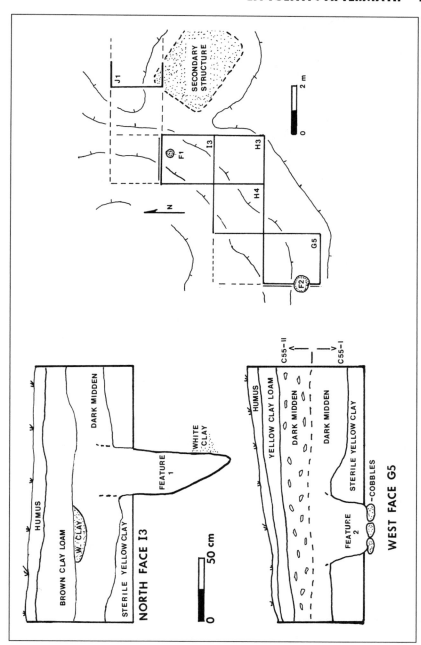

Fig. 7.5 Plan and profiles of features 1 and 2, C55.

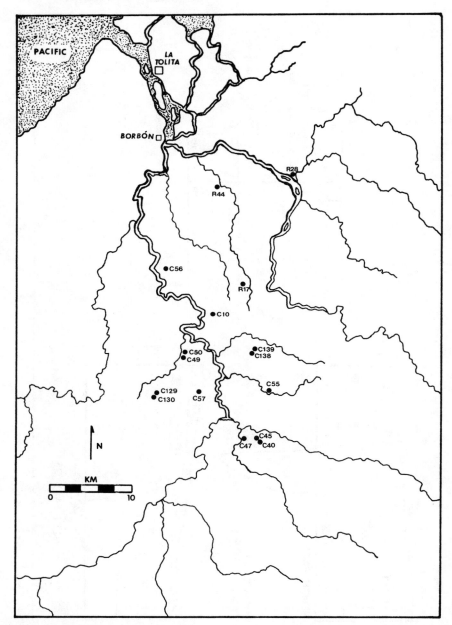

Fig. 7.6 Distribution of Herradura sites.

Table 7.1   Characteristics of Herradura sites.

SITE	ENVIRONMENTAL CODE	DRAINAGE	DEPOSITIONAL CONTEXT	SIZE (HA)	ARTIFACTS COLLECTED	COMMENTS
R17	EEIC	III	P	?	37	probable Herradura
R28	CCFC	I	P	0.3	295	in cemetery of community of Concepción; associated with 2 tolas
R44	DDF/B-C	II	P	0.04	77	in cemetery of community of Colón Eloy
C10	GEHC	III	P	0.08	426	in tagua plantation
C40	HIDD	III	P	0.02	224	mixed with Tumbaviro material
C45	HIDD	III	P	0.02	221	
C47	CIFD	I	P	0.02	178	
C49(C8-9)	GFIC	II	P&SS	0.4?	304	
C50	CFIC	II	P&SS	0.2	1141	atop a steep ridge overlooking the Camarones
C55-II	C/G-H/FC	II	P	2	17,667+	
C56	EEIB	III	P&SS	0.02	63	atop ridge
C57	HFDC	III	P	0.02	292	in abandoned garden
C129	HGIC	III	P&SS	0.1	78	
C130	HGIC	III	P&SS	0.5	51	extends along ridge top
C138	HF/H-I/C	III	P&SS	1	34	extends 400 m along ridge top
C139	HF/H-I/C	III	P	0.03	3	atop ridge

Environmental code summarizes indices defined in figs. 2.6–2.7; for example, CCGC means *C* coding for pedology, *C* for geology, *G* for agriculture, and *C* for bioclimate. For drainage, *I* means location along Santiago or Cayapas mainstream; *II*, location along navigable secondary tributary; and *III*, along unnavigable estero or in interfluves. Under depositional context, *P* means intact primary deposit; *SS*, secondary deposit found as slope wash or embedded in land-slump; and *SE*, secondary deposit found in bed of estero.

Compoteras

Compoteras are descended with modifications from the Guadual form. Direct rims are now universal, walls are somewhat thicker, and paint schemes favor vertical interior bands arranged in quadrants (fig. 7.7C–D). The clear diameter mode of 17 cm is only slightly less than that of the Guadual compotera. Although the hollow Guadual pedestal continues, the most common Herradura rendition is a largely solid pedestal with a slight basal concavity (fig. 7.7A–B, D).

Compoteras reach their greatest relative abundance in the Herradura phase, perhaps suggesting that they now subsume drinking as well as eating functions.

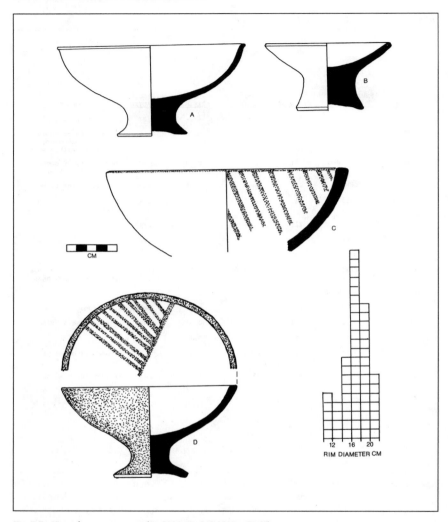

Fig. 7.7   *Herradura compoteras (A, C130; B, C49; C–D, C55II).*

The form continues as a target for painted decoration. Of sixty-three specimens, twenty-five are painted on the interior, twelve have red-slipped exteriors, and five have horizontal bands painted on the exterior. The lip is painted red in five cases. These interior, exterior, and lip paint schemes may occur on the same vessel (fig. 7.7D). Only twenty-seven vessels are seemingly devoid of any pigmentation, yet such a large proportion of undecorated compoteras would have been anathema to Guadual potters. The compotera, once so specialized in form and function, apparently becomes a more generalized category in Herradura assemblages.

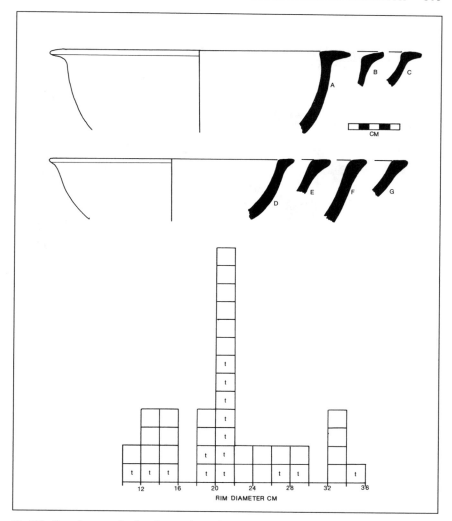

Fig. 7.8 Herradura open bowls with everted rims (A–B, C55II; C, C10) and with thickened lips (D, C50; E, C40; F–G, C55II). In histogram, t refers to the thickened lip bowls.

Open Bowls with Everted Rims

Presaged in Guadual, the open bowl with everted rim form becomes abundant in Herradura (fig. 7.8A–C). Most of the thirty-five examples are plain, but in eleven cases the upper surface of the rim eversion is painted red. There is a clear modal rim diameter of 21 cm with indications of smaller and larger size modes.

Open Bowls with Thickened Lips

The open bowl with thickened lip is almost certainly a variant of the former

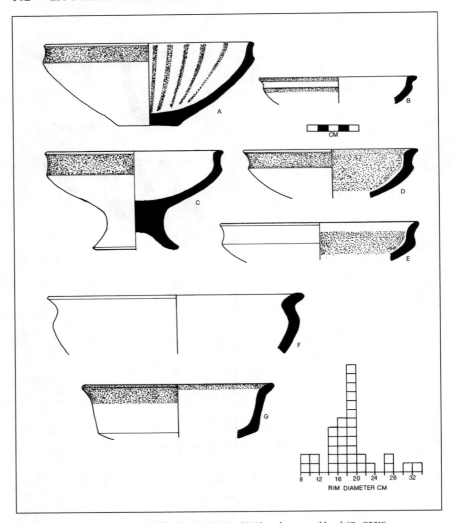

Fig. 7.9 Herradura channel rim bowls (A, C138; B–F, C55II) and carinated bowl (G, C55II).

category. Its recognition is warranted by the fact that it is absent in the preceding Guadual phase. None is decorated (fig. 7.8D–G).

Channel Rim Bowls

A rarity in earlier phases, the channel rim bowl now comes into its own. Of thirty-eight examples, nearly half are decorated with red pigment. Decoration includes five cases in which the exterior of the channel is painted (fig. 7.9A, C–D), seven cases in which the interior is slipped (fig. 7.9D–E), three cases in which

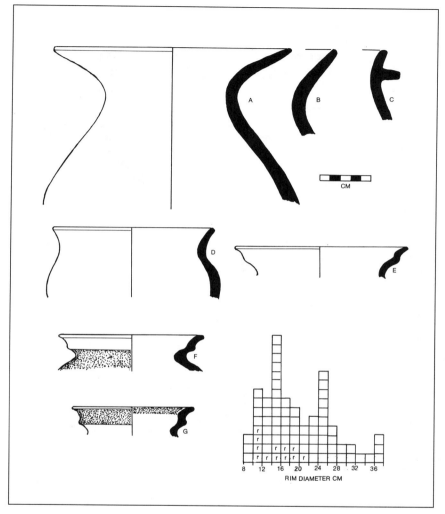

Fig. 7.10 Herradura outcurving rim jars (A and D, C50; B, C49; C, C55II) and recurved rim jars (E, C50; F–G, C55II). In histogram, r refers to the recurved rim jars.

both surfaces are slipped, and four cases of bands painted either horizontally on the exterior (fig. 7.9B) or vertically on the interior (fig. 7.9A).

Carinated Bowls

Common in earlier phases, the carinated bowl is represented by only one aberrant specimen (fig. 7.9G). It would seem that channel rim bowls, in which the carination has been shoved upward to merge with the rim profile, supplant their carinated antecedents.

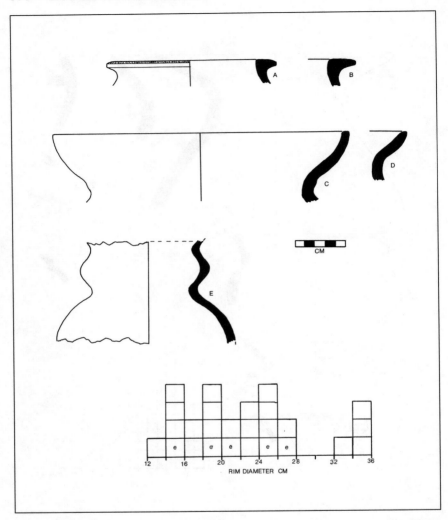

Fig. 7.11 Herradura expanded lip jars (A–B, C55II), bulbous neck jars (C, C50; D, C55II), and a biglobular jar (E, C55II). In histogram, e refers to the expanded lip jars, and blank squares pertain to the more numerous bulbous neck vessels.

Buttress Rim Bowls

Although continuing with some frequency in the contemporary Las Cruces phase, the buttress rim bowl is represented by but one example in Herradura.

Outcurving Rim Jars

To a certain extent, "a jar is a jar is a jar," and my colleagues have found this form matched in such far-flung arenas as Mississippian Moundville and the Pol-

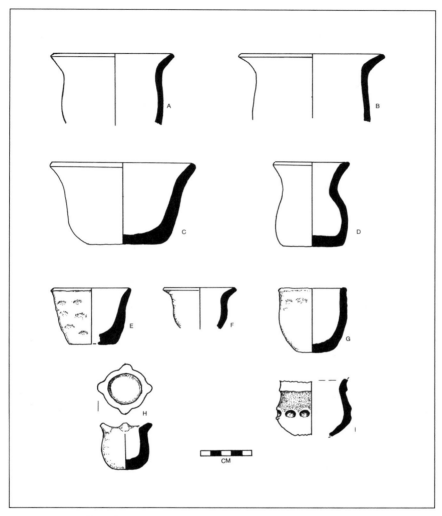

Fig. 7.12 *Rampiral cups (A, R30; B, C4; C, C53; D, C55II) and miniature vessels (E, C36II; F–H, C55II; I, C69III) from assorted phases.*

ish Neolithic. This is not to say, however, that such a general form has no comparative value. In fact, the ubiquity of the outcurving rim jar in Herradura assemblages contrasts markedly with its virtual absence in the contemporary Las Cruces phase. In Herradura, this form is undecorated. In four cases, the shoulder or subshoulder region is carbon crusted, suggesting use over a fire. In one case (fig. 7.10C), there is a prominent sublabial flange, a probable borrowing from Las Cruces where this treatment is more common. Two size modes are indicated, one at 15 cm and a larger at 25 cm.

Recurved Rim Jars

A relatively rare form in earlier phases, the recurved rim jar is a Herradura "salient" and becomes even more common in the subsequent Tumbaviro phase. Like the channel rim bowl, the distinctive profile is probably achieved by "scooping" with a calabash scraper, that virtually universal tool in neotropical ceramic manufacture. Of twelve examples, ten are undecorated, the two exceptions pictured in fig. 7.10F–G.

Expanded Lip Jars

The distinctive form of the expanded lip jar, so conspicuous and abundant in the Guadual phase, lingers in Herradura. Two of the seven examples are illustrated in fig. 7.11A–B.

Bulbous Neck Jars

In the bulbous neck jars, the scraper is applied to the interior of the neck, producing a bell-shaped or bulbous profile (fig. 7.11C–D). This nexus of tool and motor behavior is new to the Herradura phase.

Biglobular Vessel

The biglobular vessel is a rare form represented by single specimens in both Herradura (fig. 7.11E) and Las Cruces assemblages.

Rampiral Cups

First identified at C50, near the Chachi settlement of Rampiral, the Rampiral cup form is a Herradura hallmark (fig. 7.12A–D). It merges imperceptibly with the miniature vessels described below.

Miniature Vessels

Miniature vessels are "pinch pots" modeled out of a lump of clay; the finger pinches are often preserved on the finished specimen (fig. 7.12E, G). As small and crudely made vessels, these pots were likely produced for and by children. Potting is a demanding activity, one best pursued without the bother of children. I have seen Shipibo-Conibo potters give their young kids globs of clay to play with to deflect their energies away from the adult business of serious potting. Both as play and learning, the Shipibo-Conibo children's product is not all that different from the miniature vessels of Herradura. It is surprising that children, a necessary component of any viable population, are ordinarily so invisible in the archaeological record. Both "toys" and "ceremonial objects"—the joking last gasps of archaeological inference—should be reinstated in our interpretive agenda.

Although having its share of novelties, Herradura ceramics are clearly derived from Guadual antecedents through a process of simplification and "rustification." Las Cruces ceramics display the same tendencies, but with a different twist.

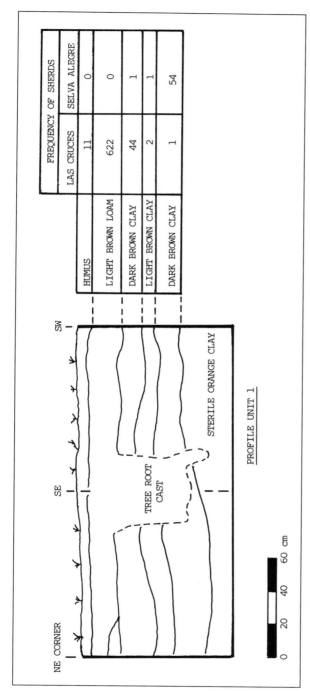

Fig. 7.13 Profile of unit 1, R30.

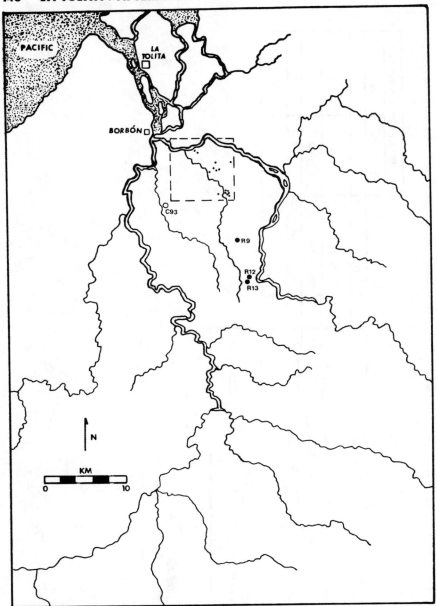

Fig. 7.14 *Distribution of Las Cruces (open circles) and Mina sites (solid circles). See fig. 7.15 for amplification of the area enclosed by dashed rectangle.*

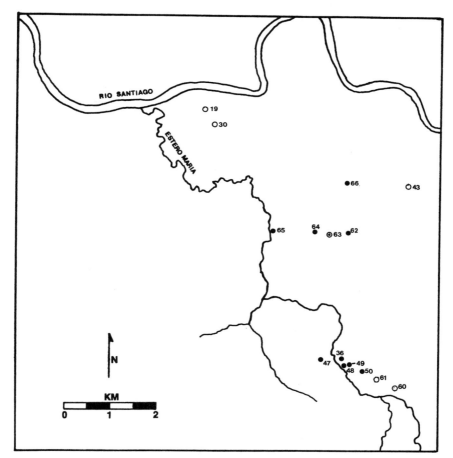

Fig. 7.15 Distribution of Las Cruces (open circles) and Mina sites (solid circles) within the inset of fig. 7.14.

The Las Cruces Phase

Whether paddling on the mainstream or hiking over the interfluves, the traveler can in one day journey from the Herradura heartland on the Cayapas to the cluster of Las Cruces settlements centering on the Estero María of the Santiago basin. Despite their proximity and apparent contemporaneity, however, the two phases are quite different in ceramic content. Furthermore, there is nothing clinal about this differentiation. A ceramic assemblage is either Herradura or Las Cruces, never some hybrid between the two. If our theory about material culture correlates were more robust, it could be argued that Herradura and Las Cruces represent distinct and bounded polities or ethnic groups, respectively occupying the Cayapas and Santiago watersheds. We could go even further to argue that relations between the two were guarded, a wariness expressed in settlements

Table 7.2   *Characteristics of Las Cruces and Mina sites.*

SITE	ENVIRONMENTAL CODE	DRAINAGE	DEPOSITIONAL CONTEXT	SIZE (HA)	ARTIFACTS COLLECTED	COMMENTS
Las Cruces						
R19	DCCB	II	P	0.25	950	
R30-II	DCCB	II	P	0.5	1269	on Estero Las Cruces
R43	EDHC	II	P	0.25	87	in platanal on Estero Delgado
R60	DDFC	II	P	0.45	40	site cut by road and drainage ditches
R61	DDFC	II	P	0.8	29	site cut by road
R63	EDH/B-C	III	P	0.05	18	site cut by road; mixed with Mina material
C93	DDEB	II	P	0.02	43	at modern settlement of El Chorro on Estero Yanayacu
Mina						
R9	CDFC	I	P	?	30	only 2 sherds definitely Mina; sherds strewn over the upper "terrace" in town of Tembiré
R12	EEFC	III	P	0.1	96	in platanal
R13	EEFC	III	P	?	87	
R36-II	DDFC	II	P	?	6+	a few Mina sherds in a much larger Selva Alegre component
R47	DDFC	II	P	0.5	148	on Estero María
R48	DDFC	II	P	0.03	131	on Estero María
R49	DDFC	II	P	1.3	165	cut by road
R50	DDFC	II	P	0.7	219	sherds concentrate on 5 natural (?) knolls
R62	EDH/B-C	III	P	0.5	79	cut by road
R63	EDH/B-C	III	P	0.05	2	cut by road; mixed with Las Cruces material
R64	EDHB	III	P	0.2	27	cut by road
R65	DDFB	II	P	1.0	38	in modern community of San Agustín
R66	EDHC	III	P	0.06	365	sherds strewn over and between 2 house mounds

Environmental code summarizes indices defined in figs. 2.6–2.7; for example, CCGC means *C* coding for pedology, *C* for geology, *G* for agriculture, and *C* for bioclimate. For drainage, *I* means location along Santiago or Cayapas mainstream; *II*, location along navigable secondary tributary; and *III*, along unnavigable estero or in interfluves. Under depositional context, *P* means intact primary deposit; *SS*, secondary deposit found as slope wash or embedded in land-slump; and *SE*, secondary deposit found in bed of estero.

located up secondary drainages, well out of sight of any would-be marauders on the mainstream. R30 is such a settlement, tucked away on the forested banks of the Estero Las Cruces, accessible by canoe from the Santiago only during high tide. At this site, the Las Cruces component (R30II) is superposed over an earlier Selva Alegre occupation (fig. 7.13). The distribution of other Las

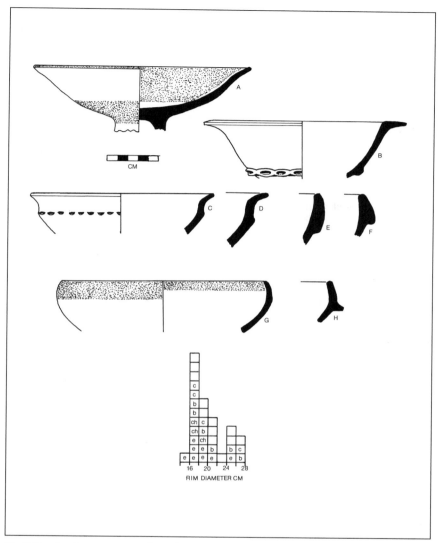

Fig. 7.16   *Las Cruces compotera (A, R19), open bowl with everted rim (B, R19), channel rim bowls (C–D, R61), buttress rim bowls (E–F, R30), and closed bowls with direct rims (G, R30; H, R19). The following key is used in histogram: blank squares, compoteras; e, open bowls with everted rims; ch, channel rim bowls; b, buttress rim bowls; and c, closed bowls with direct rims.*

Cruces sites is plotted in figs. 7.14 and 7.15; individual site characteristics are given in table 7.2.

But Las Cruces is defined primarily by its distinctive ceramics. Unlike Guadual and Herradura, Las Cruces does not emphasize the compotera. Unlike Herradura, Las Cruces eschews the outcurving rim jar; its place is taken by flaring neck jars that are frequently adorned with impressed fillets on the neck or shoulder of the vessel. Although Las Cruces vessels may be painted or slipped, pigmentation does not assume the prominence that it does in either Guadual or Herradura. A more formal account of Las Cruces pottery follows.

Compoteras

Of thirteen examples of compoteras, six are slipped or painted red on either exterior or interior surfaces. Paint schemes emphasize horizontal bands (fig. 7.16A), never the interior vertical banding so characteristic of Herradura.

Open Bowls with Everted Rims

Most of the twelve open bowls with everted rims are plain. The exceptions include one vessel with a red rim eversion and two with impressed basal fillets (fig. 7.16B).

Channel Rim Bowls

As in Herradura, the channel rim bowl is a common form, but whereas Herradura examples are often pigmented, the standard Las Cruces treatment consists of a horizontal row of impressions marking the base of the channel (fig. 7.16C).

Closed Bowls with Direct Rims

Derived from Guadual, four examples of closed bowls with direct rims linger in the sample of Las Cruces ceramics (fig. 7.16G–H). This form is unrepresented in Herradura.

Carinated Bowl

As in Herradura, the carinated bowl, so conspicuous in earlier assemblages, is represented by only one forlorn vestige.

Buttress Rim Bowls

The buttress rim bowl form continues from Guadual with some frequency. Nine of the ten examples are painted red on the exterior of the buttress (fig. 7.16E–F).

Tall Flaring Neck Jars

It is in jars that Las Cruces is most separate from Herradura. The outcurving rim and bulbous neck jars of Herradura are completely absent. In their stead, one finds a congeries of flaring neck jars that can be partitioned into tall and short variants. Likely antecedents for these flaring neck vessels can be found in the everted rim and so-called C69 jars of the Guadual phase.

Of thirty-four tall neck variants, none is pigmented, and most are otherwise unembellished. Five specimens, however, have impressed fillets midway up the neck (fig. 7.17A).

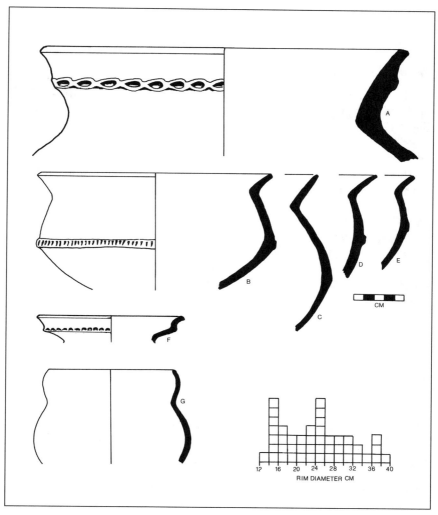

Fig. 7.17 Las Cruces tall flaring neck jar (A, R30), short flaring neck jars (B–D, R19; E, R43), recurved rim jar (F, R61), and biglobular jar (G, R19).

Short Flaring Neck Jars

Of thirty-four specimens of the short flaring neck jars, none is pigmented. The most common decorative treatment (eleven cases) is an impressed shoulder fillet (fig. 7.17B–E).

Collectively, flaring neck jars display a bimodality in rim diameter (15 and 25 cm respectively) with the possibility of a third mode at 37 cm. Occasional soot-ing of the subshoulder region of these vessels indicates use over a fire.

Cambered Rim Jar

The cambered rim jar—one last gasp for this ancient form.

Recurved Rim Jars

The recurved rim jar, a common Herradura form, is rare and is appropriately modified to Las Cruces decorative canons by the addition of an impressed fillet (fig. 7.17F).

San José Jars

The San José jar is yet another Guadual holdover lingering as a rare inclusion in Las Cruces contexts.

Biglobular Vessel

Only two biglobular vessels are known for the entire sequence: one in Herradura and the second in Las Cruces (fig. 7.17G).

Rampiral Cup

One example of a Rampiral cup surfaces in Las Cruces. Miniature vessels, relatively common in Herradura, reduce to one specimen, but we suspect that the Las Cruces population also included children.

Convergent Neck Jar

Represented by a single Las Cruces specimen, the convergent neck jar is also found in Mina and Tumbaviro.

The above survey, if clipped as the tedium of ceramic description takes its toll, nonetheless underscores a number of salient differences between what are interpreted to be contemporary and propinquitous phases. In fact, if our chronology is on the mark, this survey forcefully suggests that contemporary variability within relatively small areas (a day's travel time) may rival or exceed sequential variation in time. This totally plausible suggestion, however, should be qualified as archaeological "units of contemporaneity" may often span centuries, as they do in the case of Herradura and Las Cruces. So the issue is: were these two phases actually part of the same interactive milieu? Chapter 3 presented the basic argument for contemporaneity between Herradura and Las Cruces, and here only one more piece of supporting evidence need be mentioned. R61, a surface collection containing only "classic" Las Cruces ceramics, also yields a complex conical spindle whorl of a type more generally attested in Herradura (fig. 3.8M). This singular specimen of high specificity is almost certainly a "trade piece," although whether the whorl was actually traded or whether its Herradura owner was abducted or married into the R61 community is uncertain. Nonetheless, this small piece of evidence argues that Herradura and Las Cruces were indeed interacting contemporaries.

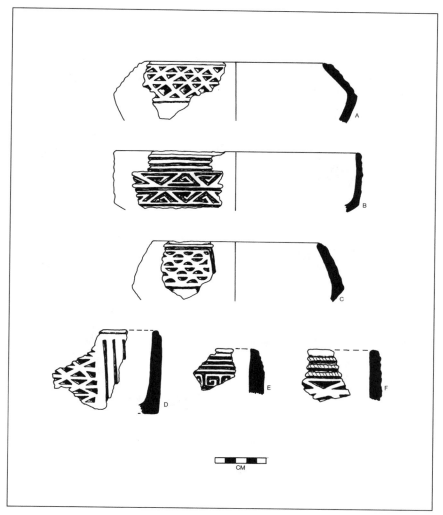

Fig. 7.18 Mina "trellis" bowls (A–B, R36II; C, R49; D, R47; E–F, R64).

These interesting and important matters of interaction among contemporary communities, however, become even more tangled when we turn to that most peculiar and recalcitrant of our cultural historical constructions.

Mysterious Mina

Mina must be introduced with apologies. It breaks nomenclatural rules by being named after a property owner at Colón Eloy (R36) rather than after a descriptive or locative feature. Second, a Mina tradition is already billed for the lower Amazon, and, closer to home, Zeidler and his colleagues talk of a Minas

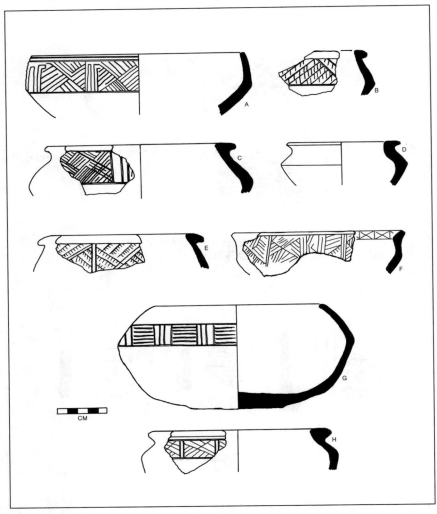

Fig. 7.19 Mina incised vessels (A, R36II; B, R50; C, R12; E, R47; F, R48); D shows a rare plain example of a form that is ordinarily incised. G–H are Bucheli vessels redrawn from Bouchard (1985: figs. 11-3 and 24-5).

ceramic style for the Jama valley in Manabí. One need not be overly perspicacious to see that terminological confusion is brewing. Third, it is not yet clear that Mina represents a coherent entity that actually ever existed. Its definition rests on two distinctive wares, one decorated with appliqué and one with incision, that always occur as minor ingredients in ceramic collections that form a pastiche of Guadual, Las Cruces, and Herradura traits. This pastiche, marked by a few Mina diagnostics, is too poorly resolved to be labeled a phase. That delightfully ambiguous (and essentially noncommittal) term "complex" will serve our purposes better. So what is this "complex" that deserves renaming once its cultural historical context is better understood?

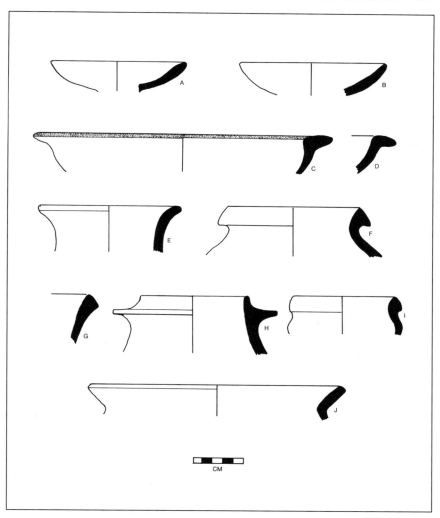

Fig. 7.20 *Assorted Mina vessels: compoteras (A–B, R47); open bowls with everted rims (C–D, R49); outcurving rim jar (E, R62); wedge rim jar (F, R50); San José jar (G, R66); convergent neck jar (H, R66); R49 jar (I, R49); and short flaring neck jar (J, R49).*

The distribution and characteristics of Mina sites have already been presented in figs. 7.14–7.15 and table 7.2, respectively. The distribution centers on the lower Estero María and is virtually coincident with that of Las Cruces. In terms of size, Mina sites encompass a range similar to that of Las Cruces or Herradura.

There are two groups of distinctively decorated ceramics that define the Mina complex. The first of these is a fine, whitish colored ware decorated with what can be called a "trellis" pattern (fig. 7.18). At first, it was thought that these trellis designs were achieved through excision or a champlevé technique. Closer inspection, however, shows that the technique is actually one of appliqué with strips of clay added to the pot surface much as one might apply icing to a wedding cake. As seen in fig. 7.18, these appliqué designs are confined to a variable set of carinated bowls and, in at least one case (fig. 7.18D), a square vessel. These trellis vessels are unique in the Santiago-Cayapas sequence, and I know of only two comparable specimens from elsewhere. The first is a boxlike vessel illustrated by Reichel-Dolmatoff (1965: plate 17) and said to be from the Quimbaya region in Colombia. Unlike the Mina specimen, this piece is decorated with a champlevé technique, and the resultant design only superficially resembles the Mina trellis pattern. A second specimen, one provenienced to the Río Mira, more convincingly resembles the Mina treatment; in fact, as near as can be seen in the published photograph (Errázuriz 1980: plate 158), this Mira piece would be right at home in fig. 7.18. This identity is not surprising given that the Río Mira is just across the Colombian border. More surprising is that nothing like these Mina bowls is recorded in the Tumaco sequence worked out by Bouchard (1985).

A second distinctive group of Mina vessels is illustrated in fig. 7.19A–F. In terms of ware, the coarse sandy, generally buff to brown-colored paste of these vessels is indistinguishable from Las Cruces or Herradura fabrics. It is the fine-line incised decoration that sets these vessels apart as a Mina specialty. This incision consists of simple geometric designs that occur in panels on a horizontal band placed beneath the rim exterior. Vessels receiving this special treatment include a carinated bowl (fig. 7.19A), a distinctively shaped bowl with an everted rim (fig. 7.19B–C, E; D shows a rare plain example), and a form that resembles a channel rim bowl as found in Las Cruces, Herradura, or Tumbaviro (fig. 7.19F).

With respect to external similarities, the Mina incised material is virtually identical to the late prehistoric Bucheli ceramics from the Tumaco area (Bouchard 1985). Two Bucheli pots are pictured in fig. 7.19G–H to convince the reader that this similarity extends to the specifics of vessel form and decoration. The Bucheli radiocarbon date of A.D. 1075 tends to confirm the late placement of Mina within the Santiago-Cayapas sequence; however, this chronological cross-tie technically applies only to the incised material. The reality of the association between the Mina trellis and incised wares, where "association" is limited to co-occurrence in the same surface collections, needs further discussion. By definition, a collection must contain either trellis or incised sherds to be assigned to Mina. In fact, however, trellis decoration never occurs in the absence of the incised material that can be so persuasively related to Bucheli. Of thirteen Mina collections, six share both diagnostics whereas seven have only fine-line incision, a pattern that is not surprising because fine-line incision, represented by twenty-two specimens, is more common than the ten cases of trellis decoration.

It is also important to mention that the two Mina diagnostics comprise but a small part of the sherd collections in which they are found. From a seriational standpoint, this major residuum of nondiagnostics behaves in a peculiar way. Only one form (the so-called R49 jar pictured in fig. 7.20I) is unique to Mina. The wedge rim jar (fig. 7.20F) and the expanded lip jar are characteristics of the Guadual phase. Small-sized compoteras (fig. 7.20A–B), everted rim bowls (fig. 7.20C–D), San José jars (fig. 7.20G), convergent neck jars (fig. 7.20H), and flaring neck jars (fig. 7.20J) are shared with Las Cruces, but the outcurving rim jar, abundant in Mina (fig. 7.20E), is completely absent in Las Cruces, even though

Mina and Las Cruces sites commingle along the Estero María. Put another way, minus the trellis and incised materials, Mina collections do not comfortably conform to any phase established on the basis of the repeated co-occurrence of attributes. The one possible exception to this pattern (or nonpattern) is the badly disturbed site of R63 where two Mina diagnostics were mixed with a "pure" Las Cruces assemblage, a fact accounting for the entry of R63 under both Las Cruces and Mina site lists (table 7.2).

Mina remains murky.

Summary

To backtrack somewhat, during La Tolita's apogee, the Santiago and Cayapas basins participate fully in the same ceramic styles, first in the Selva Alegre phase and then in the rather abruptly installed sequel of Guadual. These style zones extend northward to encompass the Tumaco area. Settlement patterns are increasingly geared to the mainstreams, and a brisk riverine trade in obsidian, gold, and perishable goods is intimated, if not securely documented by the archaeological data. Some riverside settlements such as R10 become hypertrophied in size, and it is likely that this increase is in some fashion related to the La Tolita regime, although it is doubtful that La Tolita and its hinterland ever formed a well-organized or tightly administered settlement hierarchy.

With the demise of La Tolita (perhaps preceding by a century or two the end of the Guadual phase), the Santiago-Cayapas world splinters into a mosaic of contemporary phases: Herradura on the Cayapas; Las Cruces and that messy mélange Mina on the Santiago. Settlements retire from the mainstream highways and now favor secondary, but usually navigable, tributaries. Obsidian and other evidence for interregional trade decrease in abundance. Large sites such as R10 are abandoned, although several settlements relocated on tributaries still exceed a hectare in extent and preserve traces of a well-organized community plan of several houses (C55II). Although founded in Guadual antecedents, the ceramic arts decline in elaboration and become more localized. It is significant that the ceramics of Herradura and Las Cruces are not only insular with respect to each other but also display no compelling similarities to those of neighboring regions, whether Tumaco to the north or the Esmeraldas valley to the south. In this context in which ceramic styles are involuting to small areas, the radii of which do not exceed a day's round trip travel time, the trellis and incised vessels of Mina can perhaps be seen as specialty trade items that, by transcending new boundaries, preserve the old connections between Tumaco and the Santiago-Cayapas.

But we should not be hypnotized by the pots. Ornately stamped spindle whorls and a flourishing ground stone industry in which celts and wood-working adzes proliferate at the expense of T-shaped axes belie the notion that aesthetic decline infected all material media. Basketry was almost certainly highly developed. In fact, it has been suggested that the Mina trellis decoration is a ceramic rendition of a more pliable and valued basketry technology (Errázuriz 1980: 312).

As always, trends can be thrown into relief only when their outcomes are known.

8
BACK TO BARBARISM
The Tumbaviro Phase

If Herradura and Las Cruces evince a retreat from the mainstream of the collapsing La Tolita world to the relative isolation of secondary drainages, then Tumbaviro represents a virtual hydrophobia in which the typical settlement is situated atop an interfluvial ridge away from navigable waterways. If Herradura and Las Cruces folk react against such megasized sites as R10 and retire to more modestly sized villages safely nestled along the Zapallo Grande or the Estero María, then Tumbaviro is an accentuation of this trend. Judging from archaeological traces, the typical Tumbaviro settlement consists of one to a few houses perched on a ridge top with what can be imagined as a paranoid view of the surrounding landscape (New York Owasco comes to mind as a comparative example). If Herradura and Las Cruces ceramics can be seen as simplified derivatives of the high ceramic art of Guadual, then the unadorned Tumbaviro pottery can be viewed as the nadir of this trend. If the virtual absence of imported obsidian and the near disappearance of figurines are measures of anything, then Tumbaviro sinks to new depths of insularity and aesthetic poverty. It is only in these senses and with a penchant toward alliteration that I title this chapter.

In implying that the people responsible for Tumbaviro are "barbarians," I am probably influenced by the point of view of my Chachi hosts. For it is likely that the Tumbaviro folk represent the "Indios Bravos" of Chachi legend, the allegedly cannibalistic Indians whom the Chachi claim to have supplanted in their initial colonization of the Cayapas basin. By "barbarism" I certainly do not refer to any "evolutionary stage" of the kind that has so long bedeviled archaeological reasoning. From my point of view, there are no universal evolutionary stages sequenced by "progress" or by any other inexorable forces driving toward complexity. There is only time and history, a guaranteed playful variability, and selection constrained by contingency. Increased complexity is more an occasionally successful accident than a mandated outcome; more common are the "ups" and "downs" of the Santiago-Cayapas sequence. In this scheme, Tumbaviro is not a setback so much as it is yet another quite ordinary "downer."

The distribution of Tumbaviro sites is plotted in figs. 8.1 and 8.2 (C2–3 is the "type site" situated atop a ridge locally known as Tumbaviro). Largely restricted to the Cayapas basin, this distribution maps quite closely onto that of the preceding Herradura phase. In terms of ceramic content, Tumbaviro displays many more continuities with Herradura than with the Santiago-based Las Cruces phase. This Herradura-Tumbaviro continuum centered on the Cayapas poses an interpretive problem because no Santiago phase coeval with Tumbaviro is presently recognized. Either the Santiago was lightly populated at this time or our temporal indexing of phases is in error.

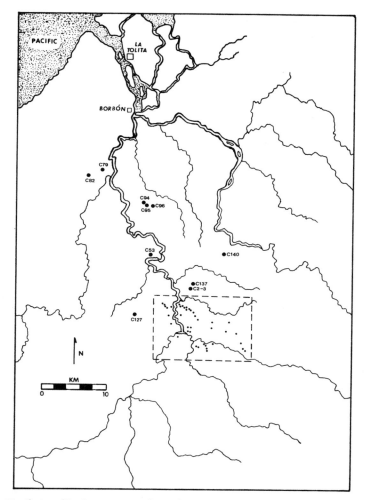

Fig. 8.1 Distribution of Tumbaviro sites. See fig. 8.2 for amplification of area enclosed by dashed rectangle.

Tumbaviro site characteristics are listed in table 8.1. Although the number of sites (forty-nine) exceeds that of any other phase, Tumbaviro settlements tend to be small, and their total hectarage is the lowest in the sequence, excepting for the historic Chachi (table 6.2). For reasons discussed earlier, however, these estimates are to be regarded with caution. First, small sites may have been selectively missed in our reconnaissance. Second, if attention is limited to the Cayapas basin where both Tumbaviro and Herradura sites are concentrated, then Tumbaviro density—measured as (site hectarage)/(area surveyed)—actually exceeds that of Herradura. Thus, during the Tumbaviro phase, the Cayapas basin may have experienced a population upswing while the combined Santiago-Cayapas basins

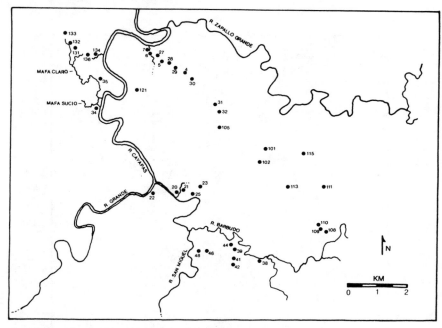

Fig. 8.2 *Distribution of Tumbaviro sites within inset of fig. 8.1.*

witnessed a downturn; yet another demographic impression might apply to the larger region encompassing these two basins.

Well over half (twenty-eight) of Tumbaviro sites are 0.06 ha or less in extent, and the modal site size is a mere 0.02 ha. Chachi archaeological middens also center at 0.02 ha, and ethnographic observations testify that the typical Chachi settlement consists of a single structure housing a nuclear family or occasionally a more extended retinue of kin. It is quite likely, therefore, that the modal Tumbaviro site consisted of a single structure. This is not to say, however, that such a small site constituted a Tumbaviro community. Tumbaviro sites often show up in clusters linearly arranged along a ridge top (C27-5-28-29-4-30 form one such cluster; see fig. 8.2). It could be that clusters of sites, often within earshot and certainly within the range of a signal gong, comprised the effective community.

Not all Tumbaviro sites are small and shallow sherd scatters. C2–3 covers a respectable 1.4 ha, and auger probes indicate a midden that reaches 50 cm depth in parts of this site. Nor are all sites confined to interfluvial ridge tops. C34 is located at the mouth of the Mafa Sucio, the Cayapas but a stone's throw away. Sherds at this latter site are sprinkled over 2.3 ha, a whopping size by Tumbaviro standards. Yet only three or four "hot spots" within this large area display respectable sherd densities, and it could be that C34 represents but a few dispersed houses or a composite produced through repeated occupations.

No soil samples from Tumbaviro contexts have yet been analyzed for pollen or phytolith content, and no direct evidence for subsistence is yet available. The

settlement and artifactual shifts, however, imply some change in dietary practices. In keeping with their interfluvial orientation, Tumbaviro assemblages virtually lack fishing gear; the one net sinker and the one fish scaler both come from
sites bordering the Río Barbudo (*barbudo* means "bearded catfish" in local parlance). Otherwise, fishing is seemingly deemphasized in the artifactual record,
although the wooden weaponry that might attest to the compensatory importance of terrestrial hunting is not preserved. Nether stones change dramatically,
although the culinary meaning of this change is not known. Whereas manos and
metates occur sporadically in all earlier phases, they are notably absent in
Tumbaviro. Instead of metates that would fit into most Mesoamerican or Southwestern ground stone assemblages, the Tumbaviro counterpart is a massive basin formed through a combination of lateral grinding and vertical pounding. On
a gigantic scale, this metate *qua* mortar resembles the *piedra de bala* used in preparing the plantain mash that is a staple in both Chachi and black households
today. As plantain phytoliths are readily recognizable and as the governing con-
sensus is that *Musa* spp. are post-Columbian introductions, the analysis of
Tumbaviro soil samples becomes even more interesting and urgent. Although
there is little doubt that Tumbaviro has prehistoric beginnings, it plausibly extends well into historic times. Still left unexplained would be the wildfire spread
and adoption of plantains throughout much of the Neotropics shortly after European contact. This remarkable story still awaits proper telling.

But I have stalled long enough: the local story of Tumbaviro ceramics, remarkable for their aesthetic poverty, needs recounting, if only to allow colleagues
working in neighboring areas to compare their distressing potsherds to a tough
Tumbaviro standard.

On the muddy trails that follow most interfluvial ridges, Tumbaviro potsherds
pop out as thick-walled, unadorned slabs—crystalline platelets protruding from
ooze that swallows boots and sucks at calves. When washed and seen, these
sherds are plain and poorly smoothed, are tempered with coarse sand with an
occasional rock inclusion, share the same color as their mud source, and, in the
case of occasional rims, intimate a limited but serviceable array of vessel forms. It
is the base, however, that is the most salient ceramic residue. Although the ancient Guadual pedigree of pedestal bases continues, Tumbaviro pedestals are bulky
and solid with flat bottoms, and are rarely pigmented or otherwise adorned (see
fig. 3.4I–J). For the first time, flat bases, which have some frequency in Herradura,
exceed pedestals as the favored way of bottoming a vessel.

The roster of Tumbaviro vessel forms reduces to 11 categories, all but one of
which have Herradura antecedents.

Compoteras

Although no complete profile linking rim and base was encountered, the
compotera can be postulated on the basis of 26 rim profiles (fig. 8.3A–E) that
roughly match, in number, thirty-two fragments of solid pedestals. Only one
specimen is pigmented with a red slip hastily applied to the exterior. Rim diam-

SITE	ENVIRONMENTAL CODE	DRAINAGE	DEPOSITIONAL CONTEXT	SIZE (HA)	ARTIFACTS COLLECTED	COMMENTS
C82	EDIB	III	P	0.04	46	beneath modern house
C94	EEIB	III	P	0.01	12	atop ridge
C95	EEIB	III	P	0.01	2	atop ridge
C96	EEIB	III	SS	?	110	washing down ridge
C101	HGDC	III	P	0.04	45	atop ridge
C102	HGDC	III	P	0.04	33	on flat-topped hill
C105	HGDC	III	P	0.04	7	
C108	IIHD	III	P	?	25	
C109	IIHD	III	P&SS	?	13	atop ridge
C110	IIHD	III	P&SS	0.06	31	atop ridge
C111	IIHD	III	SS	?	4	washing down ridge
C113	IIHD	III	P	0.06	26	atop ridge
C115	IIDC	III	SE	?	12	in estero
C121	HGHC	III	P	?	11	atop knoll
C127	HGIC	III	P	?	6	
C131	HFDC	III	P	0.02	30	atop ridge
C132	HFDC	III	P	0.02	56	atop ridge
C133	HFDC	III	P	0.06	35	
C134	HGDC	I	SS	?	3	
C136	HFDC	III	P	0.04	90	atop ridge
C137	HFIC	III	P	0.06	9	atop ridge
C140	HEHC	III	P	?	4	
C2-3	HFIC	III	P	1.4	224	atop ridge
C4	HGDC	III	P	0.7	663	atop ridge
C5	HFHC	III	P	0.1	118	atop ridge

C6	HFHC	III	P	0.02	119	atop ridge
C7	HFHC	III	P	0.4	225	atop ridge
C20-21	HHHC	III	SE	?	16	in Estero Palizada
C22	CHFC	I	P	?	206	an extensive sherd scatter at the confluence of the San Miguel and Río Grande
C23	HHHC	III	P	0.02	27	in finca
C25	HHHC	III	P	0.02	196	atop steep hill
C28	HFHC	III	P	0.02	134	atop ridge
C29	HFHC	III	P	0.02	136	atop ridge only 30 m from C28
C30	HGDC	III	P	0.02	107	perhaps outlier to C4
C31	HGDC	III	P	0.05	101	
C32	HGDC	III	P	0.04	229	in clearing
C34	CGFC	I	P	2.3	698	extensive but thin sherd scatter with several "hot spots"
C35	HGDC	III	P	?	5	in platanal
C38	IIDD	II	P	0.1	257	atop ridge overlooking the Barbudo; 3 "hot spots"
C39	HIDD	III	P	0.04	252	
C41	HIDD	III	P	0.01	303	
C42	HIDD	III	P	0.01	218	
C44	HIDD	III	P	0.02	230	
C46	HIDD	III	P	0.05	146	several "hot spots" against low-density background
C48	HIDD	III	P	0.02	176	in yuca plantation
C53	CEFC	I	(derrumbe)	?	332	
C79	EDIB	III	P&SS	0.05	17	atop ridge

Table 8.1 Characteristics of Tumbaviro sites.

Environmental code summarizes indices defined in figs. 2.6–2.7; for example, CCGC means C coding for pedology; C for geology, G for agriculture, and C for bioclimate. For drainage, I means location along Santiago or Cayapas mainstream; II, location along navigable secondary tributary; and III, along unnavigable estero or in interfluves. Under depositional context, P means intact primary deposit; SS, secondary deposit found as slope wash or embedded in land-slump; and SE, secondary deposit found in bed of estero.

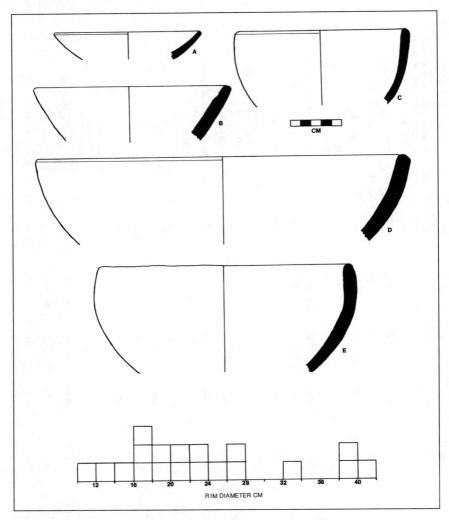

Fig. 8.3 *Tumbaviro compoteras or open bowls (A–B, C4; C, C82; D–E, C53).*

eters, formerly subject to strong modalities, now range haphazardly from 11 to 41 cm. Clearly the compotera has lost much of its former significance.

Open Bowls with Everted Rims

There are ten examples of open bowls with everted rims, none of which is decorated (fig. 8.4A–B).

Open Bowls with Thickened Lips

The open bowl with thickened lips variant or allomorph of the preceding

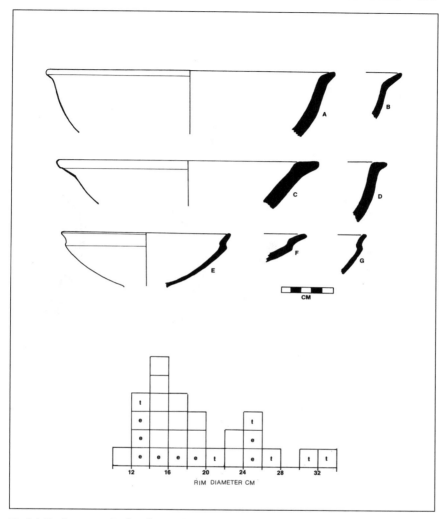

Fig. 8.4 *Tumbaviro open bowls with everted rims (A, C32; B, C53), open bowls with thickened lips (C, C46; D, C4), and channel rim bowls (E, C53; F, C2–3; G, C29). In histogram, e refers to open bowls with everted rims, t refers to open bowls with thickened lips, and blank squares refer to channel rim bowls.*

form continues from Herradura (fig. 8.4C–D). As is often the case in Tumbaviro pottery, one specimen preserves traces of unobliterated coils on the exterior surface.

Channel Rim Bowls

The channel rim bowl form is common in Herradura and Tumbaviro, but the modal rim diameter is greater in the former phase (19 vs. 15 cm). The Tumbaviro examples are thin-walled with reduced channels (fig. 8.4E–G); they are the closest thing there is to a Tumbaviro fine ware. None is decorated, however.

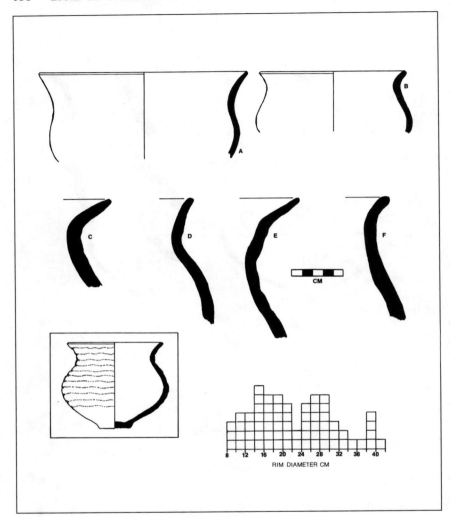

Fig. 8.5   Tumbaviro outcurving rim jars (A, C32; B, D–E, C53; C, C3; F, C82).

Outcurving Rim Jars

The outcurving rim jar is the most common Tumbaviro vessel form. It ranges from the gracile (fig. 8.5A–B) to the large and thick-walled (fig. 8.5C–F). In six cases, larger specimens preserve unobliterated coil junctures on their exterior surfaces (fig. 8.5 *inset*). Although all vessel chambers throughout the Santiago-Cayapas sequence (excepting the miniature pinch pots) were evidently made through coiling, only in Tumbaviro is this construction technique left clearly visible on the finished pot. Two lip exteriors from this form are faintly nicked;

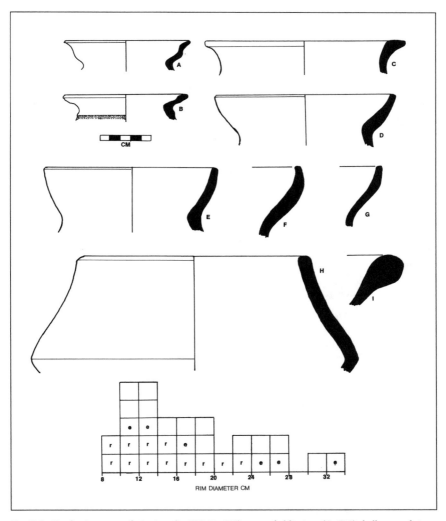

Fig. 8.6   *Tumbaviro recurved rim jars (A, C32; B, C53), expanded lip jars (C, C48), bulbous neck jars, (D, C96; E, C102; F, C4; G, C6), convergent neck jar (H, C82), and comma rim basins (I, C5). In histogram, r refers to recurved rim jars, e to expanded lip jars, and blank squares to bulbous neck jars.*

otherwise these jars are monotonously unadorned. The histogram of orifice diameters suggests three size modes of 15, 28, and 39 cm.

Recurved Rim Jar

As in Herradura, the recurved rim jar is a relatively common form. Of sixteen specimens, one carries a vestige of red paint (fig. 8.6B), a very rare decorative treatment in the Tumbaviro phase.

Expanded Lip Jars

The expanded lip jar is uncommon. Of six examples, none is decorated.

Bulbous Neck Jars

The bulbous neck jar form is uniquely shared with Herradura (fig. 8.6D–G). There is a wide range in rim diameters, and one of the larger jars preserves traces of thick coils on its exterior surface.

Rampiral Cups

Two specimens of Rampiral cups were recovered from Tumbaviro contexts (fig. 7.12B–C).

Comma Rim Basins

The comma rim basin, a rare but distinctive vessel, hopscotches throughout the sequence and is apparently of no chronological value. One of four specimens is illustrated in fig. 8.6I.

Convergent Neck Jars

Two examples of convergent neck jars occur in Tumbaviro (fig. 8.6H). This is the only form shared by Mina, Las Cruces, and Tumbaviro but lacking in Herradura. Given the total sample of four vessels, however, not too much should be made of the seeming absence of this vessel in Herradura.

Summary

With the hindsight inherent in an archaeological perspective, the trajectory from Guadual to Herradura to Tumbaviro can be delineated as follows: (1) settlements get smaller and shift in location from the mainstream waterways to the inland interfluves; (2) evidence for external trade diminishes; (3) the spatial extent of style zones contracts; and (4) decorative and other aesthetic investment in the ceramic arts declines. Except for the fourth item, none of these trends matches the characteristics that Meggers (1966: 119) posits for the post–A.D. 500 "Integration Period," nor is the Santiago-Cayapas experience the only instance where such gross evolutionary stages fail to characterize the local realities of the Ecuadorian past (e.g., Doyon 1991).

Unless we regard change to be primarily stochastic in nature, however, these local trends must, in some sense, be selected *for* and cannot be dismissed as "devolutionary" (the term is absent from the lexicon of evolutionary biology but continues as a favorite among old guard cultural evolutionists). The question then becomes, what scenario could effectively account for these trends as they unfold in specific contexts?

In seeking such a scenario, one can begin with the Tumbaviro settlement pattern, perhaps infelicitously described as "hydrophobic" and "paranoid." The

Tumbaviro penchant for small settlements dispersed along interfluvial ridge tops is difficult to explain. In terms of transportive ease or fishing or agricultural potential, the advantages would clearly seem to reside on the riparian mainstream. If the Tumbaviro settlement preferendum is puzzling with reference to the physical environment, then perhaps the social environment is a more relevant consideration. What aspect of the social landscape would prompt people to live on narrow ridges perched high above a water supply with the nearest canoe port located a long walk away?

In fact, there is a well-documented analogue for the Tumbaviro settlement pattern located quite close to home. This case is that of the Kwaiker, contemporary denizens of the densely forested piedmont of southwestern Colombia and neighboring portions of Ecuador. The traditional Kwaiker settlement pattern of dispersed houses situated atop interfluvial elevations recalls the Tumbaviro case. Cerón (1986: 81) makes it clear that the Kwaiker rationale for this pattern was defensive: "As part of their defensive strategy, the Kwaiker attempted to avoid contact with outsiders. Houses were dispersed and were located on high ground such that they commanded a view of all approaches to the settlement" [my translation]. During historic times, the feared outsiders have been European or African slavers and raiders, but there is no reason to believe that such fears were unknown in prehistory.

Contemporary with Tumbaviro, dramatic developments were taking place along the Esmeraldas shore. At Atacames, a large urban port prospered (Guinea Bueno 1984, 1988). Another major coastal center, perhaps located near the mouth of the Santiago River, was Tenumpuela, a settlement that Pizarro renamed Santiago in his 1529 *capitulación* to the queen of Spain (Nicholson 1953: 20). In a 1569 report, Carranza referred to a large palisaded settlement called Ciscala. Although yet to be identified archaeologically, Ciscala is described as a large town that "maintained peace with all the other provinces and hosted a large market. Here the Tacamas brought gold and emeralds to sell; the Campaces and Pidres [?] brought salt and fish; and the Belinquiamas brought textiles and cotton" [my translation from Alcina Franch and Peña 1979: 289].

Alas, there is no good archaeological evidence that Tumbaviro participated in this economic network (I would be reluctant to argue that the four Tumbaviro spindle whorls indicate textile production beyond domestic needs). This is not to say that the Santiago-Cayapas basins were uninfluenced by these coastal developments. The Santiago, the former sanctuary of R10 during the reign of La Tolita, was seemingly vacated, the inhabitants perhaps being "sucked into" the growing coastal settlements or, alternatively, retreating inland to join Tumbaviro populations. The Tumbaviro folk in the upper Cayapas interfluves appeared to be doing their best to stay clear of this coastal activity. Apparently the Tumbaviro attitude was that coastal intentions were not entirely neutral. It would be interesting to know how many Tumbaviro captives were secured by coastal raiding parties and how many coastal heads hung from the rafters of Tumbaviro homes.

Admittedly, the above scenario is an accommodative and speculative one, although it attempts to deal with the available evidence, however exiguous that might be. But there is a further touchstone to anchor speculation. The early Spanish accounts of northwestern Ecuador not only highlight impressive coastal ports but also contrast this urban littoral with a more amorphous background collectively subsumed under the term *Barbacoas*. As a loan word imported from the Caribbean that originally designated an elevated cooking grill (hence the derived "barbecue" of English), the term was extended to refer to the peoples of the interior who lived in houses with elevated floors (Cabello de Balboa 1945, I: 8). Stereotyped for their bellicosity, the Barbacoas were certainly not a single ethnic group but rather encompassed a number of ethnonyms that at various times included the Nurpes, Malabas, and Kwaiker (Rodicio García and Palop Martínez 1988). Thus our earlier comparison between the Tumbaviro and Kwaiker settlement patterns was not merely an illustrative analogy but also possibly a homology based on historical continuity. The distinction is an important one from the standpoint of culture history in which tradition is viewed as a reality constraining its products somewhere between entrenched inertia and free plasticity and somewhere between historical replication and the adaptive expediency of the moment.

In terms of present knowledge, Tumbaviro is but a Cayapas-based variant of a Barbacoan "field," a field that includes Bucheli in the Tumaco area and, farther northward, the Maina phase in the Patía drainage (Patiño 1993) and the San Miguel phase in the Guapi-Timbiquí basins (Patiño 1988). In all of these cases, ceramics are crudely finished and sparsely decorated, and, with the exception of Bucheli, settlements are perched atop hills with a nervous view of the surrounding landscape.

With Tumbaviro, we begin in prehistory, cross the protohistoric Rubicon, and enter the era of history. Threats from the coast will continue, but soon there will be a new threat from the Andean east. The Chachi are coming.

9
THE COMING OF THE CHACHI

For many archaeologists trained during the heyday of the New Archaeology, the terms *diffusion* and *migration* are still likely to invoke considerable antipathy. The whole agenda of the New Archaeology was to show how cultural change could be accounted for in terms of intrasystemic and local adaptations. As processes extraneous to such unfolding systems, diffusion and migration were dismissed as clumsy theoretical forfeitures.

The problem with this stance is that diffusion and migration occur regularly in the course of human affairs. They have been central processes in producing the world that we live in today, and it would be odd if past societies were insulated modules rather than nodes in similar diffusionary and migrational fields of extraregional extent. Nor does it seem reasonable to deny the existence of these processes that shunt people and things over considerable distances simply because we cannot explain why a particular case of diffusion or migration took place. In the following, I review an argument, the details of which are presented elsewhere (DeBoer 1995), that the Chachi entered the Cayapas basin from a former homeland in the Andes to the east. The historical and archaeological evidence indicates that this intrusion took place within the last two hundred years or so. It is not yet totally clear why or how this migration took place.

The case for a recent Chachi migration into the Cayapas region rests on three classes of evidence: (1) Chachi oral traditions concerning their own history; (2) western historical accounts; and (3) the archaeological record. Each deserves separate discussion.

On the basis of fieldwork carried out in 1909, Barrett (1925) summarized oral traditions that, with variations, the Chachi (Barrett's Cayapa) recount today. According to these traditions: "The original home of the people was in the mountains near Ibarra. At a time probably very near that of the advent of the first Spaniards, the Cayapas as a body moved to what is now known as Pueblo Viejo . . . in the mountains drained by the upper course of the Río Santiago. Various reasons are given for this migration, some affirming that it was because of their fear of the invaders (and, as one informant said, especially the fear of their horses), whereas others say that it was due to the general alteration in their mode of life as a result of the conquest" (Barrett 1925: 31).

Other informants claimed that this movement to Pueblo Viejo predated the arrival of the Spaniards and was in response to the Inca conquest of the northern highlands. Whichever conqueror prompted their exodus from the sierra, the Chachi were to find new enemies at Pueblo Viejo. These new and unfriendly neighbors were the *Indios Bravos* or "wild Indians," who "are said to have been cannibals. They preyed constantly on the Cayapa, killing them whenever and wherever encountered. The Cayapa, on the other hand, were then, as they are now, a very peaceable people; but after many years of these outrages they organized war-parties which descended the rivers and exterminated the enemy" (Barrett 1925: 32). The accounts, undoubtedly tendentious in part, go on to present details concerning the geography of the retaliatory invasion that installed the Chachi in their present-day territory: "The Cayapa first attacked the Indios Bravos living along the Río Zapallo Grande; next those along the Río San Miguel; next those along the Río Camarones; then those along La Herradura de Cayapas, and so on down the Río Cayapas, up the Río Onzole, and again down the Río Cayapas to its confluence with the Río Santiago" (Barrett 1925: 35). Thus the Chachi view their history in terms of a two-stage migration: the first from Ibarra (called by the Spanish loan word *villa*) to Pueblo Viejo (called *Tusac* in Chachi); the second from Pueblo Viejo on the upper Santiago to their current location on the Cayapas. The latter move involved defeat and displacement of the resident Indios Bravos. That "extermination" is too strong a word is intimated by the continuing Chachi belief that wisps of smoke seen far up the Río Grande mark lingering encampments of their foes.

The above story, abstracted from Barrett's rendering of Chachi traditions, appeals to western canons of historicity by excluding much of the idiom of the Chachi's own telling, a telling that includes jaguar guides, the shamanic capture of magical wands possessed by the Indios Bravos, and the intervention of birds that sing critical communiqués to the Chachi on their downslope trek to the Cayapas (DeBoer 1995). In summarizing Chachi traditions, Barrett (1925: 36), poised between western rationality and what a later ethnography would neologize as "alterity," cautiously concluded on behalf of the Chachi: "Their tradition cannot be taken too literally. However, it seems probable that the essential features of the tradition in large measure are based on historical facts." Let us now turn to the chronicle offered by the Europeans.

For details, the reader is again referred to the fuller treatment given elsewhere (DeBoer 1995). Here an abstract suffices. The first major encounter with the Chachi dates to 1597. In that year, the Mercedarian friar Gaspar de Torres, accompanied by thirty load-bearers and guides, descended the western slopes to the "country of the Cayapas." Five days from the Spanish outpost of Lita, the party reached the settlement headed by Don Francisco Cayapa where the mission of Espíritu Santo was established. Gaspar de Torres remained at this mission for two months, baptizing and preaching in Spanish because Quechua was not understood (Spanish missionaries frequently used Quechua as a *lingua franca*). A good case can be made that Espíritu Santo and the Pueblo Viejo of Chachi traditions are one and the same settlement. First, the location is right. A close reading of Gaspar de Torres's travel itinerary places Espíritu Santo on the upper Santiago, precisely where all Chachi accounts situate Pueblo Viejo. Second, Espíritu Santo was founded at the site of a suspension bridge passing over a deep gorge. Today's Chachi still speak of the suspension bridge that used to cross the deeply entrenched Santiago at Pueblo Viejo.

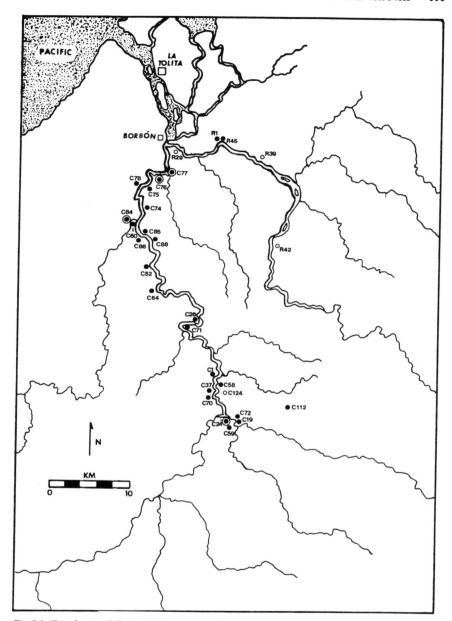

Fig. 9.1 Distribution of Chachi (solid circles) *and Cantarana* (open circles) *archaeological sites.*

Seventeenth-century references to the Chachi are scarce. When the record picks up again in the mid-eighteenth century, the Chachi were still centered on the upper Santiago, and Espíritu Santo continued to be identified as their major settlement. In accordance with the later traditions recorded by Barrett, the Chachi of this time were complaining of depredations being committed by hostile Indians, particularly those known as the Malaba. It is possible to date the Chachi movement into the Cayapas basin between 1749, when they were still based at Espíritu Santo, and the first years of the nineteenth century when several observers noted Chachi settlements on the lower Cayapas. Particularly pertinent is Stevenson's 1809 description of Punta Venado, which he called "the *new* village of Cayapas" (Stevenson 1825, II: 408–409, emphasis mine). Situated on the left bank of the Cayapas a short distance upriver from the mouth of the Onzole, Punta Venado (C52 in fig. 9.1) continues today as the premier Chachi ceremonial center. Stevenson's account is also important in locating the Malaba on the Río San Miguel, indicating that by 1809 the Chachi had not yet succeeded in completely expelling their enemies from the Cayapas basin. After Stevenson's testimony, the Malaba disappear from western history, although they survive in Chachi memory as the dreaded "Indios Bravos."

All in all, there are clear and mutually reinforcing parallels between Chachi oral traditions and European chronicles. A third body of evidence is provided by the archaeological record.

Archaeological Signature of the Chachi

Today some 2,500 Chachi live along the Cayapas and its headwater affluents, the San Miguel and the Río Grande. Disjunct populations at Tululvi, Río Verde, Canande, Muisne, and other scattered enclaves throughout Esmeraldas province probably bring the total population to more than 3500 individuals (Guderian et al. 1983). If one had to give a thumbnail sketch of Chachi ethnography, one should emphasize that they are river people, equally at home in the dugout canoe as on land, that they tend to live in single-house settlements dispersed along rivers, that plantains and fish are staples of the diet, and that they speak a language related to Colorado and Kwaiker. One would want to add that the Chachi settlement pattern also includes ceremonial centers, vacant throughout most of the year, where the residentially dispersed Chachi periodically gather for fiestas and other collective activities (DeBoer and Blitz 1991). For archaeological purposes, it is also important to note that Chachi women formerly made pottery, although this ceramic craft was abandoned during the 1950s on the arrival of Protestant missionaries, outboard motors, and cheap plastic and metal containers.

The Chachi occupation of the Cayapas can be readily identified archaeologically. This identification is based on a distinctive settlement pattern, ceramic remains that are identical to pottery formerly made by the Chachi, and the association of

Table 9.1   *Characteristics of Cantarana and Chachi sites.*

SITE	ENVIRONMENTAL CODE	DRAINAGE	DEPOSITIONAL CONTEXT	SIZE(HA)	ARTIFACTS COLLECTED	COMMENTS
Cantarana						
R29	BCCB	I	P&SS	0.35	195	atop knoll
R39	CCCC	I	P	0.1	13	extends 70 m along bluff
R42	CCGC	I	P&SS	?	31	atop knoll in town of Porvenir
C77B	DCEB	I	P	?	41	sherds eroding out of low mound beneath church of Punta de Piedra
C124	HGHC	III	SS	?	62	eroding downslope
Cantarana and Chachi						
C24	CHFC	I	P	?	132	
C76A	DCEB	I	P	0.02	6	atop knoll
C84	CCFB	I	P	0.02	68	
Chachi						
C1	CFFC	I	P	0.02	?	at modern Chachi house
C19	HHHC	III	P	?	1	1 jar exposed in estero
C26	CCFC	I	P	0.02	12	associated shell midden
C37	CGFC	I	P	0.02	612	at modern Chachi house
C52	CCFB	I	P	0.8	275	the Punta Venado ceremonial center
C58	CFFC	I	P	0.02	230	associated shell
C59	CHFC	I	P	0.04	68	associated shell midden
C60	CCFB	I	P	0.04	143	2 "hot spots", one with shell midden
C64	CCFB	I	P	0.02	31+	at town of Pichiyacu
C70	CGFC	I	P	0.02	none	at modern Chachi house
C71	CCFC	I	P	?	1	at modern Chachi house
C72	HHFC	I	P	?	none	small sherd patch at San Miguel ceremonial center
C74B	CCFB	I	P	0.02	6	associated shell midden
C75	CCEB	I	P	0.02	3	
C77A	DCEB	I	P	0.02	31	associated shell midden
C78B	CCFB	I	P	?	14	in estero
C85	CCFB	I	P	0.02	9	atop knoll
C86	CCFB	I	P	0.02	167	associated shell midden
C88	CCFB	I	P	0.02	none	associated shell midden
C112	IIHD	III	P	?	1	single complete bowl
R1	CCCB	I	P	?	none	shell midden exposed in bank
R45	CCCB	I	P	0.01	23	

Environmental code summarizes indices defined in figs. 2.6–2.7; for example, CCGC means *C* coding for pedology, *C* for geology, *G* for agriculture, and *C* for bioclimate. For drainage, *I* means location along Santiago or Cayapas mainstream; *II*, location along navigable secondary tributary; and *III*, along unnavigable estero or in interfluves. Under depositional context, *P* means intact primary deposit; *SS*, secondary deposit found as slope wash or embedded in land-slump; and *SE*, secondary deposit found in bed of estero.

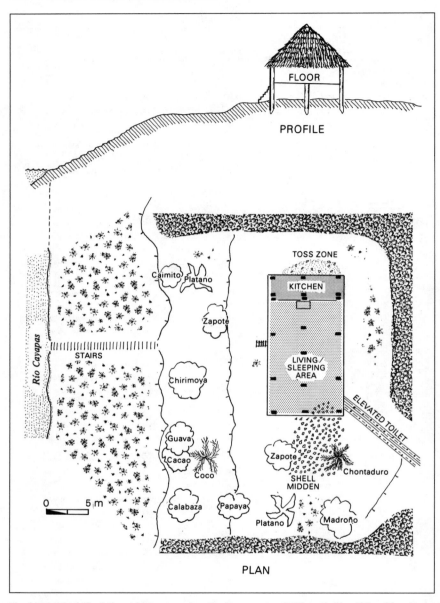

Fig. 9.2 *Modern Chachi house built over earlier Chachi occupation (C37) marked by shell midden. (From "Ceremonial Centers of the Chachi," Expedition, 1991, vol. 33. Courtesy of Expedition, University of Pennsylvania Museum.)*

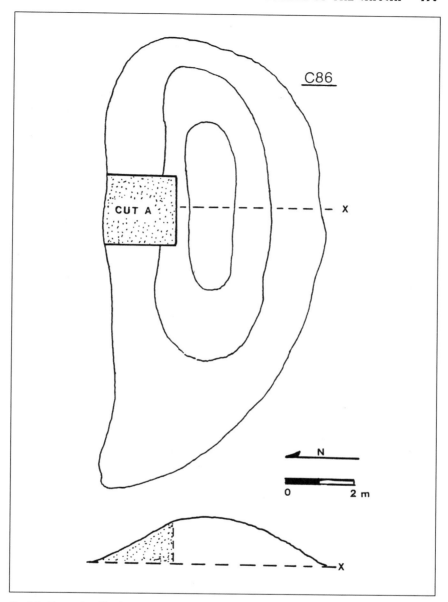

Fig. 9.3   Plan and profile of C86, a Chachi shell midden.

imported European goods dating within the last two centuries. Collectively this evidence forms a diagnostic signature that reads, "Chachi were here."

Chachi archaeological sites are plotted in fig. 9.1 and described in table 9.1 (this table also includes Cantarana sites, which will be discussed shortly). With an occasional exception, Chachi sherd scatters are small (0.02 ha is the mode) and are situated along the Cayapas mainstream. These sites conform precisely to the riparian single-house settlements still favored by the Chachi. Figure 9.2 illustrates such a contemporary house. The elevated house floor, the absence of walls, the partitioning of floor space into a living-sleeping area and a kitchen from which food scraps and other debris are tossed to the ground, and the surrounding house garden dominated by useful trees are typical. This house is built over an earlier Chachi occupation (C37) marked by a shell midden and associated sherds. Such superpositioning of occupations is not unusual because the Chachi often reoccupy abandoned house sites (DeBoer 1989). Shell middens as found at C37 used to typify Chachi settlements; however, in recent years access to the coastal shell beds has been greatly curtailed. Barrett (1925: 78) described the earlier practice: "The Cayapa make frequent journeys to the ocean, chiefly for the purpose of securing shellfish and crabs, which are abundant along the beaches about the mouth of the river. There are several species of clams and mussels, as well as oysters in large numbers. . . . Both the shellfish and the crabs are brought alive up the river, the crabs being confined in coarse baskets." That coastal resources were formerly obtained in quantities sufficient to produce substantial middens is attested at numerous Chachi archaeological sites.

C86 is a case in point. Here the shell midden, probably accumulated in the toss zone beneath an elevated kitchen, actually more resembles a shell mound (fig. 9.3). A 2 x 2 m cut excavated at the northern edge of this mound yielded abundant oyster shells, a few pieces of fire-altered rock, glass bottles and other items of European vintage, three bones from domestic pig, and an array of Chachi pottery. This pottery included several nearly complete vessels and a number of large sherds that can be readily assigned to the vessel forms described by Barrett (1925: 173–181). In 1987, Paul Tolstoy and I examined the Barrett collection of Chachi ceramics quartered in the Bronx Annex of the Museum of the American Indian. The Chachi case, therefore, affords an ethnographic opportunity to breathe life into the smashed crockery that has carried such a heavy interpretive burden in previous chapters.

The first thing to note about the Chachi ceramic assemblage is that it reduces to four named vessel categories, each associated with a specific use. Following Barrett, these are:

1. *tó palato:* a shallow bowl or plate (probably cognate with Spanish *plato*) used as a food serving vessel;
2. *piáma:* a carinated vessel used as a cooking pot;
3. *kandáro:* a medium-sized jar for carrying and storing liquids (almost certainly cognate with Spanish *cántaro*, or jar);
4. *bulum biáma:* a large jar often having an exterior coating of brea and used for the storage of alcoholic beverages.

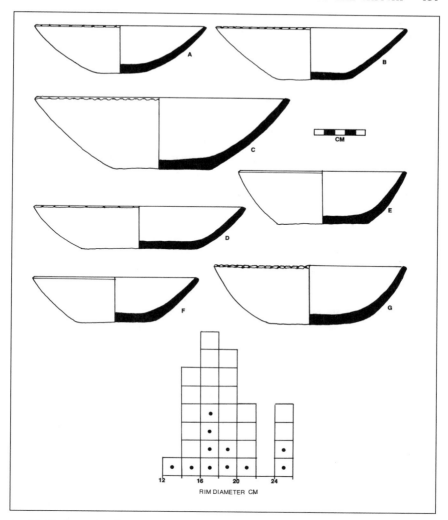

Fig. 9.4 Chachi tó palato *(A, C37; B–D, C52; E–G, C86). In histogram,* dotted squares *indicate specimens from the Museum of the American Indian.*

In addition to these ceramic containers, the Chachi used (and continue to use) bottle gourds (*wáiyu*) as light and serviceable water jugs. Calabash bowls (*cúlya*) have multiple uses: the dipping of liquids, the serving of foods, canoe bailers, caps for women, and, when perforated, colanders for straining the maize drink *champu* (Barrett 1925: 166–73).

The four primary ceramic forms manufactured by the Chachi contrast with the much larger array of vessel shapes identified in prehistoric phases. To recall:

Mafa   12+ vessel shapes
Selva Alegre   15+ vessel shapes
Guadual   17+ vessel shapes

Herradura   13 vessel shapes
Las Cruces   14 vessel shapes
Tumbaviro   11 vessel shapes

Accounting for this disparity is, to a certain extent, a resort to excuses, some more justified than others. First, it could be that the Chachi assemblage is genuinely depauperate, one invaded by European container technology and even terminology (e.g., *kandáro* = *cántaro*). Second, it could be that incomparables are being compared, namely, the emic categories of the Chachi with the etic categories of the archaeologist prone to recognize formal variability that, although real, had no conscious significance to the makers and users of the pottery in question. This possibility is another instance of the familiar "splitter-lumper" debate that infects most classificatory exercises. Third, and potentially more interesting and damaging, is that the Chachi assemblage is crisply defined and relatively spare in content precisely because it *is* an assemblage confined to a short period of time. In contrast, our archaeological phases span centuries and are accordingly less well resolved in either chronological or contextual senses. At present, there is no obvious way to assess the relative contribution of these various factors. Of great help would be a fine-grained stratigraphic sequence, one resembling French pastry more than chocolate mousse.

The following definition of the Chachi ceramic assemblage rests on both archaeological and ethnographic museum materials.

Tó Palato

A sample of *tó palato*, shallow, open bowls, is illustrated in fig. 9.4. Rims are unmodified whereas bases range from nearly rounded on smaller specimens (fig. 9.4A) to flat. Of thirty examples, half are undecorated and half bear nicked or finger-impressed lips (fig. 9.4A–D, G). Rim diameters indicate a major mode of 17 cm and a minor mode of 25 cm.

Piáma

Piáma are lithe and attractively contoured cooking vessels. The cooking function is attested by the fact that one third of all vessels (nine of twenty-seven) bear exterior carbon sooting below the carinated shoulder. Although plain examples occur (fig. 9.5D), most *piáma* are decorated, with the carination being the focus of embellishment. Decorative treatments include nicking (fig. 9.5A), rocker stamping executed with the edge of a shell (fig. 9.5B), and incised chevrons (fig. 9.5C, E). Although varying widely, rim diameters suggest three modal sizes.

Kandáro

Kandáro have flaring necks and bodies that are globular or angled at the shoulder (fig. 9.6A–D). Of thirty-five examples, nineteen have nicked lips (fig. 9.6A), whereas there are single cases of lips modified by punctations or by incised chevrons. Three archaeological vessels bear traces of a thin, maroon-colored wash on their exterior surfaces, a treatment unnoticed by Barrett, and two examples are

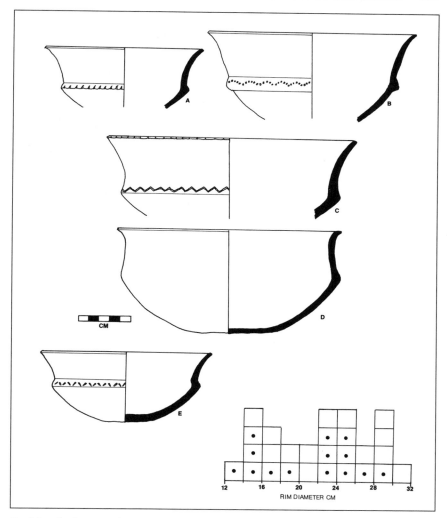

Fig. 9.5 *Chachi píama (A, C37; B, C58; C, C86; D, C112; E, Barrett). In histogram,* dotted squares *indicate specimens from the Museum of the American Indian collected by Barrett.*

textile impressed on their basal interiors, a result of the manufacturing technique described in appendix 1.

Bulum Biáma

Represented by six vessels, the *bulum biáma* form is essentially an extra-large *kandáro*. Five bear exterior traces of a brea resin. Only one specimen is decorated, this with an appliqué strip encircling the base of the neck (fig. 9.6E).

This suite of Chachi vessels is unique and could not be confused with any other ceramic phase in the sequence. Although a few general similarities such as

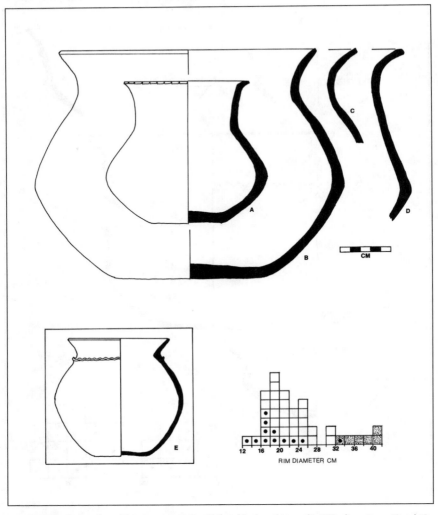

Fig. 9.6 Chachi kandáro *(A–B, Barrett; C–D, C86) and* bulum biáma *(E, C52; diameter = 40 cm). In histogram,* dotted squares *indicate specimens from the Museum of the American Indian collected by Barrett;* stippled squares *indicate* bulum biáma, *and* open squares *refer to* kandáro.

open bowls and flaring jars can be noted, Chachi and Tumbaviro ceramics are worlds apart, and one cannot regard the latter as a source for the distinctive *piáma* and its associated decorative treatments. When the ceramic evidence is combined with that of settlement pattern, a complete discontinuity is suggested. This, of course, is what Chachi oral traditions aver, and it is likely that terminal Tumbaviro represents the "Indios Bravos" of these same traditions. The origins of Chachi pottery remain unknown. Excavations at Pueblo Viejo and in the vicinity of Ibarra would be informative in this regard.

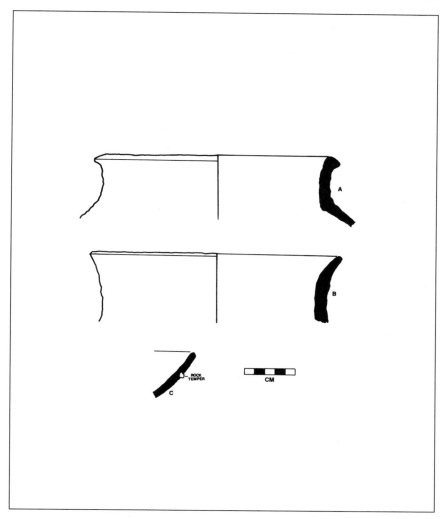

Fig. 9.7   Entire sample of Cantarana rim sherds (A, R29; B, R42; C, C77B).

But the Chachi are not the only contemporary denizens of the Cayapas who have left an archaeological imprint.

Chachi and Cantarana

Rising 40 m above the confluence of the Santiago and Cayapas, the hill called Cantarana (R29) is a local high point, at least in the topographic sense. The Ecuadorian archaeologist Presley Norton suggested to us that this prominence

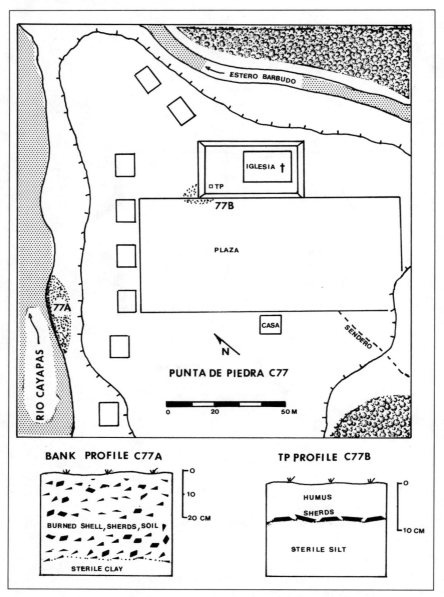

Fig. 9.8   Top, *Plan of contemporary community of Punta de Piedra showing location of Chachi (77A) and Cantarana (77B) middens. Bottom, Stratigraphic profiles (at differing scales).*

could well be a tola, or artificial mound, and ought to be investigated. Cantarana ("place where the frogs sing" in Spanish, also known as Chuchuranga, a less decodable toponym) is currently the site of a lumber mill with a port opening to the left bank of the Santiago. Houses of workmen affiliated with the mill skirt the base of the knoll, while the knoll itself sports a mosaic of secondary growth and house gardens. A sparse scatter of sherds litters the summit and extends downslope into the houseyards flanking the base. Shovel augers indicated that this cultural deposit is entirely superficial and underlain by bright orange sterile clays with a hardness approaching that of concrete. Apparently Cantarana is a natural formation, a tough and resistant gnarl separating and perhaps even directing the lowermost courses of the Santiago and Cayapas.

The pottery collected at R29 is not an impressive lot. Of 195 sherds, only one is a rim. Even when augmented by collections from other sites, the entire corpus of Cantarana rim sherds reduces to the three specimens shown in fig. 9.7, so little can be said about vessel forms. Surfaces have the texture of stucco, and the temper is shot-sized crushed rock. Even in those few sherds where patches of original surface are intact, pigmented slips or other decorative embellishments are absent.

This rather dismal utilitarian ware is not restricted to the type site. It recurs up the Santiago at the small sherd scatters of R39 and R42. It is also found on the lower Cayapas where it is admixed with, or occurs in proximity to, Chachi pottery (C76, C77, C84). A southern outlier occurs at the contemporary Afro-Ecuadorian community of San Miguel (C34) where again Cantarana ware is superficially mixed with sherds of Chachi style.

An example of a site producing juxtaposed Chachi and Cantarana remains is C77, which underlies the modern settlement of Punta de Piedra (fig. 9.8). Unfortunately our visit to this settlement was limited to a few hours. By working with a recent immigrant from Tumaco, we inadvertently offended the local establishment of old-time immigrants from the same region of Colombia. Our attempt to overcome this misunderstanding and to continue archaeological work at Punta de Piedra was rebuffed.

The port of Punta de Piedra is marked by a conspicuous midden exposed in the river bank (77A in fig. 9.8). This midden, 40 cm thick, extends for 30 m along the bank and consists of a greasy black soil laden with burned shell and sherds, the latter all vintage Chachi. One imagines a large Chachi house that burned down. Inland and upslope from this conflagration is the plaza *qua* soccer field of the contemporary community. On the northeast side of the plaza is a low rectilinear mound upon which the present church rests. Sherds eroding out of the northwest corner of this mound prompted the excavation of a 1 × 1 m test pit (77B in fig. 9.8). Beneath 8 cm of humus that included some contemporary flotsam of glass and plastic, a veritable pavement of Cantarana sherds was encountered. This pavement, one sherd thick, was superposed directly upon sterile silt.

One shallow test pit cannot resolve what might be a complex stratigraphic history, but a partial interpretation can be offered. Our initial view of the low rectilinear mound underlying the church was that this mound could well be aboriginal, as it has been Catholic policy throughout Latin America to erect church edifices over those of the vanquished. The freshly cut perimeter of the mound and the fact that rectilinear mounds with sharply angled corners are otherwise rare in the archaeological record of the region, however, cast doubt on this hunch. Although we had questionable rapport with the residents of Punta de Piedra, their own testimony on the matter carries credence. According to them, the mound was built from soil gathered from the leveling of the adjacent plaza. This operation, carried out at repeated intervals, had two practical goals. First, it created an elevated platform that lessened the impact of mud on churchgoers dressed up in their Sunday clothes. Second, it had the added benefit of leveling the playing field for the local soccer team. The lens of Cantarana sherds, therefore, could mark a former mound surface subsequently covered over during an episode of plaza clearing. This clearing obviously took place after local ceramic production had ceased. But what accounts for the pavement of sherds? Today blacks and Chachi scoop up river pebbles from beaches exposed during low water and carry them in baskets to be sprinkled as mud-resistant surfaces around houses and along paths. Our small test pit suggests that broken crockery served the same purpose in the past.

The available evidence is best interpreted to indicate that Cantarana is a relatively recent phenomenon, one overlapping with the historic Chachi. On distributional grounds alone, it is tempting to equate Cantarana with Afro-Ecuadorian occupation of the Santiago-Cayapas. African slaves, escaped from shipwrecks, settled the Esmeraldas coast as early as the late sixteenth century, intermarried with local Indians, and established a "zambo" republic that successfully resisted Spanish intervention from the sierra (Cabello de Balboa 1945, Phelan 1967). This seed population was later augmented by an influx of immigrants from Colombia during the nineteenth century (West 1957: 102). At present, the distribution of the black and Chachi populations can be summarized as follows (DeBoer and Blitz 1991: 55): "The Blacks, living in towns, dominate the Santiago basin and the lower Cayapas up to the mouth of the Onzole. Above the Onzole, the two populations share the Cayapas basin upriver to the San Miguel, above which the Chachi are demographically dominant." The current distribution maps reasonably well onto the extent of Cantarana and Chachi archaeological sites. This concordance is made more plausible by West's (1957: 183) comment that "old Negroes have told me that their grandmothers made clay pots in the days of slavery." Even in 1988, while we lived in the Afro-Ecuadorian community of Maldonado, our elderly hostess claimed that potting took place during her youth.

Cantarana, therefore, is a good candidate for marking the Afro-Ecuadorian presence on the Santiago-Cayapas. And if the archaeological record is to be trusted, Chachi and blacks have a more common and intimately shared history than their current antipathy suggests. The Chachi play marimba music of West African origin, while black curers drink *pilde* (ayahuasca), a native American hallucinogen, to see a forest filled with a syncretic cast of Afro-American spirits.

for all category III sites. Furthermore, these distinctions are maintained even if the "extra-large" mainstream occupations of R10 are deleted. In an ordinal sense, therefore, site area does as well as site counts and has the added benefit of perhaps serving as some faint measure of population.

What is problematical about the distributional oscillation between the mainstream and its backwaters is why the latter should ever be the preferred zone of occupation. As emphasized repeatedly, most advantages seemingly would accrue to the mainstream: more arable (although flood-prone) soils; richer quantities of riverine and riparian fauna; and greater canoe-based mobility. In the case of Mafa, according to the survivorship index, we may be dealing with time-sensitive taphonomic processes, but because all other phases differ just slightly in terms of this index, they can be treated without regard to differential site destruction.

An initial possibility is that interfluvial sites primarily represent farmsteads or seasonally occupied field houses linked to mainstream settlements. In this scenario, interfluvial settlements would represent a kind of "overflow" or extensification prompted by population build-up on the mainstream. There is no evidence, however, that lends credence to this scenario because occupational intensities on the mainstream and in the interfluves are totally independent. Furthermore, there is no convincing artifactual evidence that small interfluvial sites were specialized in nature. For instance, ceramic vessels from such sites are not consistently smaller, more transportable, or otherwise of the kind that one might expect to mark outlying field houses (e.g., Santley 1992).

A second possibility, one that I find more plausible and one that has been alluded to earlier, is that changing settlement patterns represent responses to a fluctuating social environment, a changing field of play in which the mainstream, as conduit to the outside world, variously acted as magnet or repellent depending on whether local perceptions deemed the outside to be enticing or sinister. In this view of the matter, Selva Alegre and Guadual were cooperative members of the riverine network whose hub centered at La Tolita. In turn, Herradura–Las Cruces phases represent a post-Tolita balkanization, a retreat from a mainstream now carrying sinister forces. Tumbaviro carried on this insulating reaction to what appears to have become an increasingly unfriendly landscape in which neighbors were more likely to be raiders than traders and usurpers rather than useful suppliers of exotic goods. But this speculative scenario is missing much of the story.

La Tolita's Local Catchment

By local catchment is meant the zone likely to have been under the administrative control of La Tolita. A comparative literature on chiefdoms suggests that the radius of effective control rarely extends beyond one day's travel from the paramount center and more commonly is limited to a day's round trip (e.g., Spencer 1982: 6–7). Beyond this distance, visits by the chief himself or by his representatives become difficult as a means of managing fragilely allied subelites who are simultaneously exposed to the outside and envious of the center. In the chiefdom arena, borders are always potential centers, a perimeter of rivals, if you will. Border maintenance, therefore, is always a concern of chiefly politics and includes a wide variety of stratagems: buffer zones that reinforce the marginality of the frontier; nepotistic appointments and marriage alliances; sumptuary goods, etiquettes, rituals, and ideologies that serve to strengthen pan-elite identity at the expense of local loyalties; and, as a resort, abject terrorism. All of these devices, however, are symptoms of stress and rapidly lose effectiveness as problems of policing an expanding perimeter mount. For chiefdoms, small is not only good, it is necessary. But can any of these considerations be grounded in the archaeological record?

As pointed out in chapter 2, canoes provide the most effective means of travel in the Santiago-Cayapas basins. La Tolita, situated a short distance below the confluence of these two waterways, was ideally placed to mediate interactions between its riverine hinterland and the maritime. Using the gauge of one day's (10 hours) round trip travel, La Tolita's catchment would have crossed the Santiago at the mouth of the Bogotá and the Cayapas at the mouth of the Onzole. Table 10.1 tracks the changing percentage of site area found inside and outside this projected catchment. Again it should be emphasized that these percentages are not to be regarded as absolute values—the intra- and extra-catchment areas are not of equivalent size, nor was survey intensity equivalent in the two areas. Therefore, the entries in table 10.1 should be viewed in an ordinal manner and read to detect the direction of change from phase to phase.

And change there was. With one notable exception (Guadual), the within-catchment trajectory parallels the previously discussed distribution-by-drainage index, suggesting that mainstream occupation and proximity to the coast are related. Thus the highest percentage of within-catchment hectarage occurred during the Selva Alegre phase coeval with the rise and initial consolidation of La Tolita. During this period, La Tolita apparently acted as a magnet, a paramountcy attracting a hinterland population. What is telling, however, is that during the subsequent Guadual phase, this centripetal effect was reversed. The major Guadual center at R10 was located two days up the Santiago. Smaller but substantial Guadual sites proliferated on the upper Cayapas, well upstream and outside the convenient "striking distance" of La Tolita. In short, Guadual was a phenomenon of the perimeter, one that overlapped the last days of La Tolita and one that may well have persisted beyond the abandonment of this regional center. What is to be made of this phenomenon?

There are several ways to address this question. One would be that during the Guadual phase La Tolita "sucked in" its catchment population, thereby creating a largely vacant zone (perhaps a kind of buffer zone) that separated the paramount settlement from a Guadual periphery. The fact that the extent of habitational refuse and the pace of mound construction at La Tolita increased during the Tardío phase after A.D. 100 (Valdez 1987: 55) is conformable with this interpretation, although why this involutionary process took place is left unexplained. The construction of raised fields at nearby Laguna de la Ciudad may suggest that subsistence intensification accompanied such a demographic implosion, but at present we cannot be certain of such links until the fields are more securely dated.

Nor is there sufficient evidence to define the nature of the relationship between La Tolita and its Guadual periphery. A La Tolita–centered perspective might view R10 and other Guadual sites as outposts designed to pump in gold or other preciosities to the chiefly core. From the upstream point of view, however, proximity to La Tolita and its growing demands for labor and goods might have been countered through the simple mechanism of spatial distancing. From the Guadual frontier, one could reach La Tolita in one day by traveling downstream. From La Tolita, in contrast, this frontier remained well beyond a day's paddling against the current. The Guadual settlement pattern, therefore, can be seen as a strategy for balancing access to, as well as autonomy from, La Tolita.

Whatever the case, the changes in settlement pattern evinced during the Guadual phase either portended or directly signaled the unraveling of La Tolita's regional hegemony. By A.D. 350, this center, which for a few centuries had been such a prominent feature of the political landscape, was abandoned. Its former catchment was repopulated in the form of the Las Cruces phase on the lower Santiago while Herradura continued the Guadual ceramic legacy on the upper Cayapas. Although quotidian artifacts survived the collapse of La Tolita, foreign imports and general artifactual "fanciness" declined, as shall be seen below.

Imports Index

Imports comprise those raw or finished materials derived from outside the Santiago-Cayapas basins and are thus but a subset of the total range of exchanged goods. At present, however, the evidence for goods procured or produced and then exchanged within the basins is sparse. Stamps and molds for figurine production were found at two rural Selva Alegre sites, and at least one case of a ceramic waster is known from C141 (based on 1992 excavations, the production of ground stone axes was also a major activity at C141). Even during the reign of La Tolita, therefore, craft production was, to a certain extent, locally based. Of course, there is no way to assess the traffic in salt, feathers, pelts, drugs, canoes, and other perishables that often play such a large role in tropical forest exchange networks.

The archaeological register of imports is slim and consists of two materials, one definitely exotic, the other probably so. Obsidian (n = 44) is clearly of highland origin, and it is even possible to identify the specific Mullumica deposit as a source. A distinctive but mineralogically unidentified green stone (n = 7) used to fashion beads is another candidate for an exotic material. Although its source is unknown, green stone is not found among the lithologically diverse cobbles that litter the low-water beaches of the Santiago-Cayapas and their tributaries.

Except in the case of the Chachi (to be considered shortly), the imports index is defined as follows:

$$\frac{(\text{obsidian and green stone}) \, (100)}{\text{phase duration in years}}$$

This index varies considerably (table 10.1). Imports have not been found at Mafa sites. If real, this absence suggests a certain insularity of the Santiago-Cayapas region during the first phase of our sequence. In contrast, imports are conspicuous during the subsequent Selva Alegre and Guadual phases. In the case of Selva Alegre, it would thus appear that the import of exotic goods played a role in the rise and consolidation of La Tolita as a regional center. More remarkable, however, is the fact that these goods did not diminish during the following Guadual phase despite the apparent withdrawal of Guadual settlements from the "inner orbit" of La Tolita's catchment. Also worthy of note is that imports, even when factored according to the volume of excavated midden, are decidedly more abundant in modestly sized components of both the Selva Alegre (C69II) and Guadual (C36II, C69III) phases than in the large mound-associated settlements (R10, R36) of the same phases. If supported by a larger sample, this result is of some interest and would be difficult to reconcile with any top-down model of material flows within the La Tolita polity. Imports declined precipitously in the post–La Tolita world of Las Cruces and Herradura, and this decline continued during Tumbaviro times, a trend that is conformable with the previously discussed evidence for an increasingly inward-turning settlement pattern.

To put the imports index in perspective, it is instructive to apply it to the archaeological record of the historic Chachi, a people in contact with the larger capitalist world. The prehistoric imports of obsidian and green stone are replaced by European crockery, containers of glass, metal, and, most recently, plastic, and by a variety of utilitarian implements including metal scissors, nails, and the all-important machete. The resultant index for Chachi and Cantarana archaeological sites is a whopping 47.33, a value nearly ten times greater than the highest prehistoric index (table 10.1). Today the major immediate source of these outside goods is the town of Borbón, the road terminus linking the Santiago-Cayapas to the rest of Ecuador. With some fifteen hundred people, mainly Afro-Ecuadorians, Borbón is strategically situated at the confluence of the Santiago and Cayapas, only a short distance upstream from the ancient center of La Tolita. The volume of goods passing through this relatively forlorn port located on the fringes of the global economy dwarfs anything known in prehistory.

Ceramic Elaboration Index

The ceramic elaboration index attempts to assess the degree to which pottery was decoratively embellished. It follows the lead provided by Feinman, Upham, and Lightfoot (1981) but differs from their "production step measure" in that only decorative elaboration, rather than total labor investment, is measured. The index, calculated separately for each vessel form, is defined as follows:

$$\frac{\text{total decorative score}}{\text{number of vessels}}$$

where the decorative score is determined in the following way. Slipping, painting, or the use of a texturing technique such as incision or brushing is coded as 1 for each surface on which it occurs. Thus, a pot with a red-slipped exterior is coded as 1, one with a red-slipped exterior and interior is coded as 2, a vessel with a red-slipped *and* incised exterior also is coded as 2, whereas a pot with a red-slipped interior and an exterior bearing resist over a red slip is coded as 3, and so on. The index thus gives the average number of decorative additions per vessel. Again, this is a simple, rough-and-ready measure to be taken in an ordinal sense rather than as a realistic absolute value of decorative investment.

The results by phase and by vessel form are given in table 10.2. In terms of phases, Guadual represents the decorative apogee of the sequence and, as expected, Tumbaviro the nadir. Mafa, Selva Alegre, and Las Cruces-Herradura ceramics are roughly equivalent to each other in elaboration, although each phase emphasizes different decorative techniques. The surprisingly high index for Chachi-Cantarana is somewhat misleading because it reflects the fact that many Chachi vessels have nicked rims, a relatively simple adornment that is nonetheless coded as 1. Turning to specific vessel forms, it is clear that there were major changes in the vessels chosen to be decorated. Thus closed bowls, frequently incised, were the decorative target in the Mafa phase. In Selva Alegre, pigmentation increased in abundance at the expense of incision, and plates and open bowls superseded closed bowls as the most decoratively elaborate of the common vessel shapes. In Guadual, the decorative target shifted to the new compotera form, a form that continued to be a focus of ornamentation during the subsequent Herradura phase.

In addition to tracking decoration over time, the ceramic elaboration index also can be used to address the possibility that "fancy" serving vessels such as Selva Alegre plates or Guadual compoteras had varying within-phase distributions. For instance, such vessels might be more abundant at large mound-bearing sites than at smaller "rural" sites to the extent that the former were the scene of elite-sponsored fiestas. Furthermore, one might expect varying vessel sizes depending on the size and composition of the consuming unit.

These possibilities are examined in table 10.3 in which the abundance, size, and elaboration of three "fancy" vessel forms are partitioned according to site size. The results are somewhat unexpected. In terms of abundance, plates are significantly more common at *small* sites. Open bowls and compoteras, however, are relatively more common at large sites, an expected pattern if these vessels were linked to elites, public feasts, or other activities where ostentatious serving

Table 10.2 *Ceramic elaboration by phase and vessel form.*

VESSEL FORM	NUMBER OF VESSELS	DECORATIVE SCORE	MAFA	SA	G	LC-H	TUMBA	CH-CA	TOTAL
Plates	100	58	.07	.67	-	-	-	-	.58
Open Bowls	200	79	.36	.66	.71	.21	.00	.48	.40
Compoteras	202	197	-	-	1.50	.74	.04	-	.93
Closed Bowls	200	128	.88	.41	.67	.40	-	.74	.64
Buttress Rim Bowls	35	38	-	-	1.17	.82	-	-	1.09
Channel Rim Bowls	67	30	-	-	.00	.56	.00	-	.45
Rampiral Cups	9	0	-	-	-	.00	.00	-	.00
Jars	1088	489	.31	.37	.79	.13	.03	.58	.45
Comma Rim Basins	37	3	.60	.00	.00	.00	.00	-	.08
Miscellaneous	12	10	1.00	.63	1.50	-	-	-	.83
COMPOSITE	1950	1032	.35	.46	.84	.33	.03	.59	.53

Table 10.3 Comparison of serving vessels from large (>5 ha) and small (<5 ha) sites.

	Selva Alegre Plates		Selva Alegre Open Bowls		Guadual Compoteras	
	Sites >5 ha	Sites <5 ha	Sites >5 ha	Sites <5 ha	Sites >5 ha	Sites <5 ha
Number of Vessels	26	59	28	16	26	74
Diameter Range (cm)	12-36	16-32	8-34	10-28	10-28	8-28
Modal Diameter (cm)	18-20	16-18	8-10	16-18	16-18	16-18
Median Diameter (cm)	18-20	20-22	16-18	16-18	16-18	16-18
Proportion of All Vessels (%)	17	30	19	8	23	9
Ceramic Elaboration Index	.88	.58	.54	.88	.88	1.72

vessels might be necessary. This interpretation, however, is not paralleled in the case of decorative fanciness. The ceramic elaboration indices for open bowls and compoteras are significantly lower at *large* sites. In contrast, plates, although proportionately less common at large sites, are more decoratively elaborated at these same sites. Finally there is no apparent size difference between vessels from large and small sites, except for the case of open bowls in which bowls from large sites have a *smaller* modal diameter.

At present, there is no unambiguous support for the idea that these fancy vessels are monitoring the workings of a settlement hierarchy. If plates were indeed food-serving vessels whereas open bowls and compoteras served as drinking vessels, then one might argue that the drinking of maize beer or some other brew was a more common activity at large sites, even if fancier beer mugs tended to occur at small sites. If forced, one could even speculate that drabber beer mugs were purposely reserved for large-scale fiestas in which the likelihood of vessel breakage was greater than usual. If so, such throwaway containers were probably provided by the host center, for vessel size (perhaps related to transportability) does not indicate any sort of "bring your own bottle" etiquette, with the possible exception of the small size mode for open bowls.

In the above discussion, several indices have been defined and individually activated to see what light they shed on the formal and distributional properties of the archaeological record from the Santiago-Cayapas. It is now appropriate to consider the linkages among these indices. To do this, we must first convert all variables (excepting site survivorship, which is exempted from the following analysis) into ordinal measures; this requires assigning a polarity to the indices of site distribution by drainage and by location with respect to La Tolita's catchment. In the former case, a shift to mainstream drainages is given a positive polarity. In the latter, a shift from outside to inside La Tolita's catchment is likewise given a positive coding. We can then ask questions of the following kind. As aggregation increases from one phase to the next, is there a covarying settlement shift to mainstream drainages (coded as +) or, in contrast, do settlements shift to the interfluves (coded as -)? Or, as a second example, if the imports index decreases from one phase to the next, does aggregation also decrease (coded as +) or, alternatively, increase (coded as -)?

The results of this mass comparison are presented in table 10.4. First consider the aggregate behavior of the entire matrix. The maximum row or column total is 150 in the case of complete positive covariation among all variables. In the absence of covariation (+ or - is equally likely), the expected total is zero. The observed total of 68 is significantly tilted toward the positive extreme, a result indicating that the overall pattern is one of positive covariation. This aggregate result, however, is not very meaningful without identifying the contributions made by specific variables.

First, note that La Tolita's catchment is the least correlated of all variables. This is not surprising given that La Tolita's occupation spanned but a fourth or so of the recorded sequence. At the other extreme, the variables of drainage orienta-

Table 10.4 Correlation matrix of phase variables.

	AGI	OCI	DRI	LTC	IMI	CEI	
AGI	/	+4	+3	−1	+3	+3	+12
OCI	+4	/	+2	−2	+2	+2	+8
DRI	+3	+2	/	+1	+5	+5	+16
LTC	−1	−2	+1	/	+1	+1	0
IMI	+3	+2	+5	+1	/	+5	+16
CEI	+3	+2	+5	+1	+5	/	+16
	+12	+8	+16	0	+16	+16	+68

AGI, aggregation index; OCI, occupational intensity index; DRI, site distribution by drainage (mainstream occupation given positive polarity); LTC, La Tolita's local catchment (within-catchment occupation given positive polarity); IMI, imports index; CEI, ceramic elaboration index.

tion, imports abundance, and ceramic elaboration form a completely correlated triad. This result suggests that the most powerful set of linkages at work in Santiago-Cayapas prehistory consisted of mainstream occupation and the subsistence and transportive advantages it afforded, access to exotic imports, and the decorative elaboration of pottery. That the first two of these are related is not remarkable. More quizzical is why ceramic elaboration should covary in such a forceful way. Seemingly access to the outside world, as evinced in settlement pattern and foreign imports, stimulated the local production of fancy pottery. This is clearly so in the case of the ornate mortuary wares of La Tolita but, to a lesser degree, also applies to the more pedestrian wares of the rustic sites encountered in our survey.

The fact that fancy pottery emerges as a central rather than peripheral player in our cast of variables is somewhat of an embarrassment to any brand of archaeology that would view decorative elaboration as mere dressing to infrastructural factors such as subsistence technology or "caloric clout." The ecologically oriented, however, could still argue that the production of fancy pottery requires access to geographically dispersed resources and, therefore, is very much related to the ways in which human populations articulate with their environments. Such an argument, in fact, has been advanced for the Shipibo-Conibo of the Peruvian Amazon, whose flamboyant polychrome pottery congeals pigments and resins having far-flung distributions along the Ucayali River (Lathrap 1973, Myers 1976, DeBoer 1984). There is no evidence, however, that nonlocal raw materials were essential to the manufacture of even the most elaborate ceramics recovered in our survey of the Santiago-Cayapas. For instance, red ochre, the pigment most used by prehistoric potters, is widely distributed throughout both basins. In terms of marshaling raw materials, therefore, the Shipibo-Conibo model does not appear to be applicable to the Santiago-Cayapas.

The presupposition that fancy pottery is an epiphenomenon to be explained (or explained away) in terms of something else, however, may be in error. It is worthwhile to entertain the possibility that our ceramic elaboration index is, in fact, a critical variable in its own right. Or, conversely, is it not a bit odd to deny processual significance to the very phenomenon (embellished material culture) that brought the La Tolita region to archaeological attention in the first place? The archaeological record makes clear that the basic ingredients of what would become the "La Tolita ceramic style" were present throughout the Santiago-Cayapas basins during the Mafa phase. Subsequently, and coincident with the rise of La Tolita as a regional center, this Mafa base was reworked and elaborated to produce the pottery that defines the Selva Alegre phase. Although found in its most flamboyant form in mortuary contexts at La Tolita proper, domestic versions of this style were widely distributed in the surrounding countryside, and there is no indication of sumptuary wares restricted to a regional elite. As pointed out previously, the same fancy pots found at large mound sites such as R10 or R36 occur in equal abundance at the smallest and most humble of settlements. The same democratic distribution seemingly applied to ceramic figurines and such imports as obsidian. To the extent that pottery can track politics, it would seem that the entire populace of the Santiago-Cayapas basins was participating in the La Tolita style and that this style was serving more to signify common membership in, rather than differentiation within, the La Tolita polity. The dramatic changes in ceramic style and settlement pattern that mark the advent of the Guadual phase undoubtedly represent a significant disjuncture in Santiago-Cayapas prehistory, a disjuncture that seemingly adumbrated the unraveling of La Tolita as a regional center. If an active voice is assigned to style, then Selva Alegre can be viewed as a phase governed by regional stylistic emulation, whereas the following Guadual phase can be seen as one of stylistic withdrawal and resistance. At present, however, we do not know what La Tolita "did," whether in the form of increasing demands or of unkept promises, to provoke such resistance and to lose its claim to being the chief style-setter.

Until a more fully described chronology of *nonmortuary* ceramics from La Tolita becomes available, it is unwise to pursue these ponderings further. The preceding sketch, however, does anticipate the kind of active role that decorated pots and other stylized artifacts, even of the most everyday sort, might play in our accounts of major sociopolitical changes occurring in the past. But these accounts will never become complete by dwelling exclusively on local linkages. Localities always engage wider fields of play.

Whatever else it was, La Tolita was a port facing the Pacific maritime. That its coastal connections were far-flung is undeniable. To the immediate north, pottery from Tumaco, the Patía, and the Timbiquí are clearly within the greater stylistic orb of La Tolita. Recently a vintage La Tolita component has been identified near Buenaventura, far up the Colombian coast (David Stemper, personal communication). That occasional contacts extended as far north as the Isthmus or West Mexico is plausible but remains indefinitely documented. To the south, the Tiaone materials of the Esmeraldas valley clearly relate to La Tolita. Farther south, trade connections certainly existed with the Jama-Coaque region of coastal Manabí. Farther afield, a gold figurine from the Lambeyeque valley of northern Peru *may* have a La Tolita source (Adoum and Valdez 1989: foto b). Inland connections were more tethered but certainly reached the Quito basin where the site of Jardín del Este could represent a La Tolita trading colony. Clearly La Tolita was a participant in, if not the hub of, an extensive zone of interaction whose major axis stretched 500 km from the Esmeraldas valley of Ecuador to Buenaventura on the central Colombian coast (the common phrase "interaction sphere" violates the geometry of this primarily coastal distribution and is thus avoided).

At this juncture, what is called for is a conceptual model that articulates what is known about the local, internal dynamics of the La Tolita polity with what is known about its regional, external workings. Unfortunately, this task is hampered by the fact that the evidence from La Tolita proper is difficult to compare with the evidence available from its hinterland. The former is dominated by mortuary goods, many indeed of a fancy nature; the latter consists of domestic debris with burials conspicuously absent. Equally impressed by the absence of burials in the Tumaco area, Bouchard (1991, 1992) has been forced to speculate that the mounds at La Tolita, in fact, were the *sole* necropoli for regional elites, if not for all members of society. On first consideration, this idea of a regional mausoleum to which the dead were hurried to be buried (corpse shelf-life is measured in hours in this humid environment) has a fancifully morbid ring (or should we say stench?) to it. Yet, on a smaller geographical scale, this is precisely what the Chachi do today.

As detailed elsewhere (DeBoer 1991b; DeBoer and Blitz 1991), when a Chachi person dies, family and neighbors conduct a quick wake immediately, after which the body is canoed to the dead's natal (which is also usually the nearest) ceremonial center for burial. These ceremonial centers, however, are more than cemeteries. Baptisms and weddings also take place there, as do the holiday celebrations of Christmas and Easter. At the latter, hundreds of Chachi gather to eat, drink, and dance over a period of several days. From an archaeological standpoint, these centers are interesting for two major reasons: although entirely vacant throughout most of the year, they are the largest Chachi sites and have the most substantial structures, today including a Catholic church; and because they are used over long periods of time (three of the four current centers were founded in the last century), these sites are associated with deep middens. For instance, a test pit at Punta Venado (C52), the largest ceremonial center, exposed 80 cm of deposits chock-full of artifacts and food remains. In contrast, Chachi residential sites are abandoned every decade or so and consequently tend to be associated with shallow middens. Furthermore, in terms of size and decorative elaboration, Chachi ceramics from Punta Venado and from single-house residential sites are essentially identical.

I am not suggesting that La Tolita was strictly a vacant ceremonial center. I do wish to question, however, the interpretive convention often employed by archaeologists in which large sites with monumental architecture, cemeteries, and substantial cultural deposits are assumed to represent large population centers and, by extension, to intimate complex political organization. This need not be the case. If the Chachi bestowed elaborate grave goods on the dead (they do not) and if their periodic aggregations at ceremonial centers included trade as a major activity (they do not), then the Chachi settlement pattern would be a fairly reasonable, if scaled-down, model of what the La Tolita archaeological record, as currently known, looks like.

These ruminations are rapidly exceeding the limits of the data. One can only specify the kinds of information needed to go further. In presenting this wish list, I find it convenient to follow the set of trenchant questions asked by Welch (1991: 20–21) in his attempt to understand the economy of prehistoric Moundville, the major Mississippian center in Alabama. I follow his wording:

1. Are the settlements within a chiefdom self-sufficient in production of food and other necessary economic goods, or is there complementary specialization in the production of these goods?

None of the sites recorded in our survey would appear to be so large or populous as to strain the productive potential of a convenient catchment, although it must be admitted that no sophisticated catchment analysis of subsistence has yet been attempted. Today communities numbering in the hundreds and equaling the prehistoric settlement of R10 in size largely maintain self-sufficiency in staple vegetables and fruits. An exception is fish, where the local catch is increasingly supplemented by purchased *salado* (salted fish) in the more populated parts of the Santiago and Cayapas. The latter dependence, however, may reflect the depletion of otherwise sustainable fish resources through dynamiting. If La Tolita were indeed a large residential center with a population of one or two thousand, then a strain on local agricultural and estuarine resources can be imagined, but Valdez (1987: 40) is only guessing when he states that "it's probable that in the late period at La Tolita, population growth had exceeded the carrying capacity of the island" [my translation].

2. If there is complementary specialization in production of necessary economic goods, how are the goods distributed? Specifically, are the goods transferred by direct exchanges between producers and consumers, or is the distribution effected by a central manager (the chief)?

At least with respect to foodstuffs, there is no clear-cut case for complementary specialization, so much of this multipart question need not be pursued. Again, however, Chachi ethnography raises a matter of possible relevance. As pointed out in the last chapter, Chachi archaeological sites are commonly marked by shell mounds. These mounds are dominated by shellfish that the Chachi obtained in periodic trips to the coast. La Tolita, of course, would have been well situated to control access to such coastal resources and to mediate the exchange of littoral and inland products. Raising a possibility, however, does not increase its likelihood.

3. Is there mobilization of subsistence goods to support the elite?

In phrasing this and other questions, Welch has the advantage of building on a century of archaeological work at Moundville. In comparison, archaeological investigations at La Tolita are still in a pioneer stage. Thus, although the elaborate metalwork, oversize hollow figurines, and other extravagant trappings might be reasonable *a priori* candidates for sumptuary items restricted to a privileged group, the very existence of an "elite," much less its exact nature, remains purely putative, something more akin to an inferential reflex than an empirically justified premise. At Moundville, a sophisticated study of mortuary remains indicates a measurable degree of social ranking (Peebles and Kus 1977). At La Tolita, despite the looting of thousands of burials (Valdez 1987: 11), only a few have been adequately described, and even in these few cases, gravelots have yet to be itemized, let alone compared.

In terms of mobilizing comestibles for La Tolita's population, elite or otherwise, a closer look at the field systems of Laguna de la Ciudad is a clear research priority. To argue that such intensification guaranteed a surplus at all, quite apart from whether it was managed exclusively by an elite, however, will require archaeological signatures that are not easily forged.

4. Is there specialization of craft items? How are craft items distributed?

As stated above, it is difficult to imagine that the more elaborate metallurgical and ceramic productions from La Tolita were not manufactured by specialists of some sort. Although the metallurgical techniques were basically simple (Bergsoe 1937, 1938), they still imply a level of technical mastery unlikely to be possessed by just any rustic farmer. Similarly, the large, hollow, mold-made vessels—typically anthropomorphic or therianthropic effigies—were certainly beyond the expertise of an ordinary potter. It should be emphasized, however, that although such spectacular pieces may dominate museum exhibits and coffee-table art books, they are decidedly uncommon finds, and the degree and extent of craft specialization, whether full-time or part-time, remain unknown.

In contrast to the occasional "masterpiece," more ubiquitous craft items, such as small figurines, ground stone axes, and elaborately decorated serving vessels, were apparently produced at all levels of society—from La Tolita itself to the most ordinary of hinterland settlements. It is not that production of these goods was "decentralized"; there were no centers capable of controlling, or inclined to meddle in, the production and distribution of these basic commodities. If such an outrage were attempted by any aspiring and meddlesome elite, this might shed light on the Guadual reaction and its sequel.

> 5. Is the mode of production and distribution of prestige goods different from that of utilitarian items?

These questions are becoming increasingly interlocked, such that failure to answer one thwarts grappling with the others. Furthermore, inferential circularities lurk everywhere. How are we to know what constitutes a prestige good? Presumably one for which distribution is limited. And how are utilitarian items to be recognized? They are ubiquitous! Clearly this single distributional criterion is insufficient without knowledge of the specific local contexts in which objects occur, and such knowledge is largely lacking. La Tolita, for instance, has been treated as a gold mine for centuries. Old-timers still talk of the gold cargo that Donato Yannuzzelli, the former owner of the site, shipped off to Italy. The bulk of this loot was sluice mined from burial mounds. In contrast, our excavations in hinterland settlements, albeit less ambitious in scale, produced but one minute leaf of gold (this from mound fill at R10). One, of course, could jump all over this singular find and claim that it represents the exceptional piece that trickled down to a rural subaltern, gold artifacts otherwise being restricted to a La Tolita–based elite. For reasons expressed previously, such a leap is unwarranted. Gold is relatively common *only* in mortuary contexts that, at present, are known *only* at La Tolita. We are comparing the dead, a putative elite marked by gold, with the living, marked by goldless demotic debris. Are we to imagine an elite that is purely necrotic?

> 6. How do nonlocal goods enter the chiefdom and how are they distributed?

In addressing Welch's final question, we can be a bit less evasive, for some germane evidence is in hand. We know that obsidian was imported to the Santiago-Cayapas. The probable source was the Mullumica deposit, located southeast of Quito, based on Isaacson's neutron activation analysis. The routes and mechanisms by which Mullumica obsidian reached La Tolita, however, remain poorly understood. Obsidian and vintage La Tolita–style artifacts are found at Jardín del Este in the Quito basin, and it is possible that this site represents a way station or trading enclave involved in the shunting of goods, including obsidian, between the highlands and the Esmeraldas coast. In a general consideration of the obsidian trade, Alcina Franch et al. (1987: 57–58) have argued for a route from Quito down the Blanco or Huallabamba to the Esmeraldas valley and then northward along the coast to La Tolita, gateway to the Santiago-Cayapas. But there is no reason to believe that this was the only route to the coast. As recently as the nineteenth century, Chachi traders ascended well-worn trails from the Upper Santiago to Ibarra, their alleged ancestral home in the Andes. By the early twentieth century, however, these trails, if not forgotten, had reverted to dense montane forest (Barrett 1925: 30). Even today, Chachi shamans maintain an elaborate toponymic vocabulary referring to specific Andean peaks to which they claim to fly during drug- and song-mediated curing sessions.

If obsidian was flown down from Andean heights on shamanic wings, there must have been limits on the weight of freight. Although most of the obsidian known from the Santiago-Cayapas consists of small flakes or chips with an occasional blade (some approaching Mesoamerican standards), large blocks of this material have been noted at La Tolita (Francisco Valdez, personal communication) and, as will be seen below, also occur as exotica which Chachi shamans retrieve from local archaeological sites. These large, multipound chunks would weigh down even the most volent of shamans and would be more safely moved by conventional land and river transport. Once received, obsidian was processed to small, sharp-edged pieces, a treatment not noticeably different from the manner in which locally available siliceous stones were reduced to expedient cutting tools.

The distribution of these cut-down chunks of obsidian is also of interest. Although the sample is small, obsidian is no more abundant at large mounded sites such as R10 or R36 than at modestly sized hamlets (this pattern is further confirmed by our 1992 excavations at C141). Thus the available evidence does not support an administered top-down flow of obsidian. Yet, with the collapse of La Tolita, obsidian imports to the Santiago-Cayapas virtually ceased, a coincidence that seemingly deserves explanation if obsidian were not a managed commodity in polity construction and maintenance. This argument, however, is misplaced, for Burger et al. (1994) have shown that obsidian imports declined dramatically *everywhere* along the Ecuadorian coast at the end of the Regional Developmental period. Any local explanation is unlikely to account for this global shakeup, after which coastal peoples either lost access to obsidian or no longer regarded it as worth having.

In the preceding discussion, Welch's set of questions has been used as a foil against which to assess the state of knowledge concerning the nature of La Tolita. Attempted answers have been admittedly evasive, in part because crucial evidence has yet to be gathered and, in part, because the questions designed for a better-documented Moundville may well be inappropriate in the case of La Tolita. In terms of all the stigmata of chiefdoms—chiefly elites, settlement or administrative hierarchies, sumptuary goods restricted to the elite, craft specialization, and so on, the preliminary evidence is either uncertain or negative. What patterning there is suggests that La Tolita might have been structured in ways fundamentally different from those expected of chiefdoms. How do we imagine chiefdoms without chiefs? How do we imagine monumentality without authoritarianism? How do we imagine complexity without hierarchy? In short, how do we imagine a past that may have been different, even weirdly so?

But total difference can never be imagined, much less comprehended. There are perforce analogic links to what is known. The ensuing question is, what are the appropriate links? There is another body of evidence that can be brought to bear on this issue. Obsidian is not the only "specialty" item that seemingly had a democratic distribution in the Santiago-Cayapas during La Tolita's heyday. Small ceramic figurines, usually found broken, comprise another example. La Tolita is famous for these figurines, and, as has been seen, they are not uncommon in rural middens. Whatever their multiple meanings and uses, these figurines were quotidian artifacts, if not utilitarian in the conventional sense. Now, what is figured in these effigies?

For starters, naivete is in order. I will assume that these figurines were not "masks" that subverted or concealed on-the-ground concerns, nor were they ideological objectifications divorced from everyday life. These assumptions seem reasonable given the dominant thematic content of the figurines. In large part, realistic, if not totally ordinary, free-standing male and female adults are portrayed (Sánchez Montañés 1981: 93). In lesser numbers, scenes of men paddling canoes (typically these paddlers have a coca quid puffing up one cheek), of women giving birth, grinding maize or fondling children, of coitus between the sexes, and of old age and illness are also represented. Bouchard (1992) has argued that the famed strapped-down bodies (personnages couchés) portray corpses in transit to burial. All of these themes convey a sense of "punctuated naturalism"—birth, the first socially significant mating (marriage?), the first grinding of maize in the case of females, the first coca-chewing canoe voyage in the case of males, illness, and death: in other words, day-to-day life tilted toward those moments of transition that anthropologists call rites of passage (Sánchez Montañés 1981).

But there is another class of figurines that stands apart from these naturalized renditions. This class consists of those rare but conspicuous figures that can best be described as therianthropic, that is, combining human and animal form. Typically transformation from human to animal is emphasized, an individual (when identifiable, invariably an adult male) assuming a snarling jaguar's mouth, serpents exuding from his body orifices, his torso transmogrifying into that of a cayman, or wings sprouting from his sides (e.g., fig. 3.10H). In the South American context, it is quite clear that this iconography represents shamanic transformation in which the shaman, through drugs and songs, acquires the ability to assume animal form, to travel widely in both natural and supernatural domains, and to become invested with the power of x-ray vision to seek out the causes of sickness. The potential political role of the shaman needs further investigation.

Mary Helms (1979, 1991, 1992) has been developing precisely the kind of theory needed to relate material trappings to social and political developments, specifically the emergence of those formations that anthropologists gloss as chiefdoms. Although having universal implications, Helms's formulation was initially based on archaeological and ethnohistoric data from Panama and perhaps can be extended most usefully to other cases from the "Intermediate Area," as Willey (1971) christened that liminal zone between Mesoamerica and the Central Andes.

The kernel of Helms's argument is that access to exotic goods or arcane knowledge, rather than merely reflecting the privileged status of already established elites, can be the means by which novel status claims are achieved and legitimated in the first place. In Helms's (1992: 323) words: "The implication seems to be that attainment of the tangible symbols of power and authority is not just an accompaniment but a useful, perhaps necessary, first step to the actual attainment and implementation of power and authority." To be effective insignia of nascent power and authority, such symbols must be of limited access. Accordingly, they must be difficult to acquire because they come from great distances, because their manufacture requires specialized skills (the metallurgy of La Tolita is a possible example), or because they are associated with the esoteric shamanic knowledge needed to contact an otherwise inaccessible "supernature." In elaborating this point, Helms (1992: 320) makes a useful distinction between "vertical" and "horizontal" axes of distance:

> Though cosmological power is believed to exist in both vertically and horizontally "distant" settings, human means of contacting these domains is not the same, for the "distance" involved in reaching these extraordinary places is traversed in different ways. As we are all well aware, the vertical cosmological dimension is attained by techniques of spiritual travel in which the soul or intangible "essence" of the actor effects communication, perhaps by "traveling" itself to otherworldly levels or spheres or, alternatively, by asking deities to do the traveling to the supplicant, while the participant himself remains generally motionless in sleep or in trance. . . . In contrast, distant horizontal cosmological locales are generally reached and explored by physical travel in which members of the home society boldly venture forth or foreigners come as visitors to the home center.

As elaborated by Helms, this scheme is hardly restricted to would-be chiefs and their nascent chiefdoms. It applies equally well to any social arena in which there is individual competition for prestige, whether it be the shaman-centered network of power gradients among the otherwise egalitarian Shuar (Harner 1972) or the differential prestige accruing to scholars of the modern academy who attend distant international, as opposed to local "regional," meetings. A contemporary example from the Cayapas can also be cited.

Until his death a few years ago, Jesusito was the premier Chachi shaman. His curing feats continue to be legendary, an ability attributed to the unrivaled repertoire of his curing songs, the hallucinogenic potency of his *pilde* (*Banisteriopsis caapi*), and the unmatched power of his *arte*, the Chachi term for shamanic paraphernalia, which in Jesusito's case included a set of carved wooden figurines, a block of obsidian, a set of ground stone axes, and several La Tolita–style ceramic figurines—all but the wooden figures undoubtedly retrieved from archaeological deposits. Even the local Protestant missionary claimed that Jesusito could make his *arte* levitate, although, unlike the Chachi, he was not sure that Jesusito himself could assume the form of a winged jaguar with x-ray vision and with the capacity to fly through the upper canopy of the forest at breakneck speed, much like a harpy eagle.

Jesusito's extraordinary powers came from afar. As a young man, he had apprenticed himself to a renowned Colorado shaman. Colorado shamans are reputed to be the most knowledgeable (and the most dangerous) on the western side of the Andes (but see Taussig 1987: 179). Later in his shamanic training, Jesusito is said to have visited the Canelos of the *oriente* or Amazonian side of the Ecuadorian Andes. The Canelos, in turn, are the power hub of a far-reaching shamanic network that extends southward into Peru (Harner 1972). It was among the Canelos that Jesusito acquired his most powerful songs and his privately tended pharmacopoeia of medicinal plants. Biographically speaking, Jesusito was a Helmsian strategist of the first order: he appropriated knowledge from afar (the Colorado and Canelos) and from "ago" (his archaeological *arte*).

By Chachi standards, Jesusito was also wealthy. He had the largest house (later to become our archaeological base camp), outlived several wives who had left him a large number of offspring, and amassed a considerable stock of European goods and money (the Chachi pay to be cured). Most Chachi assumed that our real archaeological mission was to find the "treasure" that mysteriously disappeared on Jesusito's death and that presumably lies buried somewhere along the Cayapas. Although not a chief in that he did not exercise political control over a defined area, Jesusito was an exceedingly influential shaman whose spiritual power was convertible into material rewards.

Today Chachi political organization is centered on a system of officials including *gobernadores* and *capitanes* (note the Spanish terms), whose leadership roles are activated primarily during periodic gatherings at ceremonial centers. Shamans do not directly figure in these periodic governments or "sequential hierarchies" as Johnson (1982) would dub them. In fact, the relationship between shamans and civil officials is somewhat guarded, the former controlling the supernatural, the latter the more mundane world of politics. It is not clear, however, that this division was always the case. Chachi government has every stamp of being a European imposition. Spanish priests and colonial officials and, more recently, Protestant missionaries have always correctly sensed that shamans, as custodians of Chachi core beliefs, are the real enemy. In this respect, it is significant that Chachi traditions, while emphasizing the exploits and accomplishments of their shamans, rarely assign critical roles to civic leaders. In contrast, shamans are given a shadowy, sideline role in Western historical accounts, whereas *gobernadores* and other "proper" officials figure prominently.

I am not suggesting, of course, that a contemporary Chachi model minus its European-derived governmental organization should be applied directly to La Tolita. A major point of chapter 9 was that the Chachi are relative newcomers to the Santiago-Cayapas and, therefore, are inappropriate candidates for viewing the area's prehistory in any "direct historical" or phylogenetic sense. I am suggesting, however, that the political role of shaman needs rethinking in general, that this role may have been less circumscribed in the prehistoric past, and that the shaman-priest as curer and culture broker has a ring of plausibility to it when one confronts the available facts concerning La Tolita. This suggestion is hardly novel. Hocart (1970) laid groundwork for such thinking, and, more recently, both Chang (1983) for ancient China and Burger (1992) for ancient Peru have stressed the ideological continuities between essentially egalitarian social formations and ones displaying the symptoms of nascent inequality. Elevating the age-old institution of shaman along with its primordial pantheon of caymans, jaguars, and serpents was apparently an easier task than grafting a novel system that found no basis in collective common sense, much less in collective well-being.

That there were limits to such a process is well attested by the experience of La Tolita, its reign as the largest settlement of the region having lasted but a few centuries. By A.D. 400, its monuments had been reclaimed by forest and its descendent population had dispersed inland, later to become tantalizing traces behind the Esmeraldas shore.

AFTERWORD

"Epilogue" is the more common term at this point in a book, but according to the dictionary on my desktop, *epi* in the original Greek meant "near" in either space or time and could refer to immediately above, below, before, or after. Out of a sense of symmetry to the "foreword" that opened this volume, "afterword" would seem to be the more specific and appropriate title.

Given the chronological mission of this volume, some supplementary news coming in at the last moment deserves mention. A Herradura component at C150B, a site overlooking the confluence of the Cayapas and Zapallo Grande, yielded a charcoal date of A.D. 730 ± 170 (Beta-55289), which fits in with the chronology I have suggested. C2–3, the Tumbaviro "type" site, was revisited by Arthur Rostoker in the summer of 1992. A sparse and mixed deposit of Selva Alegre and Guadual materials was found to underlie the more substantial Tumbaviro midden. The latter produced a charcoal date of A.D. 1023 ± 70 (Beta-64535). If accepted, this age estimate would push back the division between Herradura and Tumbaviro and accordingly force revision of the calendar developed in fig. 3.17.

During the final writing of this book, Earl Lubensky sent me a copy of his dissertation dealing with surface collections made by Edwin Ferdon along the Esmeraldas coast in the 1940s. Although Lubensky's seriation of these materials generally conforms to the chronology favored here, there are some discordances. For example, Lubensky (1991: figs. 17.21, 24.19, and 38) regards what he calls "excised triangles" to be a hallmark of the Formative. This treatment recalls the "trellis" designs that typify our Mina complex (e.g., fig. 7.18A). In both Ferdon's and our own collections, this distinctive Mina material appears as a rare specialty ware, the chronological placement and cultural significance of which remain murky.

Ferdon's collections include an example of a short-footed tripod vessel from Lagarto, a coastal site not far from the mouth of the Río Verde (Lubensky 1991: fig. 18). On the basis of the adage that two instances make a pattern, this additional find suggests that the short-footed theme, as playfully explored in chapter 6, is likely to have been a real and meaningful one in the past.

June 1992 was wetter than usual, and the road was a deeply rutted trace of mud. Arriving in Borbón, we were greeted by our old friend Guillermo Ayoví. His limp was much better, the wound inflicted by a manta ray well on its way to healing. Don Guillo had other good news. Under the auspices of some cultural exchange agency, his marimba band had visited Los Angeles and Paris, and he had exciting stories to tell of these strange places. Don Guillo turned wistful: "Don Ricardo, today the youngsters here don't know the marimba, they don't care. They play only radios—salsa, cumbia, and rock." It was true. I remembered my first visit to the Cayapas in 1986 and how enchanting it was when nighttime marimba music wafted along the river. Feeling very much like old men, Don Guillo and I smiled, knowing that changes, both subtle and sweeping, were nothing new in this neck of the woods.

APPENDIX 1
Textiles

Textiles are unlikely to be preserved in the rain-drenched environment of the Santiago-Cayapas, and indeed none was recovered. In addition to ceramic spindle whorls, however, other evidence for weaving is provided by three examples of textile impressions. The first comes from the interior surface of a large body sherd found at the Chachi site of C58. Unfortunately, this specimen is not presently available for study, and our field description of "impression of finely woven fabric" is hardly overly specific. It is likely that this impression resulted from the construction technique described by Barrett (1925: 178):

> In making the bottom of a large pot . . . an old pot or other object of approximately the size and form desired for the bottom of the pot to be made, is covered with thin leaves *or with a piece of cloth* in order that the clay may not adhere to the rigid surface. A large lump of clay is then worked out into a thin disc, which is laid on the form and patted and worked in such a manner as to cover it uniformly and of the required thickness. While still on this form, it is allowed to dry, since the clay required for this part of such a vessel is of such quantity that it could not stand alone.

The remaining two specimens both come from R10 and are illustrated in the accompanying figure. Bill Conklin of the Institute of Andean Studies examined these specimens and kindly made available his preliminary assessment. I quote from his letter of December 1, 1987:

> The textile patterns seem to be not literally textile impressions, but rather to have been created by actual fragments of textiles imbedded in the clay. Perhaps the rest of the textile was burned off during the firing. There is dark organic material still remaining in the locations of the textile fibers. The textiles were most certainly plain weave and appear to have been utility textiles. The element spacing (I cannot be sure of warp and weft) in the case of B371 [A in the figure] is about 8 per cm, and in the case of B340 [B in the figure] it is about 10 per cm. One would suspect that the original textiles were cotton. B371 has evidence of quite irregularly sized elements and it is the more open, widely spaced of the two, and therefore seems to have been a considerably cruder textile. I would suspect, though, on the basis of the regularity of the element spacing, that both textiles were created on a loom.

Therefore, it would seem that weaving was part of the technology during at least the Guadual occupation of Selva Alegre. In this regard, it is interesting to note the complete absence of ceramic spindle whorls in Guadual assemblages. Presumably whorls were of some perishable material. For example, Chachi whorls were made from coconut shell or hardwood (Barrett 1925: 253).

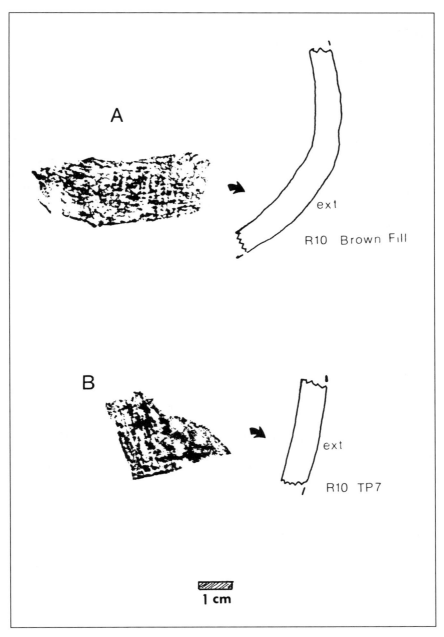

A

ext

R10 Brown Fill

B

ext

R10 TP7

1 cm

Appendix 1   Textile-impressed sherds from R10. Text describes A and B.

APPENDIX 2
Phytoliths

Deborah M. Pearsall and Warren R. DeBoer

Despite fine-mesh screening and flotation of selected excavated deposits, charcoal was the only macrobotanical remain recovered from archaeological sites in the Santiago-Cayapas. Soil samples, however, have yielded an array of microbotanical residues dominated by opal phytoliths (siliceous bodies formed in the leaves, stems, and inflorescences of plants that, like pollen, are often taxonomically diagnostic). Because these soil samples were taken from archaeological middens, their phytolith contents pertain to a blend of plants brought into a site for human utilization (as food, tools, construction materials, and so forth) as well as the vegetation growing on or immediately around a site (this flora is also likely to be human impacted).

The accompanying table condenses the phytolith evidence for twenty-three samples from five separate sites. A brief discussion of each phytolith category and its interpretive significance follows:

Gramineae

Gramineae includes grasses, bamboos, and canes. Abundance of grasses (marked by panicoid, festucoid, and chloridoid phytoliths) indicates an open, disturbed habitat. Abundance of bamboos and canes (marked by "horned towers," "flat towers," and other phytolith shapes) may indicate either a streamside setting or the import of these useful plants to a site. *Gramineae* are represented in all samples but are noticeably more common at R30 and C55. At the latter (Herradura), bamboos are particularly prevalent. Because Herradura is perched on a peninsula elevated well above the Zapallo Grande, it seems likely that the bamboos here were brought to the site.

Palmae

Palms, indicated by spinulose spheres and hat-shaped (conical) bodies, are represented in all but one sample. Of the two phytolith groups, spinulose spheres predominate. Tagua (*Phytephas aequatorialis*), widely used today for roof thatch, is one of the palms producing such phytoliths.

Chrysobalanaceae

This mouthful of a taxonomic unit, Chrysobalanaceae, includes the common tree *Hirtella carbonaria* and perhaps species of the genus *Parinari*. The abundance of the small, smooth spheres diagnostic of this group does not necessarily reflect an equivalent abundance of the corresponding trees, all of which are especially prolific phytolith producers. Nonetheless, Chrysobalanaceae can be treated as an indicator of humid forest.

Rugulose spheres

Rugulose spheres are distinctive phytoliths that occur in the Cannaceae, Marantaceae, and Helioconiaceae. These are families of robust herbs favoring moist settings. Whereas the Cannaceae and Heliconiaceae are more common in open habitats, the Marantaceae occur as understory plants in forested settings. Given the abundance of rugulose spheres in most samples coupled with the rarity of phytolith forms specifically associated with cultivated members of the Cannaceae and Marantaceae (see below), it is clear that the latter are not major contributors of rugulose spheres to our samples.

Compositae

Represented by a blackened, perforated epidermis, composites are generally open-habitat plants, often occurring in disturbed areas.

Sponge spicules

Sponge spicules are clear markers of wet conditions.

Diatoms

Diatoms also indicate wet conditions.

Cyperaceae

The presence of sedge phytoliths may be interpreted as an indicator of a moist environment.

Heliconia

Although a producer of rugulose spheres, *Heliconia* is also associated with distinctive troughed bodies. *Heliconia* prefers moist, open habitats.

Trichomanes

Trichomanes are ferns that produce distinctive troughed phytoliths and are a marker of a moist, forested environment.

Cannaceae

Producing rugulose spheres, the Cannaceae family is also associated with folded spheres. The latter are particularly common in the genus *Canna*, which includes *Canna edulis,* the cultivated root crop (achira).

Marantaceae

Another producer of rugulose spheres, the Marantaceae family is also associ-

Appendix 2 Table   Diagnostic phytolith percentages.

PROVENIENCE	Gr	Pa	Ch	Ru	Co	Sp	Di	Cy	He	Tr	Ca	Ma	Ze
C36, C2-L1	16	37	22	24	x	x	–	–	–	–	–	–	x
C36, C2-L2	20	10	15	55	–	–	x	–	–	–	–	–	–
C36, D2-L2	25	3	38	18	8	7	x	–	–	x	–	–	–
C36, D2-L2	30	8	28	34	x	–	–	–	–	–	–	–	x
C36, D1-L3	38	12	25	24	–	–	–	–	–	–	–	–	–
C36, C2-L4	23	6	16	54	–	–	x	x	–	–	–	x	–
C36, C2-L4/5	44	5	16	33	x	–	–	x	–	–	–	–	–
C36, L2-L5	41	6	31	22	–	x	–	–	–	–	–	–	–
C55, L10-dark midden	78	1	4	17	–	–	–	–	–	–	–	–	x
C55, L10-dark midden	80	3	10	6	–	–	x	–	–	–	–	–	x
C55, J1-dark midden	81	1	5	14	–	x	–	–	–	–	–	–	–
C69, 1-deposit 3	33	6	43	16	x	x	–	x	–	x	–	–	–
C69, 1-deposit 5	25	6	28	41	–	–	–	–	–	–	–	–	x
R10, Md 1A-brown fill	27	7	11	54	–	–	x	–	–	–	–	–	x
R10, Md 1A-brown fill	14	11	24	51	–	–	–	–	–	x	–	–	–
R10, Md 1A-yellow clay	19	6	26	49	–	–	–	x	–	–	–	–	x
R10, Md 1A-brown fill	20	7	16	56	x	–	–	x	–	x	–	–	x
R10, Md 1A-dark layer	16	2	8	73	–	–	–	–	x	–	–	x	x
R10, Md 1A-green clay	10	15	36	39	–	–	–	–	–	–	x	–	–
R30, 1-deposit 2	63	1	23	11	x	x	–	–	–	x	–	–	x
R30, 1-deposit 3	51	–	37	12	–	x	–	–	–	–	–	–	x
R30, 1-deposit 4	44	6	27	21	x	x	x	x	–	–	x	–	–
R30, 1-deposit 5	44	5	28	22	–	–	x	x	–	–	–	–	x

Gr, Gramineae (grasses, bamboos); *Pa, Palmae* (palms); *Ch, Chrysobalanaceae* (moist forest indicator); *Ru,* rugulose spheres (moist habitat indicator); *Co, Compositae* (open habitat indicator); *Sp,* sponge spicules (moist habitat indicator); *Di,* diatoms (moist habitat indicator); *Cy, Cyperaceae* (sedges); *He, Heliconia* (open habitat indicator); *Tr, Trichomanes* (ferns); *Ca, Cannaceae* (including achira); *Ma, Marantaceae* (including arrowroot); *Ze, Zea mays* (maize); *x,* presence at less than 1%.

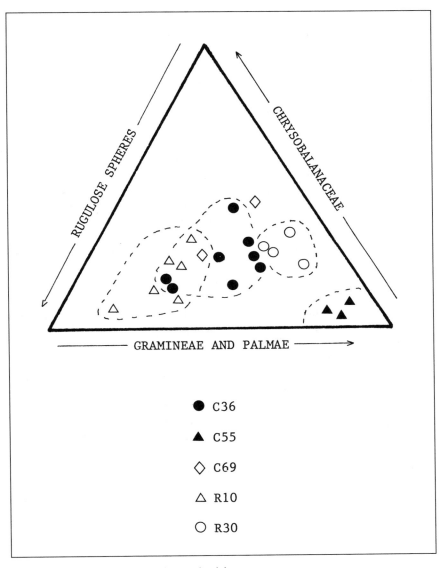

Appendix 2 Figure *Tripolar graph of major phytolith groups.*

ated with nodular spheres or seed epidermis phytoliths. The genus *Maranta,* including the cultivated arrowroot, is a possible source for these phytoliths.

Zea mays

Distinguished by its large, variant 1 cross-shaped phytoliths, maize is attested at all sites and in more than half of all examined samples. Independent confirmation of maize is provided by pollen recovered from R10 and C55 (Paul Tolstoy, personal communication).

All in all, the above roster of phytolith evidence is not surprising: humid forest studded by clearings—a reasonable description of the modern environment—is also indicated for the past; various palms, those multiuse plants of today, were also conspicuous in prehistory; maize was grown, and the cultivation of root crops such as achira and arrowroot is suggested, although not confirmed. One might also expect that manioc was present because both manioc and maize pollen have been identified in Cocotera phase contexts along the southern Colombian coast (Patiño 1988: 66). Despite negative evidence, it would also be surprising if squash and gourd were not crops throughout the Santiago-Cayapas sequence.

The preceding summary, however, fails to highlight significant variation among phytolith samples. As seen in the accompanying tripolar graph, this variation patterns according to site. Thus Gramineae (with high doses of bamboos) and Palmae (here treated as an anthropogenic category) overwhelmingly dominate the phytolith profiles for all samples from C55; they are also conspicuous in all samples from R30. One can almost see a substantial clearing flanked by houses walled with bamboo slats. In contrast, forest indicators (Chrysobalanaceae and rugulose spheres) tend to be substantially represented at other sites, and a different kind of settlement layout may be intimated. Although it is difficult to interpret these differences in a rigorous way, an important point should not go unnoticed: phytolith samples from sequent phases within one site are more similar to each other than are samples from the same phase at different sites. Locality, not temporality, is determining the Santiago-Cayapas phytolith evidence examined to date.

REFERENCES CITED

Adkins, Lesley, and Roy A. Adkins

    1989   *Archaeological Illustration*. Cambridge: Cambridge University Press.

Adoum, Rosángela, and Francisco Valdez

    1989   *Nuestro Pasado: La Tolita*. Quito: Museo del Banco Central del Ecuador.

Alcina Franch, José

    1979   *La Arqueología de Esmeraldas (Ecuador)*. Memorias de la Misión Arqueológica
           Española en el Ecuador. Tomo 1. Madrid: Ministerio de Asuntos Exteriores.

Alcina Franch, José, and Remedios de la Peña

    1979   Patrones de Asentamiento Indígena en Esmeraldas Durante los Siglos XVI y
           XVII. *Actes du XLII Congres des Américanistes,* Vol. 9-A: 283–301. Paris.

Alcina Franch, José, Alicia Alonso Sagaseta, Jean François Bouchard, and Mercedes Guinea
Bueno

    1987   Navegación Precolombina: El Caso del Litoral Pacífico Ecuatorial: Evidencias
           e Hipótesis. *Revista Española de Antropología Americana* 17: 35–73. Madrid.

Ascher, Robert

    1968   Time's Arrow and the Archaeology of a Contemporary Community. In *Settle-*
           ment Archaeology, edited by K. C. Chang, pp. 43–52. Palo Alto: National
           Press Books.

Bahn, Paul

    1989   *Bluff Your Way in Archaeology*. Horsham, U.K.: Ravette Books.

Barfod, A., B. Bergmann, and H. Pedersen

    1990   The Vegetable Ivory Industry: Surviving and Doing Well in Ecuador. *Eco-*
           nomic Botany 44(3): 293–300.

Barrett, Samuel A.

    1925   The Cayapa Indians of Ecuador. 2 vols. *Indian Notes and Monographs* 40.
           New York: Museum of the American Indian–Heye Foundation.

Bergsoe, Paul

    1937   The Metallurgy and Technology of Gold and Platinum among the Pre-
           Columbian Indians. *Ingeniorvidenskabelige Skrifter* nr. A 44. Copenhagen.
    1938   The Gilding Process and the Metallurgy of Copper and Lead among the Pre-
           Columbian Indians. *Ingeniorvidenskabelige Skrifter* nr. A 46. Copenhagen.

Blitz, John H.

    1993   Big Pots for Big Shots: Feasting and Storage in a Mississippian Community.
           American Antiquity 58(1): 80–96.

Bouchard, Jean-François

1985   Excavaciones Arqueológicas en la Región de Tumaco, Nariño, Colombia. *Revista Colombiana de Antropología* 24: 127–334.

1991   Contactos e Intercambios Entre la Región de La Tolita y la Región de Tumaco. Paper presented at the 47th International Congress of Americanists, New Orleans.

1992   El Formativo Final y el Desarrollo Regional en el Litoral Pacífico Nor-Ecuatorial. *Gaceta Arqueológica Andina* 6(22): 5–21.

Braun, David P.

1983   Pots as Tools. In *Archaeological Hammers and Theories,* edited by James A. Moore and Arthur S. Keene, pp. 108–34. New York: Academic Press.

Burger, Richard

1992   *Chavin and the Origins of Andean Civilization.* London: Thames and Hudson.

Burger, Richard, Frank Asaro, Helen Michel, Fred Stross, and Ernesto Salazar

1994   An Initial Consideration of Obsidian Procurement and Exchange in Prehispanic Ecuador. *Latin American Antiquity* 5:228–55.

Buys, Josef, and Victoria Domínguez

1988   Un Cementerio de Hace 2000 Años: Jardín del Este. In *Quito Antes de Benalcazar.* Quito: Centro Cultural Artes.

Cabello de Balboa, Miguel

1945   *Obras.* Vol. 1. Quito: Editorial Ecuatoriana.

Cerón, Benhur

1986   *Los Awa-Kwaiker.* Quito: Abya-Yala.

Chang, K.

1983   *Art, Myth, and Ritual: The Path to Political Authority in Ancient China.* Cambridge: Harvard University Press.

Damp, Jonathan

1988   *La Primera Ocupación Valdivia de Real Alto.* Biblioteca Ecuatoriana de Arqueología 3. Quito: Corporación Editora Nacional.

DeBoer, Warren R.

1984   The Last Pottery Show: System and Sense in Ceramic Studies. In *The Many Dimensions of Pottery,* edited by S. van der Leeuw and A. Pritchard, pp. 527–72. Albert Egges van Giffen Instituut voor Prae-en Protohistorie, Universiteit van Amsterdam, Amsterdam.

1989   The House that Jesusito Built. In *Households and Communities,* edited by Scott MacEachern, David J. W. Archer, and Richard D. Garvin, pp. 478–89. Proceedings of the 21st Annual Chacmool Conference, University of Calgary.

1991a   The Decorative Burden: Design, Medium, and Change. In *Ceramic Ethnoarchaeology,* edited by William A. Longacre, pp. 144–61. Tucson: University of Arizona Press.

1991b   Ceremonial Centers from the Cayapas to Chillicothe. Paper presented at the

56th Annual Meeting of the Society for American Archaeology, New Orleans.

1995 Returning to Pueblo Viejo: History and Archaeology of the Chachi (Ecuador). In *Archaeology in the Lowland American Tropics,* edited by Peter W. Stahl, pp. 240–59. Cambridge: Cambridge University Press.

DeBoer, Warren R., and Donald W. Lathrap

1979 The Making and Breaking of Shipibo-Conibo Ceramics. In *Ethnoarchaeology: Implications of Ethnography for Archaeology,* edited by Carol Kramer, pp. 102–38. New York: Columbia University Press.

DeBoer, Warren R., and John H. Blitz

1991 Ceremonial Centers of the Chachi. *Expedition* 33(1): 53–62.

Doyon, Leon G.

1991 Comments on Ceramic Style and Cultural Chronologies in the Northern Highlands of Ecuador: Contextual and Radiocarbon Evidence from La Florida, Quito. Paper presented at the 47th International Congress of Americanists, New Orleans.

Errázuriz, Jaime

1980 *Tumaco-La Tolita.* Bogotá: Carlos Valencia Editores.

Estrada, Emilio

1962 *Arqueología de Manabí Central.* Publicaciones del Museo Victor Emilio Estrada, no. 7, Guayaquil.

Feinman, Gary M., Steadman Upham, and Kent G. Lightfoot

1981 The Production Step Measure: An Ordinal Index of Labor Input in Ceramic Manufacture. *American Antiquity* 46(4): 871–84.

Ferdon, Edwin N., Jr.

1940 Reconnaissance in Esmeraldas. *El Palacio* 47: 257–72.
1945 Characteristic Figurines from Esmeraldas. *El Palacio* 52: 221–45.

Francisco, Alice E.

1969 *An Archaeological Sequence from Carchi, Ecuador.* Ph.D. dissertation, Department of Anthropology, University of California, Berkeley.

Galinier, Jacques

1987 *Pueblos de la Sierra Madre.* Mexico City: Instituto Nacional Indigenista.

Ginzburg, Carlo

1991 *Ecstasies: Deciphering the Witches' Sabbath.* New York: Pantheon Books.

Guderian, R., J. Molea, D. Swanson, R. Proaño, R. Carillo, and W. Swanson

1983 Onchocerciasis in Ecuador. I. Prevalence and Distribution in the Province of Esmeraldas. *Tropenmedizin und Parasitologie* 34: 143–48. Stuttgart.

Guinea Bueno, Mercedes

1984 *Patrones de Asentamiento en la Arqueología de Esmeraldas (Ecuador).* Memorias de la Misión Arqueológica Española en el Ecuador. Tomo 8. Madrid: Ministerio de Asuntos Exteriores.

1986   El Formativo de la Región Sur de Esmeraldas. *Miscelanea Antropológica Ecuatoriana* 6: 19–46.

1988   Valoración de las Evidencias de Intercambio en la Desembocadura del Río Esmeraldas: El Problema Cronológico. Paper presented at the 46th International Congress of Americanists, Amsterdam.

Harner, Michael J.

1972   *The Jivaro: People of the Sacred Waterfalls.* Garden City: Doubleday and Natural History Press.

Harris, Edward C.

1979   *Principles of Archaeological Stratigraphy.* New York: Academic Press.

Helms, Mary W.

1979   *Ancient Panama: Chiefs in Search of Power.* Austin: University of Texas Press.

1991   Esoteric Knowledge, Geographical Distance, and the Elaboration of Leadership Status. In *Profiles in Cultural Evolution,* edited by A. Terry Rambo and Kathleen Gillogly, pp. 333–50. Anthropological Papers 85, Museum of Anthropology, University of Michigan.

1992   Thoughts on Public Symbols and Distant Domains Relevant to the Chiefdoms of Lower Central America. In *Wealth and Hierarchy in the Intermediate Area,* edited by Frederick W. Lange, pp. 317–30. Washington, D.C.: Dumbarton Oaks.

Heras y Martinez, César Manuel

1991   La Cerámica de Integración de la Costa Nordecuatoriana: el Caso Esmeraldeño. Paper presented at the 47th International Congress of Americanists, New Orleans.

Hill, Betsy D.

1972–74 A New Chronology of the Valdivia Ceramic Complex from the Coastal Zone of Guayas Province, Ecuador. *Nawpa Pacha* 10–12: 1–32. Berkeley: Institute of Andean Studies.

Hocart, Arthur Maurice

1970   *Kings and Councillors.* Chicago: University of Chicago Press.

Holm-Nielsen, Lauritz, Lars Peter Kvist, and Manuel Aguavil

1983   Las Investigaciónes Etnobotánicas entre los Colorados y los Cayapas: Informe Preliminar. *Miscelanea Antropológica Ecuatoriana* 3: 89–116.

Holm-Nielsen, Lauritz, and Anders Barfod

1984   Las Investigaciones Etnobotánicas entre los Cayapas y los Coaiqueres: Secundo Informe Preliminar. *Miscelanea Antropológica Ecuatoriana* 4: 107–28.

Isaacson, John

n.d.   Characterization and Correlation of Elemental Concentrations of Archaeological Obsidian from Northwestern Ecuador Using Squared Euclidian Distance Hierarchical Clustering. Unpublished manuscript.

Jadán, Mary

1986 *La Cerámica del Complejo Piquigua (Fase VIII) de la Cultura Valdivia en San Isidro, norte de Manabí: un Análisis Modal.* Unpublished thesis, Centro de Estudios Arqueológicos y Antropológicos, Escuela Superior Politécnica del Litoral, Guayaquil.

Johnson, Gregory A.

1982 Organizational Structure and Scalar Stress. In *Theory and Explanation in Archaeology,* edited by Colin Renfrew, Michael J. Rowlands, and Barbara Abbott Segraves, pp. 389–422. New York: Academic Press.

Justeson, John S.

1973 Limitations of Archaeological Inference: An Information-Theoretic Approach with Applications in Methodology. *American Antiquity* 38(2): 131–49.

Labbé, Armand J.

1986 *Colombia Before Columbus.* New York: Rizzoli International Publications.

Lathrap, Donald W.

1970 *The Upper Amazon.* New York: Praeger.
1973 The Antiquity and Importance of Long-distance Trade Relations in the Moist Tropics of Pre-Columbian South America. *World Archaeology* 5(2): 170–86.
1977 Our Father the Cayman, Our Mother the Gourd: Spinden Revisited, or a Unitary Model for the Emergence of Agriculture in the New World. In *Origins of Agriculture,* edited by C. A. Reed, pp. 713–51. The Hague: Mouton.

Lathrap, Donald W., Donald Collier, and Helen Chandra

1975 *Ancient Ecuador: Culture, Clay, and Creativity.* Chicago: Field Museum of Natural History.

Lathrap, Donald W., A. Gebhart-Sayer, and Ann Mester

1985 The Roots of the Shipibo Art Style: Three Waves on Imiríacocha or There Were Incas before the Incas. *Journal of Latin American Lore* 11(1): 31–119.

Lubensky, Earl Henry

1991 *The Ferdon Collections of Prehistoric Ceramic Vessels and Sherds from Esmeraldas Province, Ecuador.* Ph.D. dissertation, Department of Anthropology, University of Missouri-Columbia.

Lyon, Patricia J.

1972–74 "Early Formative Period of Coastal Ecuador": Where is the Evidence? *Nawpa Pacha* 10–12: 33–48. Berkeley: Institute of Andean Studies.

Marcos, Jorge G.

1988 *Real Alto: La Historia de un Centro Ceremonial Valdivia.* Biblioteca Ecuatoriana de Arqueología 4–5. Quito: Corporación Editora Nacional.

Meggers, Betty J.
    1966   *Ecuador.* New York: Praeger.

Meggers, Betty J., Clifford Evans, and Emilio Estrada
    1965   *Early Formative Period of Coastal Ecuador: The Valdivia and Machalilla Phases.*
            Washington, D.C.: Smithsonian Institution.

Mitlewski, Bernd
    1985   Pesca Cayapa. *Miscelanea Antropológica Ecuatoriana* 5: 63–86.

Montaño, Maria Clara
    1991   El Manejo de los Recursos Naturales en La Tolita en su Etapa Clásica. Manu-
            script on file at the Banco Central, Proyecto La Tolita, Quito.

Murphy, Robert Cushman
    1939   The Littoral of Pacific Colombia and Ecuador. *Geographical Review* 29(1): 1–
            33.

Myers, Thomas
    1976   Isolation and Ceramic Change: A Case from the Ucayali River, Peru. *World
            Archaeology* 7(3): 333–51.

Nicholson, Henry B.
    1953   The Archaeology of Northern Manabí and Esmeraldas Provinces, Ecuador
            and Southern Nariño Province, Colombia. Unpublished paper prepared for
            Seminar on the Archaeology of South America, Harvard University.

Patiño, Diógenes
    1988   *Asentamientos Prehispanicos en la Costa Pacífica Caucana.* Bogotá: Fundación
            de Investigaciones Arqueológicas Nacionales, Banco de la República.
    1993   Arqueología del Bajo Patia, Fases y Correlaciones en la Costa Pacifica de
            Colombia y Ecuador. *Latin American Antiquity* 4(2): 180–99.

Peebles, Christopher S., and Susan M. Kus
    1977   Some Archaeological Correlates of Ranked Societies. *American Antiquity* 42(3):
            421–48.

Phelan, John L.
    1967   *The Kingdom of Quito in the Seventeenth Century.* Madison: University of Wis-
            consin Press.

Raddatz, Corinna
    1977   *Kleidung und Schmuck im Vorkolumbischen Esmeraldas.* Bremen: Ubersee Mu-
            seum.

Reichel-Dolmatoff, Gerardo
    1965   *Colombia.* New York: Praeger.
    1979   Desana Shaman's Rock Crystals and the Hexagonal Universe. *Journal of Latin
            American Lore* 5(1): 117–28.

Renfrew, Colin, and Paul Bahn

1991   *Archaeology.* New York: Thames and Hudson.

Rivera, Miguel, Emma Sánchez, Andrés Ciudad, Ana Rodríguez, and Anunciada Colón

1984   *La Cultura Tiaone.* Memorias de la Misión Arqueológica Española en el Ecuador. Tomo 4. Madrid: Ministerio de Asuntos Exteriores.

Rodicio García, Sara, and Josefina Palop Martínez

1988   Aportaciones a la Etnohistoria de la Provincia de Barbacoas. Paper presented at the 46th International Congress of Americanists, Amsterdam.

Sánchez Montañés, Emma

1981   *Las "Figurillas" de Esmeraldas: Tipología y Función.* Memorias de la Misión Arqueológica Española en el Ecuador. Tomo 7. Madrid: Ministerio de Asuntos Exteriores.

Sanford, Robert L., Jr., Juan Saldarriaga, Kathleen Clark, Christopher Uhl, and Rafael Herrera

1985   Amazon Rain-Forest Fires. *Science* 227: 53–55.

Santley, Robert S.

1992   A Consideration of the Olmec Phenomenon in the Tuxtlas: Early Formative Settlement Pattern, Land Use, and Refuse Disposal at Matacapan, Veracruz, Mexico. In *Gardens of Prehistory,* edited by Thomas W. Killion, pp. 150–83. Tuscaloosa: University of Alabama Press.

Schiffer, Michael B.

1987   *Formation Processes of the Archaeological Record.* Albuquerque: University of New Mexico Press.

Schultes, Richard Evans, and Robert F. Raffauf

1990   *The Healing Forest.* Portland: Dioscorides Press.

Shennan, Stephen

1988   *Quantifying Archaeology.* Edinburgh: Edinburgh University Press.

Spencer, Charles S.

1982   *The Cuicatlán Cañada and Monte Albán.* New York: Academic Press.

Stevenson, W. B.

1825   *A Historical and Descriptive Narrative of Twenty Years' Residence in South America.* 3 vols. London: Hurst Robinson.

Stirling, Mathew W., and Marion Stirling

1963   *Tarqui, an Early Site in Manabí Province, Ecuador.* Smithsonian Institution, Bureau of American Ethnology, Bulletin 186, Anthropological Papers 63. Washington, D.C.: U.S. Government Printing Office.

Stuiver, M., and P. J. Reimer

 1986　A Computer Program for Radiocarbon Age Calibration. *Radiocarbon* 28:1022–30.

Sutliff, Marie J., and James A. Zeidler

 1991　A Ceramic Sequence for the "Jama-Coaque" Occupation of the Jama River Valley, Northern Manabí (Ecuador). Paper presented at the 56th Annual Meeting of the Society for American Archaeology, New Orleans.

Taussig, Michael

 1987　*Shamanism, Colonialism, and the Wild Man.* Chicago: University of Chicago Press.

Thomsen, Moritz

 1989　*The Farm on the River of Emeralds.* New York: Vintage Books.

Tihay, Jean-Pierre

 1988　Aspects Géomorphologiques de L'environnement du Site Archéologique de La Tolita (Equateur). Manuscript on file at the Banco Central, Proyecto La Tolita, Quito.

Titterington, P.

 1938　*The Cahokia Mound Group and Its Village Site Materials.* St. Louis: privately published.

Tolstoy, Paul, and Warren R. DeBoer

 1989　An Archaeological Sequence for the Santiago-Cayapas River Basin, Esmeraldas, Ecuador. *Journal of Field Archaeology* 16(3): 295–308.

Uhle, Max

 1927　*Estudios Esmeraldeños.* Anales de la Universidad Central, Quito. vol. 30, no. 262.

Valdez, Francisco

 1987　*Proyecto Arqueológico "La Tolita."* Quito: Banco Central del Ecuador.

Welch, Paul D.

 1991　*Moundville's Economy.* Tuscaloosa: University of Alabama Press.

West, Robert C.

 1956　Mangrove Swamps of the Pacific Coast of Colombia. *Annals of the Association of American Geographers* 46(1): 98–121.

 1957　*The Pacific Lowlands of Colombia.* Baton Rouge: Louisiana State University Press.

White, Richard

 1991　*The Middle Ground.* Cambridge: Cambridge University Press.

Whitten, Norman E., Jr.

 1965　*Class, Kinship, and Power in an Ecuadorian Town: The Negroes of San Lorenzo.* Stanford: Stanford University Press.

1974   *Black Frontiersmen*. Prospect Heights, Ill.: Waveland Press.

Willey, Gordon R.

1971   *An Introduction to American Archaeology, Volume II: South America*. Englewood Cliffs, N.J.: Prentice Hall.

Willey, Gordon R., and Philip Phillips

1958   *Method and Theory in American Archaeology*. Chicago: University of Chicago Press.

Wolf, Teodoro

1879   *Memoria sobre la Geografía de la Provincia de Esmeraldas*. Guayaquil: Imprenta del Comercio de Carlos Kaiser.

1975   *Geografía y Geología del Ecuador*. Quito: Casa de la Cultura Ecuatoriana (reprint). Originally published in 1892.

INDEX

ABOUT THE AUTHOR

Warren R. DeBoer is a professor in the Department of Anthropology at Queens College of the City University of New York. He received his doctorate from the University of California at Berkeley.